Explore the World

NELLES

CW00507444

PERU

Authors:
Dr. Klaus Boll
Heike Mühl

*An up-to-date travel guide
with 161 color photos
and 16 maps*

Dear Reader: Being up-to-date is the main goal of the Nelles series. Our correspondents help keep us abreast of the latest developments in the travel scene, while our cartographers see to it that maps are also kept completely current. However, as the travel world is constantly changing, we cannot guarantee that all the information contained in our books is always valid. Should you come across a discrepancy, please contact us at: Nelles Verlag, Schleissheimer Str. 371 b, 80935 Munich, Germany, tel. (089) 3571940, fax. (089) 35719430, e-mail: Nelles.Verlag@T-Online.de

Note: Distances and measurements, including temperatures, used in this guide are metric. For conversion information, please see the *Guidelines* section of this book.

LEGEND

▦	Public or Significant Building	*Calca*	Place Mentioned in Text			National Border
■	Hotel	◪	International Airport			Expressway
●	Restaurant					Principal Highway
▦	Shopping Center, Market	◪	National Airport			Highway
✝	Church	☀	Beach			Main Road
∴	Ancient Site	**Volcán Misti** 5822	Mountain Summit (Height in Meters)			Provincial Road
★	Place of Interest					Railway
♣	National Park	*Abra Malaga* ⤳ 4350	Pass (Height in Meters)	10		Route number
⊨	Lighthouse			\ 25 /		Distance in Kilometers

PERU
© Nelles Verlag GmbH, 80935 Munich
All rights reserved

First Edition 2001
ISBN 3-88618-215-0
Printed in Slovenia

Publisher:	Günter Nelles	**Photo Editor:**	K. Bärmann-Thümmel
Managing Editor:	Berthold Schwarz	**Cartography:**	Nelles Verlag GmbH
Translators:	R. Rollo, A. Kelkar,	**Color Separation:**	Priegnitz, Munich
	N. Sidaway-Sollinger, J. Mayer	**Printed by:**	Gorenjski Tisk

- X02 -

TABLE OF CONTENTS

GUIDELINES

LIST OF MAPS

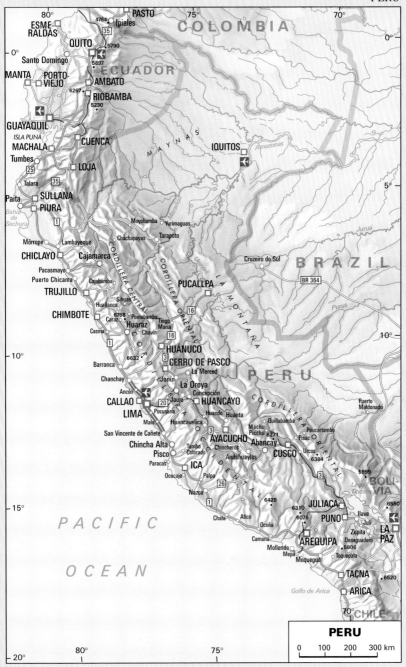

PERU

0   100   200   300 km

THE LAND AND ITS PEOPLE

GEOGRAPHY

With an area of about 1.3 million square kilometers, Peru ranks as the third-largest country in South America, after Brazil and Argentina. Some 42,000 square kilometers of the land area are designated nature reserves and thus protected by the state.

Hearing the name Peru brings to mind the fascinating, highly developed civilization of the Incas and the bloody war of subjugation by the Pizarro brothers, who were motivated by their lust for gold. Most visitors are drawn to the magnificent ruined cities of the Incas in the mountains and the mysterious ground figures at Nazca, which remain a puzzle to this day. Churches, lavishly decorated with gold, magnificent palaces, and elegant manor houses are evidence of the profound influence of the Spanish colonial masters.

Nature lovers are awestruck by the sight of the majestic, snow-covered peaks of the Andes. The largest national park in the country, the Parque Nacional Manú, covers an area half the size of Switzerland (or twice the size of Yellowstone Park) and, with its old-growth rainforests and rushing rivers, provides a number of Indian tribes and innumerable animal species with a protected habitat.

The highest summit in Peru (Huascarán; 6768 meters) towers above the distinctive vistas of Huascarán National Park in the Cordillera Blanca. All through the highlands, Indian farmers (*campesinos*) maintain their traditional

Previous pages: "Breathtaking" – the Andes at Tiobamba. Musicians at the Inti Raymi festival in Sacsayhuáman. Left: Procession in San Jerónimo near Cusco.

lifestyles. Descendants of the ancient people of the Uros have taken refuge on the floating islands of Lake Titicaca (3814 meters).

The higher regions of the Andes are home to llamas, alpacas, guanacos, shy vicuñas, and the majestic Andean condor, while the rainforests are teeming with jaguars, tiny hummingbirds, frogs, monkeys, and snakes.

Natural Regions

Peru is one of the few countries in Latin America to have all three classical landforms of this subcontinent – the tropical rainforest (*la selva*), the coast (*la costa*), here a strip of desert, and the mountains (*la sierra*).

La selva, the Amazon Lowlands, covers 60 percent of the national territory, but only one tenth of the population live here. The humid, tropical climate, with up to 200 days of rain per year, and temperatures averaging between 20° and 30°C, is very favorable to the growth of forests with giant trees, mahogany, cedars, nut trees, coffee, cocoa, orchids, manioc, and even coca.

The 2300-kilometer-long *costa*, the mostly desert-like coastal region along the Pacific, covers only 11 percent of the total area of Peru, but is home to 52 percent of the population. Driving through the coastal strip, with its gray-colored sand and cacti-covered rock outcrops, you will encounter 40 oases, in which 600,000 hectares of fertile soil is irrigation for cultivation. Cotton, sugarcane, and rice are grown to the north of Lima. In the south, you can see fruit, especially grapes, as well as olives. The enormous shoals of anchovies that at one time helped make Peru the largest producer of fish in the world have in recent years gradually moved more and more towards the Chilean coast, and because of this many Peruvian fishermen have lost their livelihood.

La sierra, the Andean highlands between the desert and the rainforest, is home to almost half the Peruvian population. Intensive cultivation of the carefully constructed terraces on the slopes of the mountains, deep ravines, rushing mountain rivers, and snow-covered giant peaks more than 6,000 meters high, have presented great challenges to the people who live here at altitudes of up to 5000 meters. *Quinua* (a native cereal), barley, potatoes, and sweet potatoes grow even at heights of more than 4000 meters. The eastern slopes of the Andes, which are carved up by tributaries of the Amazon, are called *la montaña*.

The Andes of Peru, which were formed by plate tectonic movements, upfolding and volcanism, have developed extremely deep and narrow valleys over

Above: In the land of their origin, potatoes (here a variety known as oca) can grow at altitudes above 4,000 meters. Right: The largest tropical glacial area in the world is located in the Cordillera Blanca.

the course of millions of years. Distinctive geomorphologic features include the *puna*, gigantic, flat areas of alluvial deposits in the southern highlands, and the dreary coastal desert along the Pacific. In addition, the largest glacial area in the tropics is located in the Peruvian Cordillera Blanca.

Earthquakes

An oceanic trench, up to 8000 meters deep, runs parallel to the coast, along which the Pacific Nazca plate is sliding under the South American continental plate, resulting in a highly active seismic zone. Severe earthquakes occur frequently along this "subduction zone," which the Incas accommodated with their earthquake-resistant building methods. Since the time of the *conquista*, the Spanish conquest, devastating earthquakes have repeatedly destroyed the newly established cities. On several occasions, the epicenter of the quake was located offshore in the Pacific, triggering dreaded

tidal waves (*tsunami*), as in the year 1746, when towering waves literally washed away the city of Callao, the port of Lima.

On May 31, 1970, one of the most severe earthquakes in Peru's history shook the north of the country. Numerous towns along the coast between Trujillo and Chimbote suffered heavy damage. In the highlands, tremors were felt in the Callejón de Huaylas, the idyllic Río Santa Valley, the Cordillera Blanca, and the Cordillera Negra. One entire flank of the mountain Huascarán slipped away, releasing an avalanche of rocks, ice, and mud, which then thundered down into the valley and buried the entire city of Yungay, with its 20,000 inhabitants.

Climate

Peru does not have four, but only two seasons – one wet and one dry, yet varying significantly depending on the geographic region.

On the eastern slopes of the Andes and in the lowlands of the Amazon Basin most of the rainfall occurs from January to April, whereas the drier period lasts from May to November. The Peruvians call this dry season *verano* (summer), even though it is on average somewhat cooler than the more humid *invierno* (winter).

In the Andes, too, the months of January to April are more humid and hotter than the drier and cooler "summer" from May to November, which can be accompanied by severe night-frost at higher elevations. A typical Andean day thus may seem to have all four seasons in it. The day starts as a cold winter morning, but very quickly becomes as hot as summer under the strong mountain sun. Then clouds appear and, in the afternoon, it rains briefly and heavily, as on a spring day. The early part of the evening heralds cool winds and a clear blue sky that are reminiscent of fall.

The coastal desert has real summer between December and March. The air

15

under the clear blue sky is hot and humid; and, for the Peruvians, it is time to go swimming. From May to November, in comparison, the weather becomes quite dismal along the coast, at least in the mornings. The cold deep-sea water of the Humboldt Current chills the air above the sea to such an extent that any moisture present condenses. Thick, grey fog sends drizzle , which the Peruvians call *garúa*. During this long period of climatic inversion, the smog in the capital, Lima, makes life pretty dreary.

Every four to seven years, for reasons that have not yet been fully explained, a warm branch of the equatorial current moves much further south than usual. Since this phenomenon generally occurs around Christmas time, the Peruvians have named these currents *El Niño* (the "Christ Child"). Much of the sea life can-

Above and Right: The cultures before the Incas left proof of their great artistic skill – a Mochica burial mask (2nd-6th century) and a cloth fragment of the Huaris (9th century).

not survive the unusually high water temperatures. Billions of microorganisms, which form the lowest layer of the food chain, move south with the cold water. They are followed by crustaceans, fish, seals, pelicans, gulls, and cormorants. The coastal fishermen have no work and no income. In addition, the entire climate along the Peruvian coast is thrown out of balance: where there hasn't been a single drop of rain for years at a time, there are suddenly cloudbursts that tear away bridges and roads. While the desert is converted into a sea of flowers, the fields are flooded, resulting in catastrophic consequences for the economy. The effects of *El Niño* have particular impact along the central and northern Costa. In 1983, for example, the region of Chimbote received 3000 millimeters of rain within a few weeks – whereas it normally only drizzles here on a few days in the year, and the farmers have to depend on their ancient, ingenious irrigation systems. It is not surprising that this "Christ Child" is extremely unpopular with Peruvians.

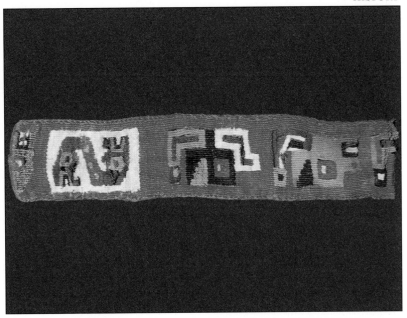

HISTORY

Cultures before the Incas

The first humans probably migrated from Asia to the Americas, crossing the Bering Land Bridge some 30,000 years ago. These nomadic hunter-gatherers reached Peru about 20,000 years ago. In the caves at Lauricocha in northeast Peru, hunter-gatherers covered the walls of the caves with primitive illustrations, dating from around 8000 BC. In the subsequent millennia, the inhabitants of the coastal valleys and the highlands developed basic agriculture and some limited herding. The sea provided rich hauls of fish. They did not yet have any metal tools. Astronomic observations and an elaborate death cult played a significant role in their religion.

Chavín

Between 1200 and 300 BC, the Chavín culture evolved in the valleys of the Cordillera Blanca, south-east of Huaraz, in which the focus was on worshipping deities that were half-human and half-animal. The original and most extensive discoveries were made at Chavín de Huántar. These, along with the Kotosh temple near Huánuco, the shrine of Cumbe Mayo near Cajamarca, the ruins of Garagay near Lima, and the related-Cupisnique style discoveries along the north coast (coastal Chavín), bear witness to the spread of this first pan-Peruvian culture. The skill of gold metallurgy is developed for the first time during this period.

Paracas

Almost concurrently, between 1300 BC and AD 200, another culture developed, albeit under totally different ecological conditions, on the desert-like peninsula of Paracas, south of Lima. The people of this culture apparently took great care to bury their men (especially those of high rank) in a worthy manner –

17

they were wrapped in the finest of textiles. The mummies were then buried in caves dug in the earth, and earthenware vessels, weapons, food, and jewelry, which they might require for their journey to the realm of the dead were laid with them in the grave.

Nazca

The next significant South Peruvian culture, the Nazca culture, was at its peak from the time of the birth of Christ till about AD 800. The Nazcas, too, buried their dead in fine cloth. They built temples of air-dried clay bricks (*adobe*), collected trophy heads in battle, and are accredited with creating the famous Nazca Lines in the desert sands, most of which mostly depict animals – probably for astronomical reasons or possibly even to pray for rain.

Above: A Chimú gold mask (Metropolitan Museum of Art). Right: The Incas were masters of architecture (here: Ollantaytambo).

Mochica

From AD 200-600, the warlike Mochica people typified the life of the fishing villages in the coastal valleys around Trujillo. They developed an ingenious irrigation system, manufactured fine ceramic pots, and built massive residential and burial pyramids. The Mochica practiced human sacrifice and used gold and copper to make jewelry. Their name is derived from the main excavation site of this culture, Moche (near Trujillo).

Huari

The former city of Huari near Ayacucho was the center of the second pan-Peruvian culture. Huari and the city of Tiahuanaco in present-day Bolivia, left a lasting influence on the civilization of the Andes highlands from AD 600-1000.

Most noteworthy discoveries include pictures of demons on fine pottery, meticulously built channels for artificial irrigation, and residential buildings and

temples of considerable height (about 10 meters).

Chimú

Like the Mochica before them, the people of the Chimú culture (AD 1000-1450) settled in the Trujillo region, but they also controlled the northern coastal region as far as the present-day border town of Tumbes. The Incas took the 10th King Minchançaman to Cusco as a hostage. His successors were still ruling when the Spaniards arrived as vassal kings on the coast.

The capital city of their empire was called Chan Chan and was surrounded by a massive wall. The central element of their religion was the worship of a moon-god, which included the worship of "lunar animals".

Minor Regional Cultures

Apart from the pre-Incan cultures mentioned above, there were several lesser cultural centers in Peru, such as: Cuélap near Chachapoyas; Antisuyo near the Río Marañon; and Pajatén (or Abiseo) between the Ríos Ucayali and Huallaga. Some of these, however, were only discovered in recent years and have not yet been excavated sufficiently to ascertain their significance in Peruvian history.

The Incas

According to legend, the Sons of the Sun – the Incas, emerged into daylight from a cave in 1200 AD. Yet their demise was already decided by 1533, with the conquest of Cusco by Pizarro's troops. The culture of the Incas is particularly well known and respected for its achievements in a country with a highly variable ecology and extreme variations in climate and altitude.

Clearly defined social structures made it possible for the Incan rulers to establish their power and to employ their knowledge and technologies to the best advant-

19

the time of the last independent Inca ruler, Atahualpa, the empire of the Incas included parts of today's Peru, Colombia, Ecuador, Bolivia, Chile, and Argentina.

The Incas did not destroy the peoples they conquered, or their culture – quite the contrary. They integrated them into their empire, forced them to learn the Quechua language and to adopt their religion of sun worship, and relocated the princes of the defeated tribes to Cusco. In addition, the Incas adopted the positive elements of the defeated culture, its knowledge and technologies, especially in agriculture, ceramics, bronze metallurgy, weaponry, and the making of jewelry.

The Incas furthermore were master architects – they designed their doors and niches in trapezoidal form, so that they were able to carry as much weight as the European Romanesque or Gothic arches of the same period. The quality and stability of their structures of granite, andesite, porphyry, adobe, wooden beams, and straw roofs was influenced by the megalithic culture of Tiahuanaco in Bolivia.

The Incas acquired crop irrigation technologies from the tribes along the Peruvian coast and developed them further. Methods employed in construction of canals are comparable to modern techniques and requirements, and have withstood the centuries well. Facilities for water supply and fertilization, granaries, and storage of food in clay pots, made the Incas less susceptible to the perils of drought.

The sophisticated 15,000-kilometer road network developed by the Incas connected the most important cities and fortresses of the Empire. This enabled *chasqui*, fast relay runners, to deliver messages and goods in astonishingly short times. Llama caravans transported immense loads from place to place along narrow trails – a single llama can carry loads up to 45 kilograms. Since the Incas

age. The introduction of the *mita*, a form of forced labor, in which the farmers had to work for the priesthood and nobility – in effect they had to give up two-thirds of their harvest – ensured that there was sufficient food for everyone.

The 13 successive Incan rulers, of whom the first to be recorded historically was Pachacutec Yupanqui (the ninth in succession and founder of the vast empire), attached a great deal of value to mastery of the art of warfare, and on politically prudent marriages of their young noblemen and aristocrats. By the age of 15, youths had to demonstrate their proficiency in the use of weapons and, upon passing this test, they were given the title of "Son of the Sun." It was thanks to this art of fighting that the Incan rulers were able to expand their empire to an area of about 1.7 million square kilometers. At

Above: An "Inca warrior" at Inti Raymi, the traditional solstice festival near Cusco.
Right: In 1532, the Inca Atahualpa encounters the Spaniard Pizarro.

did not use the wheel (but did know of it, since they used it in religious ceremonies), the llama was an excellent substitute. In any case, the topography of Peru would hardly have been suitable for wide roads. With breathtakingly long and high suspension bridges across raging rivers they overcame the obstacles of nature.

The medical knowledge of the Incas was also considerable: brain surgery in the form of trepanation (the process of boring a hole in the skull); the use of quinine as a medication, especially against fever-causing diseases like malaria; and the sterilization of wounds, would have been met with admiration in the Europe of that time.

Though the Incas (presumably) did not possess a script, and therefore no alphabet, they did have a sophisticated system of intricately colored and knotted cords called *quipus*, which they used as a kind of coded memory aid.

As in the Aztec Empire of Mexico, within the Inca Empire there were groups and peoples that no doubt suffered under the incontestable power of Cusco, and when Pizarro appeared on the scene, they supported the Spanish invasion, and indeed made it possible.

Pizarro and the Conquista

In the year 1531, two sons of the Inca Huayna Cápac (1493-1527), Atahualpa and Huáscar, were fighting over the succession to their father. This was at the time the Spanish adventurer Francisco Pizarro landed in northern Peru, near Tumbes with about 200 "conquistadors." After Atahualpa had defeated his half-brother, however, he fell into a trap laid by the Spaniards near Cajamarca, was taken prisoner and had to watch helplessly as strange bearded riders, equipped with horses and firearms, killed several thousand of his bravest warriors in a single night.

Pizarro demanded a ransom from the Incas for the release of Atahualpa, consisting of a whole roomful of gold. The

21

Túpac Amaru I, the last Incan ruler of the Vilcabamba Empire, was finally executed in Cusco in 1572. Well before, in 1541, Francisco Pizarro himself had become a victim of the greed of his former comrades. The Spanish knights then established a political system in Peru, which made it possible for them to endlessly plunder the treasures of the country. In 1542, Charles V (King of Spain and Holy Roman Emperor) had elevated the entire South American *Nueva Castilla* to the Viceroyalty of Peru, which was then ruled by a succession of 40 viceroys in the following 300 years. The "success" of the Spanish colonization can be attributed to the ceaseless and unscrupulous work of the missionaries, the insatiable greed for gold and money of the new masters of Peru, and the perfectly developed sytem known as *encomienda*. The latter deemed that the new lords, the *encomendero,* could exact tribute from the Indians in gold, in kind, or in labor, while receiving in compensation the "right" to Christian instruction – whether they wanted it or not. The *corregidores* were ruthless in claiming their dues, and lived a life of luxury.

Incas did their best, but Pizarro did not keep his word. On the contrary, under the pretext that Atahualpa had ordered the killing of Huáscar, he had the Incan leader executed in 1533. Shortly thereafter, the Spaniards conquered the Incan capital of Cusco, plundered it and installed Manco Inca, a half-brother of Huáscar who was initially submissive towards them, as the successor of Atahualpa. In 1536, Manco Inca rebelled against his new masters but, two years later, was defeated by followers of Diego de Almagro, who had just returned from Chile.

The Spaniards obtained additional profit by extracting mineral resources: an entire hill of silver in Potosí in present-day Bolivia; and mercury from mines near Huancavelica. The working conditions in these mines were worse than inhuman and cost thousands of enslaved workers their lives.

The Indian Uprising of 1780, lead by José Gabriel Condorcanqui – who called himself *Túpac Amaru II* – was crushed mercilessly by the Spanish in the following year. However, after these bloody incidents, the viceroy in Lima ensured that the exploitation of the *indígenas* became less severe. One change was the establishment of the *audiencia,* which was a court representing exclusively the interests of the native population.

Colonial Peru

In the decades that followed, by virtue of several rebellions, the cream of the Incan hierarchy was all but wiped out.

Above: In 1780 Túpac Amaru II led the last revolt of the indígenas against the Spanish.
Right: Parade on the occasion of a national holiday in Cusco, Plaza de Armas.

Independence

The revolt of the white masters of Peru against the Spanish colonial power, at the start of the 19th century, would have been inconceivable without the inspiration from other events such as the American War of Independence, the French Revolution and Napoleonic Wars, and the secession attempts of other Spanish colonies. The Creole upper class, born in Peru, increasingly resisted the administrators and tax collectors sent from Spain. As Republicans, they fought against the Royalists and, after the military successes of the Argentinean General José de San Martín, who had been called upon for help, proclaimed the formation of the Republic of Peru on July 28, 1821. After renewed unrest in Lima, it took victories over the Spanish Royalists by the Venezuelan freedom fighter Simón Bolívar and his army of 10,000 soldiers on August 6, 1824, near Junín in the highlands, and by General Sucre on December 9 of the same year near Ayacucho, to finally decide the war in favor of the Republicans.

Then came a period of upheaval and reforms: the highlands, with hardly any connections to the cities along the coast, received telegraph and railway connections; the capital Lima was modernized; and a new administration system was set up. Within a short period, the *encomienda* had been canceled and slavery abolished. However, the War of the Pacific broke out in 1879, setting the already debt-ridden Peru back considerably. The country joined with Bolivia against Chile in a war for the rich nitrate deposits in the region, which is now northern Chile. The war ended in 1883, with Peru losing three of its provinces to Chile.

The 20th Century

Following many years of dictatorship under President Augusto Leguía, from 1919 to 1930, Peru was plunged into the turmoil of the worldwide economic de-

23

pression. But the country recovered quickly and the economy started to look up again.

The 20th century also brought about major changes in housing styles in urban Peru. Prior to the turn of the century, the *casonas* (literally: large houses) were built almost exclusively using the Quincha style. This consisted of panels held within a wood frame, using some type of cane as infill, which was covered on both sides with mud (*barro*) and then finished with a thin layer of plaster. This was gradually replaced with imported styles and methods, similar to English country manors, French castles, Italian villas with an atrium, or even Greek temples and Oriental palaces. However, the *celosía* of the first story, the magnificent wood-carved balcony, survived this change. To this day, one can see these when strolling

Above: Migration from the rural areas results in slums on the outskirts of Peru's large cities. Right: Former President Alberto Fujimori.

through the old town quarters of Lima, Arequipa, Cusco, or other cities – a characteristic of the colonial architecture of Peru. The wealthy inhabitants of the suburbs now built elegant bungalows, while the newly arrived *campesinos* (farmers) had to make do with huts of corrugated sheet metal.

In the 1980's the dreaded Maoist terrorist group *Sendero Luminoso*, the Shining Path, was formed in the region of Ayacucho, under the leadership of Abimael Guzmán Reymoso, a philosophy professor (see page 78). The attacks on innocent *campesinos*, and the acts of retaliation by the police and military – which were often just as bloody, plunged the country into a maelstrom of violence. Even President Fernando Belaúnde Terry could do nothing to change that. Earlier, between his two terms in office (1963-68 and 1980-85), left wing generals had seized power, nationalized private business and had carried out reforms in the areas of agriculture, industry, health and education.

24

In 1990 the era of Alberto Fujimori began. In the presidential elections, Fujimori, a descendant of Japanese immigrants and Rector (president) of the La Molina National Agrarian University in Lima, won a decisive majority against the internationally acclaimed novelist Mario Vargas Llosa, and candidate of the Democratic Front. Fujimori's economic policies emphasized free-market reforms, privatizing state enterprises, and encouraging foreign investment. Initially his reforms were deemed to be too drastic, above all for the poor, but soon achieved significant success. These successes included the capture of Guzmán in 1992.

In 1994 President Fujimori's wife, Susanna Higuchi, made headlines all over the world. She moved out of their home and publicly criticized the social policies of the government, and the new election law that forbade blood relations to stand for political office, or to criticize it.

In mid-January 1995, the border conflict between Peru and Ecuador, which had been smoldering for 100 years, erupted again. During the war in the Cordillera del Condor, both sides used grenade launchers and air assaults, and more than one hundred lives were lost. In the Treaty of Río de Janeiro (1942), the border through the mountains had been defined, but 78 kilometers were still disputed. Both sides suspect there are mineral resources in this disputed area.

Three weeks after hostilities broke out in the border areas, Peru and Ecuador called a cease-fire on February 17, 1995 and singed the Peace Treaty of Itamaraty in the Brazilian capital, Brasilia. The treaty provided for a permanent cease-fire, the creation of a demilitarized zone, and the deployment of 40 observers in the area of conflict. On October 26. 1998 Peru and Ecador signed a peace accord ending their border conflict.

The official rationale for the border war, according to a statement by an Ecuadorian diplomat, was the fear that his country would lose access to the Amazon. On the Peruvian side it looked as if re-election tactics of President Alberto

25

Fujimori played a role – the elections being scheduled for April 9, 1995. Fujimori won that election with 64 percent of the votes. Many Peruvians, especially small, independent entrepreneurs, were counting on Fujimori to sustain Peru's economic recovery.

In September 1995, an open conflict broke out between Fujimori and the leadership of the Peruvian Catholic Church. The Cardinal of Lima, Augusto Vargas, condemned Fujimori's state program for family planning and limiting population growth, and encouraged civil disobedience among Peru's Catholics.

Peru has been in the headlines because of the Maoist terror group *Sendero Luminoso* (Shining Path), but this was defeated in 1992. More recently, in 1996/97, members of the smaller guerilla organization *Túpac Amaru*, took hostages and barricaded themselves in the Japanese embassy in Lima for four months. In the April 2000 elections, and the resulting run-off against Alejandro Toledo in May 2000, which gave him a third term in office, Fujimori was accused of electoral fraud. In November 2000 Fujimori resigned from office while on a visit in his ancestral homeland, Japan, where he remained, aginst a background of rumours that he would ask for asylum there. Congress sacked him on grounds of "moral incapacity" and new elections took place in April 2001, which were undecided. The run-off vote is to be held in May 2001, between Alejandro Toledo, a former shoeshine boy, with native Indian roots, and Alan Garcia, a former President of Peru in the 1980's.

CULTURE

It is said that the people of a country are its most valuable resource, and it soon becomes apparent to every visitor that

Right: About five percent of Peruvians still speak the old indigenous language Aymara.

this particularly applies to Peru. All through this Andean country, whether in the cathedrals, the markets, the archaeological sites, or during an excursion to the jungle, you will encounter these extremely polite and courteous, albeit sometimes very shy, people.

Population

Peru's 24.5 million inhabitants are concentrated in the large cities along the Pacific Coast; the Amazon lowlands, which comprises 60 percent of the country, is home to less than 10 percent of the population. This translates into an overall population density of 19 persons per square kilometer. The true population of the densely populated areas around the capital can only be estimated, but the city's population is believed to be around seven million. Every year more than 100,000 people migrate to the city and cause rapid expansion of the squatter settlements which stretch out into the desert.

The official languages of Peru are Spanish and Quechua. Ninety-three percent of the population is Catholic; six percent Protestant. The annual per capita gross domestic product is about US $1490, similar to that of neighboring Ecuador, Brazil, and Bolivia. The descendants of the Incas are referred to as *indígenas* (literally: indigenous, or native) or, in rural areas, as *campesinos*. The term "*indio*" is generally considered to be demeaning. The religion of the *indígenas* tends to be a blend between Christianity and their ancient ones.

The *indígenas* comprise the largest ethnic group in Peru, some 47 percent, followed by the *mestizos* (mixed race) at 32 percent. Most of the *indígenas* are small farmers and live in the highlands from agriculture and herding, in difficult conditions. The Amazon lowlands are still inhabited by some 50 indigenous ethnic groups, which total about 300,000 people. In addition there are about 12

percent whites (Creoles, the descendants of the Spaniards, Europeans, and North Americans), about five percent blacks (descendants of slaves), and about four percent Japanese and Chinese (20th century immigrants), who make up the racial mosaic of Peru. Such a statistical breakdown by race is becoming increasingly immaterial, since the various groups have intermingled a great deal since Pizarro's days. Now one's cultural affinity is a more important criterion.

Average Peruvian life expectancy is currently 65 (63 for men; 67 for women) and is thus about five years below that of industrialized nations. These figures are significantly influenced by the shorter life expectancy in the poor highlands of Peru. People frequently appear to be much older than they actually are, with the Andean sun, the tropics, or the hard work exacting their toll on the body. Forty percent of the population is under 15 years of age.

The infant mortality rate is 4.3 percent, and the child mortality rate is six percent, which is clearly much higher than the industrialized nations average – and can be attributed to the lack of sufficient medical care in the rural areas. At 2.1 percent, the growth rate of the Peruvian population is similar to the average of the developing countries and will create huge problems in the coming decades; hundreds of thousands of new jobs would have to be created every year.

The ratio of the urban population to the total population, at 72 percent, is as high as Australia's. This extremely high degree of urbanization, compared to the rest of the world, is the result of economically motivated migration from the rural areas. For some time, terrorism activities of the Shining Path in the central highlands around Ayacucho, also caused people to move in droves into the coastal cities.

Almost all the large cities are situated along or near the Pacific coast: Lima with seven million (Greater Lima: about eight million); Callao with 700,000; Arequipa with 650,000; Trujillo with 550,000; Chiclayo with 500,000; Piura with

350,000; and Chimbote with 300,000 inhabitants. At center of the highlands lies the old Incan capital of Cusco, with a population of 300,000. Iquitos, located on the Amazon, is experiencing rapid growth; with its population of 450,000, it has become one of the largest cities in Peru.

Language

Peru has two official languages, Spanish and Quechua. Spanish, spoken by 60 percent of the population, dominates in the urban areas along the coast, while Quechua, the language of the Incas, is spoken in the highlands of Peru by about 35 percent of Peruvians. Of those who speak Quechua, about 80 percent can also speak Spanish. About five percent of Peruvians communicate in the old, in-

Above: School uniforms are expensive – eleven percent of Peruvian children remain illiterate. Right: Often, girls in rural areas are only trained to look after livestock.

digenous language Aymara, which is mainly heard around Lake Titicaca. In the Amazon lowlands, a number of Indian dialects have survived the rubber and oil booms, the deforestation of the rainforests by the huge influx of settlers, and the missionaries – among them: Shipibo, Yagua, Pano, Tupi, and Jivaro. There are many differences between Peruvian Spanish (referred to as *castellano*) and European Spanish, as far as pronunciation, vocabulary, and idiomatic expressions are concerned, but not so much the syntax. Several outstanding Peruvian writers like César Vallejo and Mario Vargas Llosa, have demonstrated by their great success, even in the linguistic motherland, Spain, that they have an excellent artistic command of this language.

The *serranos* (mountain dwellers) often accuse the *Limeños* of swallowing the ends of words, or of joining all the words in a sentence together. The inhabitants of Lima counter that in the jungles the speakers draw out their vowels, and tend to lazily sing their speech, rather than speak it.

The Incas spread the use of Quechua throughout their Tahuantinsuyo Empire, so that even today it is still spoken not only in Peru, but also in some regions of Argentina, Bolivia, Ecuador, and Colombia.

Some language experts believe that Aymara, which is spoken by approximately 500,000 *indígenas* in the Departamento Puno along the shores of Lake Titicaca, is one of the most logically structured languages in the world and would be more suitable than any other as a computer language. In the hinterland of Puno, there are some villages in which most of the inhabitants still speak Aymara exclusively, but the language is faced with extinction sooner or later.

Education

Already at the time of the Incas, education was restricted to the priesthood and noble classes. This changed very little with the arrival of Pizarro; for several centuries after the conquest, the church and its monasteries dominated education. Not until well after the end of the colonial period was a reasonable school system established, with state-run schools and compulsory schooling for 6 to 15-year-olds. Even though there are enough schools and teachers in the large cities, the children from the poor families who live in the slums of the suburbs must often start earning money at a very young age, instead of going to school. Consequently, about 11 percent of Peruvians are illiterate (a percentage similar to that of the USA). In some rural areas, as many as 30 percent of the *campesinos* cannot read or write, while the official figure for Lima is just four percent.

In the countryside there are other problems: a huge shortage of teachers (not least because of the miserable pay); long distances to the schools; and the inability

to purchase the mandatory school uniform. Nevertheless, there are a large number of dedicated, idealistic young teachers who, in addition to their jobs, also function as social workers for the respective families. However, since only about 70 percent of the children finish secondary school, Peru is planning changes to the school system.

Parents from the middle and the upper classes tend to send their children to private schools, are run by churches or foreign institutions, because of their higher standards.

Only 36 percent of all youth attend post-secondary schools. Occupational training, in particular, is in a sorry state. There are only a few professions that offer apprenticeship programs. Training for skilled workers is rare and expensive, and projects by international development agencies in the area of occupational training are simply a drop in the bucket.

The Spanish established one of the first Latin American universities in Lima – the Universidad San Marcos. Today, there

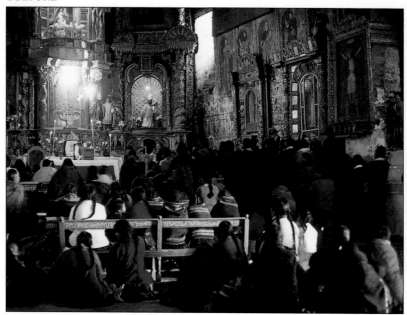

are 32 state-run and private universities in the country, of which 14 are in Lima. However, most subject matter is in the arts; for the technical disciplines, there is a dearth of professors, knowledge and funding. A large percentage of university graduates are unemployed.

Apart from the population in the country, women are at a great disadvantage. In the rural areas, girls are trained to become housewives and herders, and few other options are open to them after completing primary or secondary school. The children of the *campesinos* in the highlands are also neglected: of these at least 10 percent can neither speak nor understand Spanish, but communicate only in their mother tongue of Quechua or Aymara. Spanish language instruction, using inadequate text-books written in big-city Spanish and with contents that

Above and Right: Catholicism has replaced the old religions of the indígenas – Mass in Chinchero; Fiesta de la Virgen del Carmen in Paucartambo.

are scarcely relevant to Andean life, are not adequate to meet the needs of these people.

Religion

During the pre-Incan regional cultures, and into the Incan period, religion, piety, and work were inseparably woven into the fabric of daily life. This started to change with the missionaries and, to a much greater extent, with the influx of the Western culture at the beginning of the 20th century. The Spanish padres of the Catholic Church, first Dominicans, later also Franciscans, were primarily henchmen of the *conquistadors*. They had no aversion to torture, inquisition, and murder. The Dominican padre Vicente de Valverde distinguished himself as an enthusiastic supporter of the murder of the Inca Atahualpa; he and many of the monks in his order were in no way squeamish in their treatment of the Indians. More than anything else, they wanted to report missionary suc-

cesses to the Pope and often resorted to un-Christian methods of "conversion."

The monks, however, soon recognized that the natives retained many elements of their traditional religion even after baptism. The sun god *Inti*, whose representative *Inca* descended to earth much like Jesus, continued to be secretly worshipped, and the worship of *Pachamama* (Mother Earth), was transposed to Mary, Mother of God. The *indígenas* considered the *apu* (mountain tops) and *cocha* (lakes) to have souls and believed that these expected sacrifices from them, as did the many *huacas* (sacred places). Even the systematic destruction of the *huacas* by the missionaries could not change that. *Illapa*, the Indian god of thunder, was transposed into the Christian *Santiago* (Saint James). The *indígenas* continued their death cult worshipping, but doing so on November 1 and 2 in concession to the Christian All Saints' Day and All Souls' Day holidays. The remoteness of many of the Andean villages was a favorable factor in preserving their religious traditions, especially if the priests only came once a year to carry out ceremonies, such as weddings, baptisms, and the like. With heavy hearts, the monks had to make theological compromises in the very first decades of their missionary work.

Large annual religious festivities are not restricted to little Andean villages; even in Cusco, Puno, and Arequipa, among others, kilometer-long processions made up of thousands of believers moving through the streets for hours on end, while singing and praying, are sometimes even accompanied by a military band. While the women recite litanies with fervor, pray the rosary, and sing hymns, large numbers of men use the festival as a chance to drink *chicha* (corn beer) in earnest.

The Roman Catholic Church, to which 93 percent of Peruvians belong today, (6 percent claim to be Protestant), has been trying for a few years to rid itself of the image of conqueror, and now tries to take the position of a mediator between the

31

poor and the rich. The Peruvian, Gustavo Gutierrez is considered to be the father of "Liberation Theology", which is now widespread in Latin America. First referred to publicly in 1968, this belief attempts to link political involvement with a Christian mission within the Catholic Church and to fight for recovery of the rights of the poor and the disadvantaged. This results in recurring power struggles with the conservative Vatican.

Pope John Paul II, already under frequent criticism from Latin American bishops because of his views on family planning and emancipation, felt compelled, on the occasion of his visit to Peru in 1985, to make some considerable concessions. During his visit he beatified the Prioress of the monastery of Santa Catalina in Arequipa, Ana de los Ángeles Monteagudo y Leon, who was born in 1602 and died on January 10, 1686 – a

Above: The prioress of the Santa Catalina monastery in Arequipa – beatified in 1986.
Right: Peruvian women in Miraflores / Lima.

very significant gesture for the patriotic Peruvians.

Even though Roman Catholicism is the official religion of Peru, the constitution has guaranteed complete religious freedom since 1973. The state and the church have been separated since 1980, and religious instruction in schools is limited. Nonetheless, and in spite of an already-high national debt, the state is under considerable pressure to restore at least some of the numerous lavish churches built by the Spanish – if only because of its interest in the growth of tourism.

Attitudes and Opinions

Although one must be careful of generalizations, a few trends are discernible in the attitudes of Peruvians. To have many *amigos* (friends) from your own class of society is eminently important. Men, but even more so women, attach a great deal of importance to a well-groomed appearance in public. A sophisticated neckline, high-heeled shoes or high leather boots, elaborate makeup, and an expensive haircut can consume a large part of the household or personal budget.

Peruvians avoid being alone at work or in their leisure time, and seek out entertaining company. They have extremely strong connections with their extended family. Peruvians often share their homes with many relatives, and not necessarily out of economic necessity.

Whereas the whites and *mestizos* are generally open and sociable with strangers, the *indígenas* tend to be rather shy and reserved. One should always treat them with respect. Particularly when taking a close-up photograph, it is important to ask for permission first. A friendly greeting such as *Buenos dias!* (Good day!) or *¿Qué tal?* (How are you?), even if you don't speak the language, smoothes the way and opens doors. Many travelers to Peru are especially surprised by the humor of the In-

dian women. The saleswomen and *campesinas* in the markets laugh together over many humorous and silly situations.

Interpersonal contact in Peru is typically very polite and diplomatic. People address each other formally with *Señora* and *Señor* or yet more respectfully as *Doña* and *Don*, and generous compliments are in order. An elderly lady, whether in a shop, post-office, bank or in a restaurant, would always be addressed as *Señorita*, even if she is long since a grandmother.

Among the men, hearty shoulder slapping and the *abrazo* - the embrace, are common. Women with whom one is already acquainted, can be given a kiss on the cheek; shaking hands is obligatory. A Peruvian will invariably make some friendly inquiries about your family, and then interject positive comment,s such as "How nice!" or "Very good!" into your answer.

In Peru it is considered to be good manners to arrive at least a quarter of an hour late for an engagement, in order not to be too imposing upon the host. Another aspect of civility, however, can at times be rather inconvenient for travelers: ask a Peruvian for directions, for instance, and rather than profess ignorance if he does not know, he will offer up something just to be polite. Despite the usual goodwill and sincerity towards foreign visitors to Peru, some individual local people – in the markets, in taxis, etc. – will at times try to cheat them, on the assumption that tourists have a lot of money anyway.

Relationships between husbands and wives are heavily influenced by traditional Spanish and Indian values – by behavioral codes and emotions such as pride, honor, and jealousy. The oft-quoted Latin American machismo has become less intense in the last few decades, but in schools and at home, daughters continue to be groomed to become good mothers and subservient wives. In upper-class families the wife does not normally work outside the home. She is the head of the family at

home, but not in society, where she has to be seen to be subordinate to her husband. In middle-class families, the roles of husband and wife are much less clearly defined. Here women work at least as much as men, and often outside the home. In comparison, the wife in purely indigenous families has the least advantageous role. She has to work hard looking after the household and raising the children, and often has to earn money on the side, all the while remaining subordinate to her husband.

People's interests are revealed by how they spend their free time. Peruvians love both melancholic and lively music, and dances. They like to sing together in social situations and optimistically take their chances in gambling. People buy lottery tickets in the street and play the popular pools on horses several times a week. Bullfights, especially those held in

Lima's Plaza de Acho, in which the Torero kills the bull during the fight, and cockfights that also end in death, continue to be the most popular "sports" among Peruvian men (after soccer) – despite vigorous protests from animal-rights activists.

Visual Arts and Theater

As with Peru's early cave paintings and the artistic drawings of a few Inca princes, the detailed drawings and accompanying comments by Felipe Guamán Poma de Ayala, depicting scenes from the everyday lives of the Incas, have become very well known. During the colonial period, *La Pintura Colonial*, the painting school of Lima, as well as the *Escuela Cuzqueña* (Cusco School) adopted painting techniques and motives from Europe and integrated them with local characteristics. This is particularly noticeable in a depiction of the Last Supper in the cathedral in Cusco in which the customary lamb set in front of Jesus is re-

Above: The mural "The History of Cusco" by Juan Bravo Vizcarra. Right: Mario Vargas Llosa, Peru's most famous writer.

placed by the Peruvian specialty *cuy* (guinea pig).

The 20th-century painters Sérvulo Gutierrez and Fernando Szysko depicted specific Peruvian elements in their mostly abstract paintings. Other artists, such as Juan Bravo Vizcarra, patterned their large wall paintings after the Mexican muralism of Diego Rivera, Orozco, and Siquieros.

Despite the lengthy tradition of drama amongst the Incas in Cusco and the Spanish viceroys in Lima, the theater is not very highly developed here. Apart from performances at major festivals, such as the Inti-Raymi festival in Cusco (June 24), and the occasional theater in Lima, theatrical productions are confined to the "Café Teatros" in the Liman suburbs of Miraflores, San Isidro, and Barranco. These take the form of sketches and popular comedies.

Literature

Peruvians can look back upon a very long literary tradition. Apart from the Incan poets, the first Peruvian writer of note was Garcilaso de la Vega, the son of a Spanish knight and an Inca princess, and author of *History of the Incas*, written in the 17th century. Ricardo Palma's *Tradiciones peruanas*, a narration of the cultural traditions of Peru published around 1900, is also very well known in Peru.

Social criticism is the theme of the classic *El Mundo es ancho y ajeno* ("Broad and Alien is the World"), by the *Mestizo* Ciro Alegría (1909-67). It describes the day-to-day struggle of the Indian *campesinos* (small-scale farmers and farm workers) of Northern Peru, against the greed of the large landowners. The lyricist César Vallejo (1892-1938) became world-famous with his poems on the Spanish Civil War.

The works of José María Arguedas (1911-1969), especially the novel *Drink My Blood, Drink My Tears,* about the sheer hopelessness of the situation of the *campesinos* in the highlands of Peru are really worth reading. Another great hope of Peruvian literature, Manuel Scorza, died in a plane crash at the age of 55. His satirical novels (*e.g., El Jinete insomne* – The Sleepless Rider) deal with concerns of the *indígenas* of Peru using almost surrealistic fantasy.

Mario Vargas Llosa, born in 1936, has achieved an international reputation as Peru's best-known author, as the first Latin-American president of the International PEN Club, and as presidential candidate in 1990. His works are filled with social criticism and almost all are set in Peru, e.g., *The Green House, The Real Life of Alejandro Mayto, Conversation in the Cathedral*, and *The Story Teller*. His most recent books, such as the erotic novel, *In Praise of the Stepmother*, the exciting and yet very humorous mystery thriller *Who killed Palomino Molero?* and his political novel, *Death in the Andes*, enable outsiders to obtain some

excellent insights into everyday life in Peru.

ECONOMY

Peru has, by virtue of its geography and lack of infrastructure, two independent economic systems operating side-by-side. The population of the rural areas, particularly in the valleys and on the *altiplano* (highlands), have a nearly currency-free barter system and have managed to retain their self-sufficiency. Since the *campesinos* rarely produce any excess, they also do not have any purchasing power, and are therefore of little interest to merchants of consumer goods.

Political unrest and insecurity have hindered foreign investment for decades, and Peruvian private capital is scarce. Until recently, the government was the

Above: Shoeshine boy by profession – but it is hardly enough to survive. Right: Thirty-four percent of those who are gainfully employed work in the agricultural sector.

largest investor. World market conditions are also unfavorable for Peru. Prices for exported raw materials from mining and agriculture are dropping, while prices for necessary imports (cars, electronic equipment, household appliances, etc.) are rising year after year.

About 40 to 50 percent of Peruvians live below the poverty line (40 percent in cities, 60 percent in the rural areas) including, of course, those who receive the state-prescribed minimum wage of 100 US$ per month. The distribution of wealth could hardly be more unequal: half of the entire income in Peru goes to only 10 percent of the population. Unemployment was at 28 percent in 1992; by 1997, with the implementation of Fujimori's economic reforms, it had dropped to below ten percent. Officially it is only six percent in the city of Lima, but this is precisely where many "hidden" unemployed live, such as shoeshine boys, street vendors, lottery vendors, black marketeers, and the seasonally employed. In the highlands, the numerous

campesinos without full-time jobs are also not registered as unemployed.

The problem of high inflation (in 1990 the rate was 7000 percent!) appears to have been solved. With unemployment at less than 10 percent since 1996, Peru is better positioned than most of the other Third World countries. The high foreign debt of 29 billion US$, on the other hand, will continue to be a big problem for Peru. In 1995, economic growth in real terms reached a respectable 7 percent, which enabled Peru to obtain a special credit of one billion dollars from the World Bank.

Thanks to the export of natural resources and income from fishing, the balance of trade is more or less balanced. Peru's imports in 1995 were valued at four billion dollars (almost 30 percent from the USA), at an average import duty of 12 percent, and exports amounted to 3.5 billion dollars. About half of the exports were accounted for by mining (zinc, copper, lead, and silver), about 15 percent by fish and fish products (fish-meal), and nine percent by textile products. A quarter of Peru's exports go to the USA, 10 percent to Japan, and 20 percent to the European Union.

International development projects have been trying, since the 1950's, to improve the power supply, irrigation, sewage, and garbage disposal in the large cities, mines, fisheries, and basic health services. Particular emphasis continues to be placed on education.

Agriculture

Agriculture, which yields only seven percent of the gross domestic product, employs 34 percent of Peru's workforce, due largely to the low level of technical development in many places. In comparison, industry achieves 37 percent of the GDP, but employs only 17 percent of the workforce.

Sugarcane, cotton, coffee, and alpaca wool are the chief export commodities. It is estimated that about 60 percent of the world's coca crop originates in Peru.

Corn, beans, potatoes, wheat, and sheep's wool play a significant role in meeting the needs of the population. The working conditions for agricultural laboreres are often very harsh. Terraces are built at extreme heights, still using the same methods employed by the Incas. The seasonal rainfall further limits the harvest. In the end, Peru still has to import wheat, cattle feed, soy oil, and milk.

In the highlands of Peru, about 900,000 families live from agriculture, cultivating 35 percent of the total agricultural land. The soil, however, is often not very fertile. The long frost, the short growing period of the Andean summer, and long transportation distances contribute to making the work of the *campesinos* particularly difficult. The shortage of land has led those *campesinos* not wishing to migrate to cities to re-activate old, almost inaccessible terraces and irrigate

Above: Oil and gas are produced in the Amazon lowlands. Right: Peru earns about one billion dollars per year from tourism.

them. During the colonial era, about 50 % of the terraces from Incan times were allowed to all into decay.

Industry

Peru's industry, which is very efficient in certain individual areas, makes up 39 percent of the GDP, however it employs only 17 percent of the working population. The oil resources currently supply arounfd half of the local energy consumption. However, the oil reserves, mainly located in the lowlands of the Amazon, are estimated at only around 700 million barrels and likely to be exhausted by the year 2005. On the other hand exploration of the Camisea gas fields has just begun, and this is expected to yield in the order of seven times the equivalent amount of oil.

About 80,000 mainly indigenous, poorly paid laborers work in miserable conditions in the large mines. They produce copper, iron ore, zinc, lead, silver, and gold and process the ores in the large

smelters situated along the north coast. The most significant export ports – Callao, Paita, Talara, and Chimbote – are all located north of Lima. Yet, two-thirds of Peruvian industry is located in the Greater Lima area. This includes the final assembly of automobiles, buses, and trucks, and production of small electrical appliances, textiles, chemical, and pharmaceutical products, as well as confectionery and beverages. Peru is currently the world's largest producer of fishmeal, at 1.2 million metric tonnes, just ahead of Chile. However, the fish stocks of the Pacific have been severly decimated by over-fishing and changes in sea currents.

President Fujimori had followed a policy of privatizing the large public-sector companies, and attracting more foreign investment. Corruption, the illegal coca market, and the black market economy, remain hindrances to Peru's economic development. However Peru (at least at present) could scarcely suvive economically without the income from coca and this very flexible, informal sector.

Tourism

Foreign visitors come to Peru not so much for the sun, the beaches, or the sea, but more out of interest in the old Peruvian cultures, the grandiose Inca sites, the Spanish colonial architecture in the cities, and, naturally, because of the people. The more adventurous tourists are drawn by excursions into the tropical rainforests, and mountaineering and trekking tours into the Cordilleras of the High Andes.

After a major setback in the number of visitors in the 1980's, resulting from the political instability of Peru (caused mainly by the terrorism of the *Sendero Luminoso* and its rival group *Túpac Amaru*), the number of tourists visiting Peru annually has increased again to around 500,000 – the majority being from Europe. Of these European visitors, Germany makes up the largest share. Peru earns just about a billion dollars a year from tourism; it is thus an extremely important factor for the underdeveloped economy.

LIMA

A TOUR OF THE OLD CITY
PUEBLO LIBRE
OUTSIDE THE CITY CENTER
MIRAFLORES
AROUND LIMA

It used to be that after landing in **Lima**, when you drove from the airport to your hotel in the district of Miraflores, or downtown, you could rather shocked by the dusty gray of the concrete and adobe houses, and by the numerous beggars, the garbage in the streets, and the seemingly chaotic traffic – with thousands of old buses and trucks spewing pitch-black exhaust smoke into the air. "Lima the Horrible" is the epithet that the author José María Arguedas used for the capital of his country at the beginning of the 1960's. And the Peruvian winner of the Nobel Prize for Literature, Mario Vargas Llosa, facetiously states in his novel *Historia de Mayta*, "When one lives in Lima, one must either get used to the poverty and the dirt, or go crazy or commit suicide."

The *garúa* (coastal fog) that hangs over the city for many months on end, makes Lima look rather dreary at times. To this day, there are still sprawling poor districts, which the "average tourist" hardly ever gets to see. Lately, thanks to Mayor Alberto Andrade, there have been a lot of positive aspects to report on the

Previous Pages: The cathedral of Lima in the Plaza Mayor. Casa Oquendo de Osambela in Lima's old city. Left: The changing of the guard at the Government Palace.

"reincarnated" metropolis of over 7,000,000, which lies on a plane that gently slopes from the foothills of the Andes to the Pacific coast. The garbage collection system now functions and it is possible to walk safely on the sidewalks again. The wide avenues have been planted with greenery and, thanks to new roads and traffic signals that work, even the traffic seems to be surprisingly civilized. In the well-maintained suburb of Miraflores, pretty little street cafés, discos, and good hotels beckon. In the historic old city of Lima, there are many magnificent, carefully restored colonial buildings, numerous churches, and an imposing cathedral. Beautiful plazas, a lively pedestrian zone, and several world-renowned museums make a visit to Lima an almost obligatory part of any trip to Peru. The coastal region has been, for millennia, home to a great variety of cultures. Though the city, sprawling on both banks of the Rimac River, from which it gets its name, lies in the tropics, really hot and humid days are limited to three or four months in the summer. Surfers give a high rating to the persistent waves of the Pacific, which is not really all that "pacific," that pound the long pebble beaches of Lima.

The cities the Spaniards established in Latin America were intended to avoid the

45

LOS OLIVOS

Avenida Angelica Gamarra de Leon

Avenida   Tomas

Avenida

Aeropuerto Internacional
"Jorge Chávez"

SAN MARTÍN
DE PORRAS

C
La

Avenida   Pe

Avenida

Avenida

Avenida   y   Agrales   Dua

J. Biglu
y Carillo

Avenida

Elmer

LA LEGUA

Atr

Rio   Rimac

República

Edisor

Avenida

(Avenida Colonial)

Ave. Germ
Amecaga

CALLAO

J.

Universidad
Nacional
de San Marcos

Cemeterio
Baquijano

Faucett

Ave. Jose

P. Zoológico
Las Leyendas

Ave.

Guardia

BELLAVISTA

SAN MIGUEL

Ave. 2 de Mayo

Saenz

Peña
Aires

P. Zonal
Yahuar Huaca

Chalaca

Ave.   de   la   Marina

Ave.

Buenos

Ave. Jose Galvez

LA PERLA

★ *Mus. Histórico*
del Real Felipe

Ave.

Ave. Huascar

Colegio Militar
Leoncio Prado

Feria I
nacion
del Pa

Avenida   la   Paz

Ave. Bolognesi

Ave. Grau

Escuela
Naval

La Punta

PACIFIC

OCEAN

GREATER LIMA

0   1   2   3 km

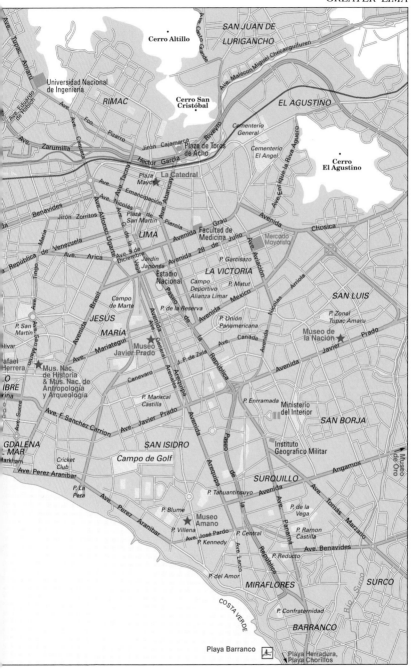

feeling of the cramped and unsightly medieval Spanish cities. Therefore the city planners in the Viceroyalty of Peru drew the roads of the new settlements with a ruler. The streets intersected at right angles and the blocks were mostly of equal size and square. Surrounding the city center, the equally square Plaza de Armas, were churches, the City Hall, the governor's palace, and other public buildings. Only the aristocracy was allowed to settle in the vicinity of this main square.

As well as several parks, the Spanish conquistadors always left enough space for monasteries, additional churches, hospitals, and similar institutions. Small merchants, craftsmen and day laborers set up their modest houses at the outskirts of the city. Indians, who had lost their land, built their meager huts outside the city limits.

Above: "Lima Colonial" – a painting by Vejarano. Right: Lima today – with a population of several million.

Pizarro founded the city of Lima, known as *City of Kings*, on January 18, 1535, following the wishes of his advisers to shift the new capital city from Jauja in the central highlands to the coast. It is said that Pizarro himself drew the plan for his city on the ground with his sword. The decision to choose Lima over Jauja must have been made on a dry, sunny day; had Pizarro known about the fog that shrouds the coast for half the year, he might well have made a different decision.

The original *Lima Cuadrada* (as the old city of Lima is still called today) was subdivided into 117 *manzanas* (blocks) which, shortly thereafter, in 1562, had to be expanded with a new district to the north. At the beginning of the 17th century, Lima already had a population of 20,000 inhabitants, consisting largely of Indian servants, craftsmen, African slaves, and a few hundred family members of the conquistadors. In 1680, the *Limeños* built a massive protective wall around the city, with twelve gates, to pro-

tect themselves from attacks by British pirates. In 1687 and 1746, powerful earthquakes destroyed the majority of the buildings. Subsequently, growth was significantly reduced until the middle of the 19th century. At the same time, new vice-royalties were founded in Bogotá and Buenos Aires, which ended the monopoly that Lima enjoyed in overseas trade with Europe and ending the bountiful sources of money. Thus the days of glory came to an end.

The first railway line to the Pacific port of Callao (today, Peru's largest port) was built in 1851. Parts of the old city wall were taken down and another bridge was built across the Río Rimac. During the War of the Pacific, Lima was plundered by Chilean troops in 1881.

A wide avenue and later even a street-car route, led to the exclusive beach resort of Miraflores, which Lima continually encroached upon and eventually encompassed. The working class settled in the eastern part of Lima, in particular on land belonging to the *hacienda* of the

wealthy Pardo family. Lima acted like a magnet for many of the highlanders. Though the city's population was only 250,000 as recently as the 1920's, the massive migration from the countryside starting in the 1960's caused Lima to grow virtually overnight into a city of millions.

A TOUR OF THE OLD CITY

Plaza Mayor

The **Plaza Mayor** (previously known as Plaza de Armas) is the historic heart of the city and the place with the most significant past. This was where grand processions ended, where the heads of decapitated rebels were exhibited and where those that were sentenced to death by the Inquisition were burnt at the stake.

Colonial buildings that are really worth seeing, such as the cathedral, the Archbishop's Palace, the Presidential Palace, and City Hall are located here. The plaza was dedicated on September 8, 1651 and

49

underwent a major renovation in 1997. Other magnificent historical buildings are just a few minutes' walk from here. A considerable number of the buildings in the old city were constructed in the pompous Spanish Baroque style that has been favored by Peru's various dictators since independence. The three-story bronze fountain, dating from 1650, splashes in the middle of the plaza.

The **Palacio de Gobierno** on the northeastern side of the Plaza Mayor, also known as the Pizarro Palace or Government Palace, is not open to the public. The building, completed in 1938 in the neo-classical style, sits on the foundation of the former Pizarro Palace. Every day (except Sunday), around 11:45 a.m., a spectacle unfolds. The Presidential guard, the Junín Hussar Regiment, goose-steps the changing of the guard in

Above: The Palacio Arzobispal is famous for its balconies with filigree carving. Right: A tiled wall with sensual motif in the Convento de Santo Domingo.

their blue-and-red uniforms and glistening gold helmets.

In a small square near the Government Palace, there is an **equestrian statue** of the conquistador **Francisco Pizarro**. Although he has been shown sitting proudly and steadfastly in the saddle here, Pizarro, the dare-devil, is supposed to have been only a moderately skilful rider.

On the southeastern side of the Plaza Mayor, the **Cathedral**, whose foundation stone was laid by the great Pizzaro himself, towers into the sky. The original church building was soon found to be too small, and the decision was made to expand the cathedral. The work started in 1564 but, soon after its consecration in the year 1625, an earthquake caused so much damage that it had to be completely rebuilt. The interior of the imposing Renaissance structure, renovated in 1996, is alive with color. The choir-stalls, carved by the Spanish sculptor Pedro Noguera around 1623, are considered among the finest in the world. The high altar appears to be almost completely covered with silver decoration, the many side altars are not too far behind. To the right of the entrance, moving toward the first side chapel, one can marvel through a window at the wooden coffin of Pizzaro, which was only discovered during excavations in 1977. Some parts of the chapel walls are decorated with mosaic work depicting the coat of arms of the city of Lima and of Pizarro. To the left of the high altar is the entrance to the Museo de Arte Religioso.

The special features of the **Palacio Arzobispal** (Archbishop's Palace), which is to the left of the cathedral, are its wide balconies with filigree carving. The upper classes of Lima used to invest considerable amounts in such balconies. The Archbishop's Palace was constructed in the High Baroque style.

The **Municipalidad de Lima** is located opposite the cathedral. After the original City Hall burnt down, it was reconstructed in 1944 in the neo-colonial

style. The building is worth seeing because of its beautiful wooden balconies and for its art gallery.

Next to the City Hall, politicians and businessmen meet in the rooms of the **Club de la Unión**. The elegant colonial façade of this noble and tradition-rich clubhouse completes the picture of the Plaza Mayor in great style.

West of Plaza Mayor

Right next to the Pizarro monument is the main post office (*serpost*). In the stylish neo-classical arcades, one can find postcards of all of Peru. There is a special counter for collector postage stamps as well as the small **Museo Filatélico,** with an interesting exhibition dealing with the messaging system of the Incas. On Sunday mornings, there is a brisk trade in stamps here.

The black market or "Polvos Azules" used to be located behind the main post office. Since Mayor Alberto Andrade had the itinerant street-vendors driven out, they now meet in the fourth block of the Paseo de la República, 1.5 kilometers farther to the east. The **Alameda Chabuca Granda** has now been set up in place of the former black market. Here, on weekends, the *Limeños* enjoy their most popular performers of the *Música Criolla* in open-air concerts.

One block down the street between the Pizarro monument and City Hall (Jr. Conde de Superunda), one comes to the **Convento de Santo Domingo**. The church, which was consecrated in 1599, only retains a few figures of saints and the magnificent cedar choir stalls from the original interior decorations and furnishings of the church. Everything else fell prey to the classical obsession for renovation of the 19th century. The neighboring monastery, which, in the 17th century, was among the biggest and richest in the city, was founded by the Dominican Father Vicente de Valverde, a confidant of Francisco Pizarro. The first of the three cloisters that has survived is particularly worth seeing. Tiles brought from Seville (1604-1606) and paintings illustrating the life of Saint Dominic decorate the walls. Beginning in the year 1551, the lectures of the first Peruvian university were held in the Baroque chapter room in the cloister. At the passage to the second inner courtyard, a staircase leads to the crypt of the three Peruvian saints, Santa Rosa, the dark-skinned St. Martín de Porres and the Blessed Juán Masias.

In the same street (Jr. Conde de Superunda 298) the blue façade of a colonial manor house catches the eye. The interior of the **Casa Oquendo de Osambela** from the late 18th century is impressive because of the elegance of the renovated rooms with their old furniture and the Moorish roofs with recessed paneling. The house is used as an art gallery.

Continuing for two more blocks, one crosses the Avenida Tacna, with its busy traffic, and comes directly to the **Santuario de Santa Rosa**. From the outside, this "holy place" appears to be a pretty but insignificant little church. However this is where one of the most well known saints of the Catholic world, Santa Rosa of Lima (1586-1617), is revered. The chancel that is dedicated to her was constructed on the site of the clay house in which she was born. Santa Rosa always returned here for her daily prayers after she had worked herself to exhaustion on behalf of the city's suffering people. She was the first saint of Latin America to be canonized and is now the patron saint of the New World. In the garden, there is a small lodge built of air-dried clay bricks, and a little well, into which Rosa threw the key to the iron chains that held her penitential robe together. Today, 380 years after her death, many pilgrims still come here every day. They write about their sufferings and desires on a piece of paper, and then throw this into the 19-meter deep well.

Every year, on August 30, the parish celebrates the festival of Santa Rosa with a large procession and a festive church service.

Continuing three blocks south along the Avenida Tacna, one comes to the **Iglesia de las Nazarenas**, which has an interesting tale to tell. At one time, liberated black slaves lived in this district of the city, which was then miserably poor. One of these slaves had painted an image of the crucified Jesus on a clay wall. When the earthquake of 1655 shook the entire city, this picture was the only thing that remained undamaged. Of course, this was understood by the believers as a great miracle. A new church was subsequently built and the picture was placed in it. Magical powers are attributed to this picture to this day. According to another legend, many years ago this portrait was held up against the rising waters of a catastrophic flood – and, naturally the flood waters receded.

Las Nazarenas, thoroughly renovated in the 1950's, is the starting point of what is the most spectacular procession in Lima. From October 1, the *Limeño* believers start to wear violet as a sign of repentance, or at least to wear a violet tie. Then, on October 18, 19, and 28, the painting of the "Lord of the Miracles" (*El Señor de los Milagros*), mounted in a silver frame, is carried through the streets on a carriage that weighs 1000 kilograms. It makes ceremonial stops at hospitals, fire stations, and other public buildings. The prayers and the songs of thousands of believers are accompanied by the heart-rending brass tones of a military band. A picture of the crucifixion of Jesus Christ, said to be a copy of the original wall painting in the Iglesia Las Nazarenas, has been supposedly healing the sick and providing succor to the despairing since 1670. Bitterly poor street traders and shoe-shiners, starving Indian women with their mal-nourished children, and even rich businessmen, powerful politicians, and unscrupulous military men go down reverentially on their knees

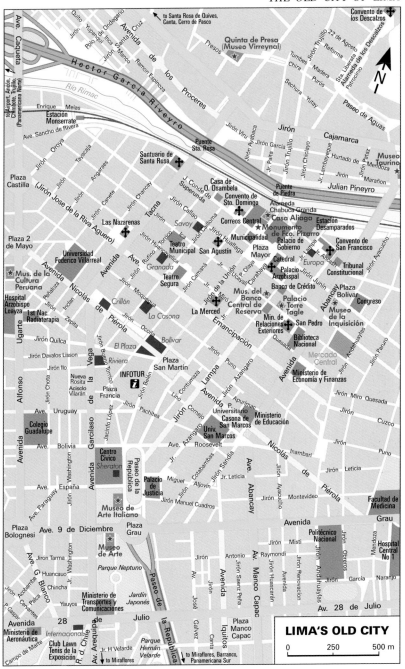

LIMA'S OLD CITY

0   250   500 m

before the *Señor de los Milagros* while the procession is passing, and pray for his help.

The brotherhood of *Hermandad del Señor de los Milagros* leads the procession, which indicates that it has a position of some honor among the Limeños. The *Turrón de Doña Pepa*, a sweet pastry with colorful sugar pearls is baked on the occasion of this festival and it's not only the children who start looking forward to it weeks in advance!

South of Plaza Mayor

Now, it is best to hail one of the many taxis and have it drive one via the Plaza San Martín to the **Parque Universitario**. The tasteful colonial **Casona de San Marcos** on the southern side of the Plaza was originally the center of the oldest

Above: Plaza San Martín. Right: In October the festival of the "Señor de los Milagros" (Lord of the Miracles) is celebrated in Lima-for days on end.

university in South America. It very soon became too small for the many students from the Spanish-Creole upper class. In the park you will notice a clock tower from Germany. At one time, its clockwork would play the Peruvian national anthem every day at noon. Unfortunately, the mechanism was stolen during the Chilean occupation during the 19th century.

The wide Nicolás de Pirola Street leads back to the **Plaza San Martín**. This pretty square is named for the Argentinean general and liberator San Martín, who, in 1821, proclaimed the independence of Peru in Lima. The Spanish sculptor Mariano Benlliure sculpted the central bronze monument, erected in 1921. It depicts the General mounted on a horse and the massive base of this statue has memorial plaques with information on his deeds and battles. Participants in political demonstrations often collect in the Plaza San Martín. In the evenings after work and on weekends, clowns, entertainers, and musicians try to earn some

extra money here, whereas Indian maids and young recruits come here "to try and find a match."

The **Jirón de la Unión**, the most important pedestrian zone in the old city, starts on the opposite side of the square, next to the venerable **Hotel Bolívar**. During the day, this is a very busy street, crowded with leisurely strollers, businessmen in a hurry, moneychangers, and street vendors – that is, those vendors who still dare to do their business here despite the ban imposed in 1996 by the new mayor. Movie theaters, jewelers, bookshops, watchmakers, banks, and boutiques offer their wares or services on both sides of the street.

At the end of the fourth block is the Church of the Order of Mercy, **La Merced**. Its construction was started as early as in 1534, one year before the official founding of the city. It was built exactly where the first missionaries used to hold mass, in what later became Lima. The church was completed in 1639 in the purely Baroque style. It has a monastery

attached to it and is conspicuous on the outside because of its reddish-colored façade. It also has Fayence tiles on the inside walls. The focal point of the church is the statue of the Mother of God of Mercy (*Merced*) with its precious robe. Resplendent above it is the Band of the Grand Marshal of Peru. The Mother of God is the patroness of the army. It is believed that, in the 17th century, she protected Lima from an attack by pirates and, in the 19th century, helped the Peruvian freedom fighters against the Spanish colonial rulers.

If one continues from the La Merced den Jirón de la Unión in the same direction and turns left after the next block into the Jirón Ica, one comes to the **Iglesia de San Agustín**, which is among the most worthwhile sights in the city. The Baroque façade is in the Churrigueresque style and was completed in 1720. Its stylized grapes, leaves, small figures, geometric decorations, and curved niches make it a typical example of the work of the Spanish family of architects, the

Churriguera (17th to 18th century). Their style influenced the art of church-building in Latin America for centuries, even though not a single member of the family ever visited Latin America. The church, built in the 16th century, suffered severe damage during the earthquake of 1687, was restored during the 19th century, and again was damaged by the earthquake in 1970. Art historians consider its façade to be the most impressive in all of Lima. The interior is simple, but the sacristy has a *Mudéjar* ceiling with very detailed working, and the "Assassin" is considered to be one of the most valuable carved Baroque figures in Peru.

From San Agustín, take the same road back to the pedestrian zone, cross it and follow the Jirón Ica, which is now called Ucayali. At the corner of the second crossroad (Lampa), one can see the

Above: The Palacio Torre Tagle, a jewel from the colonial period. Right: Practical souvenirs from Lima – re-usable Easter eggs made of minerals from the Andes.

massive granite structure of the **Museo del Banco Central de Reserva**, the museum of the Central Peruvian Bank. In 1982, the bank set up a museum for pre-Columbian art in its basement. The permanent exhibition displays ceramics, gold figures, and jewelry from Lambayeque, as well as findings from the Inca period. In the upper story, a collection of paintings by Peruvian artists ranges from the 18th to the 20th century up to the present.

One block further is the **Palacio Torre Tagle**, which is justifiably considered to be the colonial jewel of Lima. It was built in 1735 for the *caballero* (knight) José de Tagle y Brancho, who later became the Marquis de Torre Tagle. It is also the birthplace of his son, the second President of the Republic of Peru.

In many ways, the patrician's house with the lion's head symbol is a masterpiece of its time. The yellow ochre walls and the bright white main entrance with its bronze-plated doors alone have a really majestic appearance. The elegance of the sweeping, wide, bay windows, magnificently carved out of dark brown precious woods, is simply without rival. In addition, the balconies had a very practical use: the noble ladies of the upper classes of Lima could follow the activities on the street through the grilles of the balconies, undisturbed and unobserved. Naturally, the carpenters used only the best wood inside and out, including cedar, mahogany, and coca bolo.The inner courtyard is also worth seeing. It is paved in the *Mudéjar* style, and has a fountain. Today, the palace serves as the seat of Peru's Foreign Minister and the diplomatic corps and, unfortunately, is no longer accessible to visitors.

At the next street corner, one can see the **Iglesia de San Pedro**. Built by Jesuits as a cruciform Baroque basilica it later served as the last resting-place of the Viceroy O'Higgins. Consecrated in 1638, it has miraculously survived all the

earthquakes almost undamaged. Even the unusually large vault above the crossing and the small cupolas above the ends of the aisles withstood the earthquakes. Outstanding tile work, gold-plated altars, and valuable paneling with inset oil paintings all make the church a historical treasure-chamber of art. The large wooden balconies on each side of the high altar were reserved exclusively for the use of the viceroy and high religious dignitaries during the services. The Moorish influence is apparent, as is so often the case in the churches in Lima, in the wood carvings. The bell of San Pedro which was given the affectionate name of *La Abuelita* (Little Grandma), rang out to proclaim the beginning of the struggle for independence in the year 1821, a parallel to the Grito de Dolores of Miguel Hidalgo in Mexico.

Numismatists will be sure to want to make an excursion to the **Museo Numismático de Banco Wiese** at Jirón Cusco 245. Here the comprehensive coin collection displays Peruvian money. But no coins are required to visit the museum, as there is no entrance fee.

Those interested in street markets, on the other hand, would be drawn to the **Mercado Central** at the intersection of the Avenida Ucayali and Jirón Ayacucho. The many stands have long since expanded into the side streets, beyond the block originally allocated. The market is full to the point of bursting every day as a result. One may certainly find a bargain here once in a while, but the goods sold there are mainly intended for local households.

If one goes two blocks north on the Jirón Ayacucho, one comes to the green **Plaza Bolívar**, on the right-hand side of which is the monumental **Palace of Congress**.

The dreaded Inquisition courts met in the **Museo de la Inquisición** on the southern side of the Plaza. After the inquisition was abolished in 1813, the building was completely destroyed by survivors, but later rebuilt. Thereafter, it was used first as the Senate building and

57

today as part of the University Library. However, the spine-chilling torture chamber in the basement is likely to be of much more interest to most visitors. Wax figures, whose heads are covered by hoods, lie on the stretching rack, the way the defendants once did, who – whether guilty, having confessed or not – were subsequently flogged, quartered, burnt, or throttled with the Spanish garrote. The museum also serves up reminders of a piece of recent Peruvian history, because it is easy to imagine and very likely that the henchmen of the numerous military dictators were inspired here.

If one follows the wide Avenida Abancay in a northerly direction and turns left into the Jirón Ancash, one will immediately see the yellow Baroque towers of the **Monasterio de San Francisco**. The monastery, built in 1546 by Franciscan

Above: In the library of the Monasterio de San Francisco. Right: Bullfights in the Plaza de Toros de Acho still awaken the passion of the spectators.

monks, is today on the UNESCO world cultural heritage list. The imposing structure, with the two distinctive wooden domes of the monastery church, was only completed in 1674. A large earthquake caused damage in 1970. In this Baroque monastery, one can see Arabian-Andalusian influences on some of the wall decorations. One can gain some insight into the wealth of the order at that times by viewing the: choir stalls (with 132 seats), carved from dark brown cedar, in the gallery of the church; golden monstrance, set with jewels; and several valuable paintings of the Spanish painters Francisco de Zurbarán and José de Ribera, from the middle of the 17th century. The 71 carved panels of Panama cedar, depicting Franciscan saints, are a precious heritage today. In the monastery's cloister, tiles imported from Seville in southern Spain very clearly depict tales from the life of St. Francis.

In the catacombs, which are also worth seeing, the bones of about 70,000 epidemic victims of Lima have found a

resting-place. The bones are carefully arranged on shelves, and sometimes even in geometric patterns. The magnificent, but less well-known library is also worth a visit. It has 25,000 ancient leather-bound books and 6000 parchments from the colonial times of Peru. A guided tour takes one to the catacombs, the library, and the monastery buildings.

The **Casa Pilatus**, opposite the San Francisco monastery, is one of several typical 18th century manor houses scattered throughout the city. These belonged to the Peruvian upper classes and have remained to the present. Peru's constitutional court, the *Tribunal Constitucional*, has its seat in this house with the biblical name.

If one continues down the Jirón Ancash, right after the next block, one comes to the green and white painted façade of the main train station, which is significantly called the **Estación Desamparados**, "Station of the Abandoned." Since passenger traffic via the spectacular Andean route to La Oroya has been stopped, the station serves as a temporary art gallery.

The **Río Rimac**, from which the Spanish conquerors derived the name of the city, Lima, runs parallel to the railway tracks. At the time of the *Conquista*, it provided the best connection and hence the easiest route from the Costa to the Sierra, in the heart of central Peru. The Río Rimac carries large quantities of water from the mountains to the densely populated coast. But even the river has not been equal to the growth of Lima to a city of seven million. In the dry period there is an extreme water shortage, particularly in the poorer residential districts.

The **Puente de Piedra**, the "stone bridge" to the west of the station, was the first bridge over the Río Rimac. Built in 1610 in the Romanesque style, it has a remarkable feature that is not apparent from the outside – the masons apparently mixed the mortar for the bridge with hundreds of thousands of sea bird eggs. This unique mixture is supposed to have made it more durable and it seems to have worked – the bridge has so far withstood all the earthquakes and floods. Two blocks to the north of the river and 500 meters to the east of the bridge is the **Plaza de Toros de Acho**, which has served as the bullfighting arena for several centuries. It is said to be one of the three oldest arenas in the world. On Sunday afternoons, during the October to December season, the stadium is jampacked with passionate spectators, whose cheers for *toro* or *torero* can often be heard outside.

The **Museo Taurino,** which is located here, tells the history of bullfighting (not only in Peru) and displays the skin-tight, richly decorated clothing of the matadors and their weapons, such as rapiers, *capa* (cape), and *banderillas* (skewers with barbs). Numerous historical paintings of bullfights also serve to illustrate this extremely dangerous way of earning a living.

From the bullfighting arena, one can take a short detour to the **Convento de los Descalzos**, situated in the same district of the city (Rimac). This monastery of the "Barefoot Order," which was founded in 1592 and is still inhabited by monks, is located in the eastern part of the Alameda de los Descalzos, a promenade with parks and statues. On a guided tour through the monastery (only available in Spanish), one can see more than 300 valuable religious paintings, a large refectory, the cramped monks' cells, and two richly decorated chapels. The order once ran a school for boys here, and was also intensely engaged in one of the loveliest sidelines in the world: the making and enjoyment of wine. In the 17th century kitchen of the monastery, one can see a variety of equipment that was used in wine making. The small church in the middle of the park, **Santa Liberata**, was

Right: Modern architecture along the Paseo de la República.

built in 1549 and is held to be the oldest in Lima.

Paseo de la República

Two long blocks to the south of the Plaza San Martín, the narrow streets of the old city open out into a spacious park. On the lawns, below the imposing royal palms, there are a few noteworthy statues, among them, an Indian farmer with two oxen harnessed in a yoke. The buildings around the park could hardly contrast more. On one side, there is a modern skyscraper and the concrete tower of the Sheraton Hotel, whereas on the other, there is the sedate classical Palace of Justice (which houses the Supreme Court) and, next to the Sheraton, the **Museo de Arte Italiano**, a dainty building decorated with large mosaic walls in the style of the Italian Renaissance. Cynics say that the museum is more beautiful on the outside than on the inside, but perhaps good intentions are more important than the execution. In 1921, on the 100th anniversary of Peruvian independence, the Italian inhabitants of Lima presented this building, which includes twelve wings hung with paintings by little-known painters of the previous 200 years, to the art-loving public of Peru. A large number of the works of art however are not originals, but rather reproductions.

The traffic circle of the **Plaza Grau**, at which the freeway to the southern parts of the city starts, is the most chaotic traffic intersection in the city. In the center of the Plaza there is a monument dedicated to Miguel Grau, who is honored as a national hero due to his heroic combat in the War of the Pacific.

The **Museo de Arte** is located in a sprawling building in the classical style on the southwest side of the Plaza Grau. The exhibits provide a comprehensive overview of the artistry from the pre-Columbian Indian cultures to the present

day. One of the highlights is the large number of paintings from the famous Cusco School, which, over the course of several centuries, developed a unique painting style in the one-time heart of the Inca realm. More than seven thousand items from the history of Peru, including pottery, gold work, colonial furniture, and pre-Columbian artifacts round out the exhibition.

The magnificent eight-kilometer-long **Avenida Arequipa**, which stretches to the south towards the exclusive suburbs of **San Isidro** (the diplomatic quarter) and **Miraflores**, starts behind the art museum.

Here is a hint for fans of specialty museums – a destination somewhat off the usual tourist routes.

The **Museo de la Cultura Peruana** is located at the edge of the old city, on the Avenida Alfonso Ugarte 650, and is best reached by taxi. The façade, which was inspired by the ruins of Tiahuanaco (on the Bolivian side of Lake Titicaca), promises a little more than the interior

can deliver. However, the ethnological section, dealing with the rich variety of folk art and the excellent handicrafts of Peru, is definitely well worth a visit. Ceramics, carvings, modern art, folkloric art, traditional costumes, and even valuable altar pieces and crosses made in the syncretistic style of the "christianized" Indians from the Ayacucho region, illustrate the old Peruvian cultures. Jewelry and ceremonial objects of the Indian tribes from the Amazon, as well as silverwork and colonial furniture, complete the exhibition.

PUEBLO LIBRE

In the district of Pueblo Libre, in the Plaza Bolívar, is the well-known **Museo Nacional de Antropología y Arqueología**. Innumerable exhibits from all the millennia of Peruvian history provide evidence of how long Peru has been settled. The Museum of Anthropology and Archaeology presents stone reliefs of the Chavín culture, excellent ceramics of the

Mochica and the Chimú, the finest materials from Paracas, the best woven work in all of Latin America, and evidence of professional skull operations, known as trepanation, from pre-Incan times. The famous Raimondi stela, the Tello obelisk, and a large, detailed model of the ancient Incan city of Machu Picchu that fills a whole room, make the visit through the old rooms of the museum a memorable experience.

The **Museo Nacional de Historia** is located in an elegant manor near the National Museum. In what used to be the residence of Generals Simón Bolívar and José de San Martín, late colonial furniture and paintings from the early times of the Republic – symbols of the freedom struggle – serve as a reminder of these troubled times in Peru's history. As well as personal belongings of the heroes of the freedom struggle, there are exhibits of

Above: Mochica pottery (Museo Nacional de Antropología y Arqueología). Right: A holy animal set in gold (Museo de Oro).

transcripts, portraits and uniforms, which bring alive the long and bloody process by which Latin America gained its independence from Spain.

The privately owned **Museo Rafael Larco Herrera** (on the Avenida Bolívar 1515, also in the district of Pueblo Libre) has specialized in the exhibition of pre-Columbian ceramics. The first glance into the large exhibition rooms gives the visitor an idea of what awaits him here: an extremely comprehensive collection of almost 60,000 items. There are marvellous woven fabrics, including a cloth with 157 (!) strands per centimeter, *fardos funerarios* (wrapped mummies), and a treasure chamber of gold jewelry (behind a safe door that is as thick as a man's body), making this one of Peru's most valuable collections. While it is doubtless a very lovingly and expertly organized depiction of pre-Columbian art, the Larco Herrera collection, in common with other museums, sometimes feels – at least in part – rather like a warehouse of exhibits.

A visit to the separate erotic ceramic collection, in a hall on the other side of the courtyard, is particularly entertaining. Here, one can get a very clear picture of some of the sexual practices of the pre-Columbian cultures. However, first impressions may be misleading – while the Mochican culture can be accredited with a certain level of sexual freedom, it also had strict sexual taboos, the breach of which could bring about harsh punishments.

OUTSIDE THE CITY CENTER

During a stay in Lima, it is worth visiting the **Museo de Oro del Peru** in the Avenida Alonso Molina 100, in Monterrico. This world-famous, privately owned gold museum is housed in underground vaults. Its innumerable display cabinets exhibit ceremonial objects, various tools, and jewelry made of gold, silver, precious stones, and feathers. Some of the most beautiful gold objects have, however, been replaced by reproductions. Ponchos decorated with gold paillettes and jewelry combinations of lapis lazuli, emeralds, and pearls illustrate the advanced skills of the early pre-Columbian cultures of Peru.

The collection of weapons on the first floor is said to be one of the best of its kind but, as with the gold exhibits, it is rather over-filled with valuable artifacts. Thousands of ancient firearms, pistols, rapiers, swords, suits of armor, and coats-of-arms conjure up a bloody picture of the battles that have taken place since the arrival of Pizarro in Peru. Articles of clothing of the colonial nobility are also on display on the first floor. The upper floor houses an exhibition of pre-Columbian textiles.

Another museum not to be missed is the **Museo de la Nación** (Av. Javier Prado Oeste 2465, San Borja, in the former headquarters of the Banco de la Nación). It provides an excellent overview

of Peruvian history, including painstakingly detailed models of Machu Picchu and the grave of Sipán.

Anyone planning on trekking in the Amazon jungle, on the Inca trails, or in the Cordillera Blanca, and wishing to familiarize themselves with the animals that inhabit these areas, should visit the **Parque Zoológico Las Leyendas**, to the north of the Avenida de la Marina. The layout of the zoo corresponds to the geographical regions of Peru; here animals of the *costa* (coast), the *sierra* (mountains) and the *selva* (jungle) lead a wretched existence in cages.

En route from the inner city to Miraflores, a worthy stop is at the **Museo de Historia Natural Javier Prado** in the Avenida Arenales 1256. This houses the only museum style collection of animals in Lima worth mentioning. Fauna, flora and natural medicine are presented in the building, which is a part of the Universidad San Marcos.

At the **Mercado Artesanía Indígena** (along the Avenida de la Marina, with ad-

dresses between house numbers 600 and 1000), the focus is on something different: a long line of shops offers a large selection of Indian art and craft work from throughout the country. Here one can find a wide variety of clothing, leather goods, woodcarvings, furniture, musical instruments, etc. There is a broad range of prices and differences in quality too. The market does not only cater for tourists; the local people also enjoy shopping here.

MIRAFLORES

The palm-lined Avenida Arequipa, which leads straight as an arrow southwards from the old city, ends after about six kilometers at the Ovalo, the center of Miraflores, which is gradually developing into the commercial heartland of the country. Banks, travel agencies, depart-

ment stores, gourmet restaurants and fast-food joints, discotheques, street cafés, and most of the good hotels are all concentrated here within walking distance.

Turning left at the Ovalo and left again two blocks later, brings one to the **Mercados de Artesanía** (Av. Petit Thouars). At this market one can purchase anything that the country has to offer in terms of art and craft work, and at far more reasonable prices than in the souvenir shops: hand-embroidered sweaters; warm ponchos; jewelry of all types; artistically decorated gourd bottles; wonderful crooked clay churches from Ayacucho; wall hangings made from alpaca skins; colorful Indian hats, altars fashioned from salt dough; and highly imaginative ceramic figures.

In the **Parque Kennedy**, to the southwest of the Ovalo, local artists sell their paintings, and concerts take place on weekends. All around the park, people young and old, largely from well-to-do families, meet to enjoy an espresso or

Above: The beach at Miraflores, a weekend destination. Right: La Rosa Naútica, built on stilts above the Pacific.

pisco sour at the *Café de la Paz, Café Tigre* or *Café Haiti.*

A few blocks beyond Parque Kennedy, one comes upon a road that winds its way along the steep escarpment high above the coast. To the left, near a bridge that spans a deep gorge, is the small **Parque del Amor**, which owes it name to a sculpture of a kissing couple. From this park there is a magnificent view of the wide curving bay and the ocean, in which, even on cool foggy days, a few undaunted surfers challenge the waves. At the foot of the hill, built on a pier, is the restaurant **La Rosa Náutica**, which is very well known for its excellent seafood dishes.

The beaches at **Barranco** and **Chorillos,** located to the south of Miraflores, are among the most popular bathing resorts of the *Limeños*, who have given this stretch of coastline the colorful name of **Costa Verde**, or "green coast." The coastal road ends at the **Playa La Herradura** and leads through the suburbs of Chorillos and Barranco – Lima's artists' district, back towards the old city. Following the trend set by Miraflores, this area is developing into a second night-life center.

But Miraflores has more to offer than avenues for strolling and beaches for swimming. There are also cultural attractions such as the **Museo Amano** (Calle Retiro 160), which specializes in pre-Columbian artifacts. The founder of the museum, the Japanese engineer, Yoshitarao Amano, ensured that only really special grandiose exhibits are presented here. The Peruvian postal service has depicted several of the exhibits in special-issue stamps. Anyone who is interested in pre-Columbian textiles should not miss the Museo Amano – it has the largest collection of textiles and pottery of the Chancay culture, as well as unique materials from the graves of the Paracas peninsula. Visitors are admitted only if tey make an advance reservation, and only in small groups. There is no entrance fee for the museum, however photography is not allowed.

AROUND LIMA

The **Harbor Town of Callao**, with a population of 700,000, once served as an outpost of Lima against the attacks of pirates like Francis Drake, but has long since been assimilated into the country's capital city. The earthquake and the subsequent devastating tidal wave of 1746 cost 5000 lives but Callao experienced a revival with the guano boom. In 1940, an earthquake again destroyed the city. Apart from the large industrial port, the **Fort Real Felipe**, built in 1774 with massive natural stone blocks, is worth seeing. Defeated Spanish soldiers held out here for an entire year after the end of the War of Independence, before they finally surrendered to the Peruvian troops. The **Museo Militar** narrates the history of the fort and the Peruvian struggle for freedom.

Above: The Museo Amano houses the largest collection of pre-Columbian textiles – weaving work from the Chancay culture.

The small towns of **Chaclacayo** and **Chosica** (30 and 34 kilometers from Lima, respectively) have developed into fine resorts. Winter temperatures here (May to October) at 700 to 850 meters above sea level, are on average 10°C higher than on the foggy coast, and in the summer they are pleasantly cool. The villas of rich *Limeños*, exquisite restaurants and charming picnic spots in green settings, attest to the elegant clientele of these locations, from which one can make pleasant trips to tropical valleys.

For trips out of Lima, the choice is between the Panamericana highway, which transects the city from north to south, and the Carretera Central, which winds its way through narrow, dry valleys and quickly reaches great heights in the mountain region.

About 10 kilometers east of the city center (in the suburb of Ate) a road branches off from the Carretera Central, and one kilometer later, reaches the pre-Columbian **Ruins of Puruchuco**. An adobe building, reconstructed in 1953 and probably once an Inca palace, stands out among the complicated system of passages and streets. The small museum at the entrance exhibits ceramic vessels, stone tools, textiles, local plants, and mounted animals such as *cuys* (guinea pigs) and hairless dogs. The pre-Incan adobe city of **Cajamarquilla** is near the village of Huachipa and was once a settlement of the Cuismancu Empire, which the inhabitants must have had to leave in a terrific hurry. Labyrinthine streets pass through the site, which has some depressions whose significance nobody has yet been able to explain. Three groups of houses, terraces and pyramid bases can still be seen. Other interesting excursions in the vicinity of Lima are to the oracle ruin of **Pachacamac** (31 kilometers south) and the popular beach town of **Pucusana** (70 kilometers due south), which are described in the chapter "The Southern Coastal Region," pages 158 and 161.

LIMA (Area Code 01)
Accommodation

LUXURY: **El Pardo**, Miraflores, Av. Independencia 141, tel: 4442283, fax: 4442171. **Oro Verde**, San Isidro, Av. Santo Toribio 173, tel: 4214400, fax: 4214422, new, quiet, heated pool, room safes. **Gran Hotel Bolívar**, Plaza San Martín, tel: 4287672, fax: 4287674, historical atmosphere, worth visiting just for the décor, centrally located in the old city. **Sheraton**, Paseo de la República 170, tel: 3155000, fax: 3145015, high-rise building from the 1970s, pool, disco, casino, room safes.

MODERATE: **Boulevard**, Miraflores, Av. José Pardo 771, tel: 4446564, fax: 4446602, new, comfortable, small pool. **El Marqués**, Calle Chinchón 461, San Isidro, tel: 4420046, fax: 4420043, between Lima and Miraflores. **Savoy**, Jirón Cailloma 224, tel: 4283520, fax: 4330840. **El Plaza**, Avenida Nicolás de Piérola 850, tel: 4286270, fax: 4235744.

BUDGET: **El Patio**, Miraflores, Av. Diez Canseco 341, tel: 4442107, colonial building with a pretty courtyard. **Hostal Lunar**, Av. Angamos O. 310, Miraflores. **Residencial Inn**, Calle General Borgoño 280, tel: 4471704, friendly service. **Albergue Juvenil**, Miraflores, Casimiro Ulloa 328, tel: 446-5488, good location, near the ocean, for small budgets. **Hostal Barranco**, Malecón Osma 104, Barranco, tel: 4671753, old mansion near the ocean, has a garden and pool. **La Casona**, Calle Moquegua 289, near Plaza Mayor, has a beautiful lobby.

Restaurants

La Mansión, Avenida Nicolás de Piérola 560, tel: 4250952, first-class Peruvian cuisine, esp. dishes from Arequipa. **Astrid y Gaston**, Miraflores, Calle Cantuarias 175, dishes from around the world, elegant atmosphere. **Rinconcito Cajamarquiño**, Rimac, Calle Micaela Villegas, Creole cuisine. **Café Domino**, Galería Bozas/corner of Jirón de la Unión, a charming café in the old city's pedestrian zone. **La Rosa Naútica**, Espigón 4, Costa Verde, tel: 447-0057, built on wooden stilts above the Pacific, excellent fish dishes. **La Ermita**, Barranco, Bajada de los Baños, Peruvian specialties.

Sights / Museums

Cathedral, Plaza Mayor, Mon-Fri 10 am-1pm and 2-5 pm, Sat & Sun 10 am-4 pm. **Museo Nacional de Historia**, Plaza Bolívar, tel: 4632009, Tue-Sun 9 am-5 pm. **Museo de Oro**, Calle Alonso de Molina 1100, tel: 4350791, daily noon -7 pm. **Museo Nacional de Antropología y Arqueología**, Plaza Bolívar, tel: 4635070, Tue-Sun 9 am-6 pm. **Museo de Arte**, Paseo de Colón 125, tel: 4234732, Tue-Sun 10 am-5 pm. **Museo Amano**, Calle Retiro 160, tel: 4412909, Mon-Fri afternoons, by appointment. **Museo Larco Herrera**, Avenida Bolívar 1515, tel: 4611312, Mon-Sat 9 am-6 pm, Sun 9 am-1 pm.

Museo de la Inquisición, Calle Junín 548, Mon-Fri 9 am-7 pm, Sat 9 am-4 pm. **Museo Nacional de la Cultura Peruana**, Av. Alfonso Ugarte 650, tel: 4239932, Mon-Fri 10 am-6 pm, Sat 9 am-12 noon. **Convento de San Francisco,** Plaza San Francisco, tel: 4271381, Mon-Sun 9:30 am-5:45 pm. **Museo de la Nación** (Peruvian history, paintings), Av. Javier Prado d'Este 2465, tel: 4769890, Tue-Sun 9 am-8 pm.

Souvenirs

Handicraft markets flourish in Miraflores (Av. Petit Thouars) and along Av. de la Marina (towards the Aeropuerto). In the Camino Real shopping center in San Isidro, **Alpaca 111** specializes in high quality alpaca-related products, **El Artesano** also has a large selection, Av. Diez Canseco 498, Miraflores. The shop at the **Museo de Oro** has a large selection of traditional, old-style Peruvian jewelry.

Transportation

AIRLINES: **Aero Continente**, Av. José Pardo 651, tel/fax: 2424260. **TANS**, Av. Arequipa 5200, tel: 4457327. All domestic airports have daily connections to/from Jorge Chávez International Airport in Callao (15 km from Plaza Mayor). Take a *micro* or taxi (ca. US \$10-15; incl. registration at taxi stand ca. US \$20) from the airport into the city.

MICROS: Mini-buses for up to 12 people can be rented from **Alejandro Maldonado**, tel: 4450564; **Flores**, tel: 4771518; **Pedro Longa**, tel: 4815639.

COLECTIVOS / BUSES: Buses follow set routes, but the colectivos will stop almost anywhere.

LONG-HAUL BUSES: Lima has no central bus station. Each bus company has a different departure point, which can be found in the phone book's yellow pages under *Transportes Terrestres.* **Ormeño** offers services to all cities in Peru, Terminal Nacional, Av. Carlos Zavala 177, tel: 4275679. **Roggero**, Av. Bausate y Mesa 1050, La Victoria, tel: 4276271. **Cruz del Sur**, mostly southern routes, Jirón Quilca 531, tel: 4277366.

TRAINS: In 1999 trains were still not running along the famous *Ferrocarril Central* line, from the Desamparados station in Lima to Huancayo in the mountains. Only on Sundays (in summer) trains do travel 70 kilometers to San Bartolomé; depart 8:30 am, return 4 pm.

RENTAL CARS: **Avis**, Hotel Sheraton, tel: 4335959, and at the airport, tel: 4524774. **Budget**, Calle Canaval y Moreya 514, San Isidro, tel: 44-11129. **Hertz**, Calle Arístides Aljovin 472, tel: 4444441, and at the airport.

Tourist Information

Infotour, Pas. Pancho Fierro 131 (behind the city hall), tel: 4390117. **24-Hour-Hotline** for assistance tel: 42247888. **Tourist Police**, Javier Prado d'Este 2465, in Museo de la Nación, tel: 4769896.

CENTRAL HIGHLANDS

FROM LA OROYA TO
TINGO MARÍA
FROM TARMA TO OCOPA
HUANCAYO
HUANCAVELICA
AYACUCHO

Just a few large cities, like Huancayo and Ayacucho, but rather more small towns and villages, pretty old inner cities, churches and monasteries with colonial charm and the highest lake in America – that is what characterizes the central highlands of Peru. As compared to Lima, Cusco, Machu Picchu or Arequipa, foreign tourists visit the central highlands only very rarely. The region is poor and underdeveloped; a single railway line, bad roads and only a few isolated airports are evidence of an inadequate infrastructure. The *Sendero Luminoso* also repeatedly tried to draw attention to this situation, but by using very violent means, which was often to the disadvantage of the local people.

Since the leader of the terror group, the former professor of mathematics and philosophy Abimael Guzmán, was arrested in 1992 things have quietened down. People have become optimistic, and feel that there is a future again after the end of the massacres of the *Sendero* and the bloody reprisals of the police and the military, which often affected innocent campesinos. If you are prepared to rough it for a night, without the usual

Previous Pages: Village near Tingo María. Left: "El Nazareno," a painted wooden figure in the Santo Domingo church, Ayacucho.

comforts, you can see what the "real" Peru is like in the central highlands.

FROM LA OROYA TO
TINGO MARÍA

Until it was attacked in 1991 by terrorists, a passenger train used to travel from Lima through the highest train pass in the world (4843 meters, near Ticlio) towards Huancayo and after hundreds of curves, numerous tunnels and bridges, it reached the first large intermediate station, **La Oroya**, an industrial city, surrounded by desert. If you travel this route today, you have to cover 190 kilometers of road and the Anticona Pass (4850 meters). Near La Oroya, the Río Yauli and the Río Mantaro unite at a height of 3750 meters above sea level. The majority of the population of about 40,000 works in the state-owned Centromín Mines and Furnaces, which smelt lead and copper here. Smoking copper furnaces symbolize the not very picturesque countenance of the town. One feature that seems a little out of place is a golf course, the highest in the world, an inheritance of the Americans who independently ran the mines and smelting works for a long time.

A sometimes bumpy and winding road leads north to the picturesque little town of **Junín**. Here, General Sucre, fighting

71

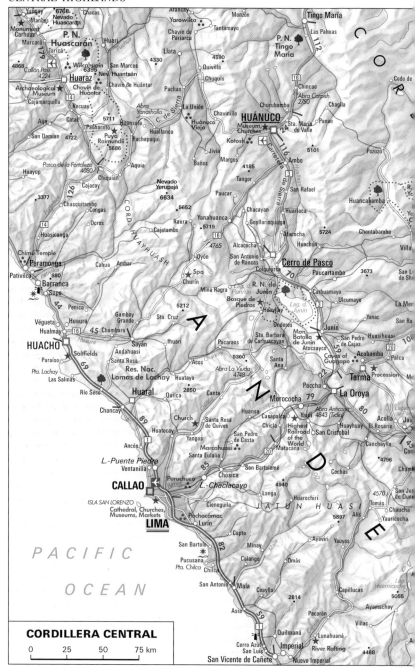

CORDILLERA CENTRAL

0   25   50   75 km

on behalf of the Venezuelan freedom fighter Simón Bolívar in 1824, defeated the Peruvian royalists and the Spaniards on the Pampa de Junín. A simple obelisk provides a reminder of this historic battle.

Nearby is the lake, **Lago de Junín**, which, with an area of about 300 square kilometers, is Peru's second-largest lake, after Lake Titicaca and is located about 200 meters higher than the latter. It is a paradise for flamingos, Andes geese, common herons, ibises, toads, frogs and other water-loving animals and plants. However, it is as yet rather underdeveloped with regard to tourism.

To the north of the Lago de Junin, a short turn-off (nine kilometers) runs through the rather unattractive mining city of **Cerro de Pasco**. The capital of the Departamento Pasco, home to 35,000 inhabitants, is distinguished, in the most depressing sense of the word, by the smelting of lead, zinc and copper. The smoke from the chimney-stacks has practically destroyed the surrounding natural environment. The nights at an altitude of 4350 meters are bitterly cold, and there is nothing worth seeing.

One hundred kilometers north of Cerro de Pasco, on the upper course of the Río Huallaga, and at a moderate height of 1850 meters, is the peaceful Andean town of **Huánuco** with its colonial churches of San Francisco and San Cristóbal which can be seen from far and wide. The 95,000 inhabitants of Huánucos make their living from the cultivation of sugarcane and the manufacture of rum. Also worth a visit in the capital of the *departamento* (administrative district) of Huánuco is the **Museo de Ciencias** in the Avenida General Prado 495. A lovingly organized natural history collection provides information about the geology, topography, fauna and flora in the region. The exhibits have all been described in several languages with particular care – which is unfortunately all too rare in Peru.

Just five kilometers from Huánuco, near the road to La Unión, Japanese archaeologists uncovered in 1963 remains of one of the earliest Andes cultures in Peru: the **Templo de Kotosh**. The people of this culture had developed sophisticated social structures, and made some of the earliest ceramics in the Andes. Since the completion of the excavation work, the remains of the temple have become more and more overgrown, so that it is only a question of time until it vanishes again. For better security and conservation, scientists have moved a stone plate discovered here, which is probably between 3000 and 2500 years old, to the archeological museum in Lima. The plate shows two crossed human forearms, formed out of clay.

Westwards, after another 140 very winding kilometers, you reach **La Unión**, whose main attraction are the ruins of the

Above: Railway bridge on the La Oroya route. Right: The La Oroya region lives from copper – the mines in Morococha.

Inca town of **Huánuco Viejo**. A badly built road leads 11 kilometers to a high plateau with temples that are more than 500 years old, fortifications, living quarters for administration officials, storage rooms and the remains of a narrow Inca road. From La Unión, 3250 meters high, it is about 40 kilometers, as the crow flies, from the well-known ruins Chavín de Huántar, along a bumpy road to the Cordillera Blanca – the Direttissima of mountaineers.

The city of **Tingo María**, with a population of 30,000, is 136 kilometers north of Huánuco, on the eastern slopes of the Andes at a height of just 650 meters. The town is thus civilization's border to the Amazon lowlands. The climate here is always very hot and humid. For many decades now, Tingo María has been the trans-shipment center for coca leaves and marijuana, as also for coffee, corn, bananas and sugar cane, and was avoided by tourists for a long time because of the activities of the *Sendero Luminoso*. Apart from a university, a zoo and a botanical garden, the city does not have any other places worth visiting.

FROM TARMA TO OCOPA

About 60 kilometers to the east of the railway junction of La Oroya is **Tarma**. Its approximately 60,000 inhabitants live, at a height of 3000 meters, mainly from the agricultural harvests of the fertile valley soil. Tarma, named after the original inhabitants of this region, the Tarama, does have an Inca tradition and was founded afresh by the Spaniards as early as around 1540, as a frontier post in the central Andes, but none of the colonial buildings have been preserved.

Many modern buildings have been constructed in the last few years, not always adding to the beauty of the town's appearance. The religious celebrations during the Holy Week and the big Good Friday procession over carpets of flowers

around the new cathedral of Santa Ana in the Plaza de Armas attract most visitors to Tarma.

From Tarma, it is worth making a short excursion to the village of **Acobamba**, eight kilometers away. A kilometer and a half outside Acobamba, you can visit the shrine of **El Señor de Muruhuay**, a depiction of Christ painted on the rocks in the early 19th century. In 1972, the faithful built a small chapel with a bell tower, which calls the Christians in the vicinity to church services and processions, especially during the month of May.

From Tarma, a well-paved road leads southwards to **Jauja**, which was the first capital of Peru till Pizarro shifted the capital of the Viceroyalty in 1535 for strategic reasons to the Pacific, to Lima. If the statistics are to be believed, Jauja enjoys the maximum number of hours of sunshine of all the Peruvian highland cities and has a magnificent cathedral with an amazing 15 side altars. Many of the occupants of the local tuberculosis sanatorium have prayed to get cured here.

At a height of 3250 meters, the road to Huancayo goes through the town of **Concepción**, which is known for its colorful Sunday market and the subsequent bullfights in the Arena de Toros. Five kilometers to the northwest, in **Ocopa**, is the **Convento de Santa Rosa de Ocopa**, a monastery built in 1724 by Franciscan monks. Here preachers were trained for missionary work in the primeval forest. The well-preserved library of the monastery with thousands of dusty volumes, numerous valuable, religious paintings of the famous Cusco school, and a small collection of mounted animals from the nearby primeval forest make this excursion from the main route worthwhile. If you don't mind somewhat unconventional lodgings, you can use the simple guest rooms in the former monks' cells and the good restaurant in the monastery.

HUANCAYO

The 400,000 inhabitants of the university city of **Huancayo**, which is also the

75

capital city of the Departamento Junín, make their living mainly from agriculture. Almost half of the Peruvian crop of wheat is cultivated in the 3250 meter-high region in the beautiful valley of the Río Mantaro.

The city of Huancayo, founded as early as 1572, is an ideal destination for fans of Peruvian handicrafts. A large selection and good prices are a characteristic of the Sunday **Mercado** (market) for woolen articles in the Avenida Huancavelica. The best time for strolling through the market is immediately after sunrise, until around 10 a.m. In the pale morning light, Indian women, warmly clad in several layers of blouses, jackets, skirts and shawls sell engraved calabashes, silver jewelry made in old Peruvian designs, alpaca and llama pullover, wall carpets, woolen blankets and woolen ponchos.

Above and Right: The calabash engravers of the Huancayo region are known for their artistic skills.

Being the seat of an archbishop, Huancayo is also a religious center. Numerous religious festivals are the highlights of the otherwise very hard daily life, of the inhabitants of the city: colorful events on Epiphany (January 6), a big procession on Good Friday and several days on the occasion of the Fiesta de San Juan on June 24, provide some variety in the routine of the year. The most important festivity in Huancayo is the week-long *Fiesta de La Virgen de Cocharcas* (Festival of the Holy Virgin of Cocharcas), which begins on September 8.

HUANCAVELICA

Just 150 kilometers further to the south of Huancayo, after numerous curves and potholes, you come to the next large settlement in the central highlands: **Huancavelica**, the capital of the departamento of the same name. The name of the town is a Spanish word play on a Quechua word meaning something like "stone idol." Huancavelica is located at 3680

meters and in the last few decades, has grown from a small, sleepy mountain town into one with a population of 40,000.

Founded in 1572 by Spanish prospectors, who were sent by the Spanish viceroy to look for silver and the mercury that was required for the smelting of silver from Potosí, the mines of the region still employ many miners in the silver and copper galleries. Through the centuries, the inhuman working conditions that existed earlier in the mines have improved considerably. Only a few whites or mestizos live in and around Huancavelica, the inhabitants are almost exclusively Quechua Indians who cultivate wheat and potatoes, and sell leather and alpaca products in the nearby markets.

Huancavelica is pleasantly tranquil and has charm. The nearby mountains are an inviting prospect for trekking and walking, e.g., to the summit of the **Cerro de Santa Barbara**, from where you have a lovely view of the harmonious cityscape of Huancavelica. The Río Ichu (usually called the Río Huancavelica by the locals) divides the city in two. To the south are the **Plaza de Armas**, the historical town hall or **Municipalidad** and eight rather badly maintained colonial churches. **La Catedral**, the cathedral from 1633 in the Plaza de Armas, has a finely worked altar from the Spanish colonial era; the **Iglesia San Francisco** from the year 1774 (three blocks to the west of the Plaza) can proudly claim to have as many as eleven altars from the colonial period.

North of the river, in the district of San Cristóbal, there are hot springs – the **Baños Termales** has hot showers and a very warm swimming pool. They are accessible to the public for a small entrance fee.

The daily **Mercado** for agricultural and handcrafted products has its colorful zenith on Sundays. On that day, many of the older men wear black and brightly coloured pompoms on their caps, hips and knees. They also decorate the animals that they sell in the market with vivid red woolen tassels. The red woolen

balls, are a particularly photogenic spot of color, contrasting with the snow-white llamas and alpacas, and symbolize the oneness of the animals and their owners with *Pachamama*, or "Mother Earth."

The old narrow-gauge railway from Huancavelica to Huancayo, which had been finished in the 1920s, and had been closed down some decades ago (to the regret of not only the tourists, but also of the locals), may possibly become operational again in the coming years by means of privatization. This would be a huge step forward in the attempts to renew tourism in this region – which is so little known, but which has extraordinary natural beauty.

AYACUCHO

The southernmost point of the central highlands is marked by the venerable and

Above: Farmers' market on a hill near Ayacucho. Right: Heavily loaded trucks on the gravel roads of the highlands.

historic city of **Ayacucho**. The capital of the Departamento of Ayacucho, founded by the Spaniards in 1539 lies at 2700 meters and is home to 100,000 inhabitants. Ayacucho has one of the oldest universities in Peru (founded in 1677, but closed from 1886 to 1958) and is one of the colonial cities in the Peruvian highlands that is most worth visiting. Many of the 33 mostly colonial churches in Ayacucho are still open to worshippers and tourists during mass; others are not accessible because of their badly dilapidated state. Ayacucho is also considered the "birthplace" of the Maoist terrorist group *Sendero Luminoso* in the 1980s, – an attribute of which only a few of its inhabitants are proud. After all, more than 5000 Ayacuchanos were murdered during the course of the violence. Since the end of the Sendero terror (1992), this attractive Andes town has ambitions to become the second most important tourist metropolis in Peru – after Cusco.

The heart of Ayacucho is the **Plaza de Armas**. Because of the tall equestrian

statue of General Antonio José de Sucre towering over the square, the locals also call it the *Parque Sucre*. It is flanked by the cathedral, the Palacio de Gobierno (the Government Palace), the Municipalidad (town hall) and the Prefectura (district administration).

The **Prefectura**, in which the administrative offices of the Departamento are located, was built in the middle of the 18th century and almost exactly 200 years later, was sold by its private owner to the state. Another example of the magnificent colonial buildings in Ayacucho is the **Municipalidad**, particularly because of its halls with stucco work and antique furniture.

In the 17th century **cathedral,** the **Museo de Arte Religioso** presents religious paintings, figures of saints, monstrances, incense bowls and the liturgical vestments of the priests. From the outside, the appearance of the cathedral is very simple, but inside there are nine magnificent altars, several of which are plated with fine gold leaf, testifying to the former wealth of the Catholic church in Peru.

The churches near the Plaza de Armas **La Compañía de Jesús, Santo Domingo** (erstwhile location of the Spanish Inquisition), **San Francisco de Asís** (in the Avenida 9 de Diciembre), **Santa Teresa** (with valuable paintings of the Cusco school), **San Cristóbal** (the oldest church in the city) and **Santa Clara** were all built at a time when an extreme variant of the European Rococo – the art of the Spanish master builder family (especially José-Benito Churriguera, 1665-1725) – was popular. In its pure form, the Churrigueresque style is characterised by churches filled with opulent art work of every kind. Every wall, every ceiling, every façade is covered with decoration, figures of saints, religious symbols or paintings. Even the gleaming gold altars and the finely-carved pulpits, benches and confessionals are integrated into this total composition. Observers can hardly see even a square meter of free, undecorated wall.

Outside the city center, one kilometer to the north of the Plaza de Armas, along the Avenida Assemblea (which later becomes the Avenida Independencia), is the **Centro Cultural Simón Bolívar**, a generous present from Venezuela to the city of Ayacucho (the "Liberator of Latin America" grew up in Caracas).

One part of this building houses the **Museo Histórico Regional** with numerous artifacts of the Huari-culture. The Huaris buried their noblemen lavishly in graves in the vicinity of Ayacucho, for example there is one site along the road to Quinua. The exhibits – mostly ceramic urns and stone figures – largely date from the first millenium AD.

The processions around Easter time are particularly important in the life of the very poor inhabitants of the city, of whom only one-third can read and write and who, because of the miserable living

Above: In Quinua the ridges of roofs are decorated with small clay churches, which you can also buy in Ayacucho as souvenirs.

conditions, seldom live past the age of 50. This is also the only time of year at which the number of Peruvian and foreign tourists staying in Ayacucho is worth mentioning. The **Semana Santa**, Holy Week, begins with a large procession on Palm Sunday. Most of the participants and spectators then experience the *Procesión del Encuentro* on the Wednesday evening of Holy Week. In this "Procession of the Encounter," thousands of believers, among them numerous indígenas from the surrounding countryside, walk in procession, with flaming torches and sacrificial candles in their hands, through Ayacucho and thus symbolically reenact Jesus' journey from the court of Pilate to Golgatha. With stirring music from the local brass bands and the deafening noise of numerous *cohetes* (fireworks), the faithful carry large wooden figures of Jesus, Mary, John, Veronica, Judas, Peter and various other saints.

But the Semana Santa has more than just processions to offer: traditional dance evenings, art exhibitions and handicraft markets with the pretty clay churches from nearby Quinua, engraved pumpkins, *retablos* (three-dimensional miniatures of scenes of daily life), wall hangings and silver jewelry. The Latin American zest for life finds expression in the townspeoples' love of concerts and parades, in their fascination for horse racing, in their cooking competitions and during the annual agricultural fair.

About 30 kilometers to the north of Ayacuchos, a monumental statue, which can be climbed on the inside, in the **Pampa de Quinua** serves as a reminder of the battle of December 9, 1824, when 6000 soldiers of the Bolivian General Sucre defeated the army of the Royalists – which had 3000 more soldiers – and thus achieved Peru's independence from the Spaniards. A small historical museum in the nearby village of Quinua illustrates the other circumstances around the battle, with the help of old pictures, weapons and flags.

From Ayacucho, you can follow a route that is breathtaking in places, leading via Andahuaylas and Abancay over mountain roads at dizzy heights and through very steep valleys into what was once the heart of the Inca Empire: the city of Cusco. A visit to Cusco and its surroundings would be an ideal continuation of your travels through the Central Peruvian Highlands.

Some tourists miss the usual comforts while traveling in the central highlands of Peru. The development of accommodation and restaurants, in fact, of the entire tourist infrastructure, remained stagnant for more than 15 years, beginning from 1980, with the start of the terrorism by the Sendero Luminoso group. Tourist facilities cannot satisfy high expectations. On the contrary: at present, getting to know the authentic Central Peruvian Highlands requires a large portion of pioneering spirit and endurance. Nonetheless: things are looking up.

HUANCAYO (Area Code 064)
Arrival

Several times a day by bus from Lima via La Oroya and Jauja with the company Ormeño from the Terminal Nacional at Av. Carlos Zavala 177. The train from Lima via La Oroya has been discontinued.

Accommodation

MODERATE: **Hostal América**, C. Trujillo 358, tel. 242005, modern, quiet, at the edge of town. **Presidente**, C. Real 1138, tel. 231736, good service, well maintained, no restaurant. *BUDGET:* **Hostal El Sol**, Calle Mantaro 888, Tarapaoá, tel. 224010. **Hospedaje Suizo**, C. Huancas 473, family-run pension, great service, clean.

Restaurants

Olímpico, Av. Giráldez 199, Peruvian cuisine, local specialties of the Ayacucho region, highly recommended. **Martín Fierro**, C. Ayacucho 165, tel. 671366, delicious meat dishes.

HUANCAVELICA (Area Code 064)
Accommodation

MODERATE: **Presidente**, Plaza de Armas, Calle Manco Capac, tel. 952760, in a lovely colonial building. *BUDGET:* **Mercurio**, Av. de Angulu, Calle Manco Capac, hot water, bath tubs. **Tahuantinsuyo**, Av. Muñoz, C. Baranca, tel. 952968, hot water, well equipped.

Restaurants

Restaurant Hotel Mercurio, Plaza de Armas, internationa cuisine, acceptable standard **Restaurant La Japonesita**, Calle Baranca, Japanese dishes, good fish from all the rivers and lakes of the mountains, above all *trucha* (trout). **Hotel-Restaurant Presidente**, international cuisine.

AYACUCHO (Area Code 064)
Arrival

Daily by bus from Lima via Pisco and from Cusco via Andahuaylas; by air from Cusco and from Lima (not daily).

Accommodation

MODERATE: **Hotel Plaza**, Avenida 9 de Diciembre 184, tel. 912202/03, fax 912314, north of Plaza de Armas, beautiful colonial building, noisy. *BUDGET:* **Hotel Samary**, Jr. Callao 335, tel. 912442, two blocks west of the church Iglesia San Francisco, pleasant atmosphere, central location. **Hotel Colmena**, Calle 140, tel. 912146, well equipped, delightful patio.

Restaurants

Restaurant Los Portales, Plaza de Armas, both light and large dishes; dine with a view of the bustling Plaza, chicken, beefsteaks, spicy soups. **Restaurant Urpicha**, Jr. Loudres 272, tel. 913905, good regional cuisine.

CUSCO AND THE SACRED VALLEY OF THE INCAS

CUSCO
AROUND CUSCO
THE SACRED VALLEY
OF THE INCAS
THE INCA TRAIL
MACHU PICCHU

CUSCO

Cusco, at the lofty height of 3330 meters above sea level, was for 300 years the "Navel of the World" for the Incas. This was the center of the 1.7 million square kilometer "Land of the Four Quarters," known as Tahuantinsuyo and it was here that the most important temples and palaces were built. Today visitors from all over the world are fascinated by the magnificent colonial buildings as well as by the remains of the breathtakingly skilful Incan architecture. It is therefore no wonder that Cusco is the undisputed tourist center of Peru. Because of its magnificent church architecture this Andean city is rightly known as the "Rome of Latin America.".

If you walk up from the Plaza de Armas to the ruins of Sacsayhuamán and look down on Cusco, the city looks like a red-brown sea of roofs in the wide valley basin. The few modern buildings have so far not destroyed this extremely homogenous effect. Although few people can be seen in the main square or in the narrow streets in the evenings – even during the warm summer months – Cusco,

Previous Pages: Machu Picchu towers like an eagle's eyrie over the Urubamba Gorge. Left: A young woman from Ollantaytambo.

with a population of 300,000 is very lively place during the daytime. There are many markets, plenty of small shops, a bustling train station, a busy airport, and countless sights worth seeing. The *Cuzqueños*, mostly Quechua Indians and *mestizos*, have had to endure numerous destructive earthquakes in the long history of the city, but the will of the people to reconstruct their city was always stronger.

Different small tribes, often numbering only a few hundred members, used to live in the valley of Cusco, even in the years before Christ. According to legend, the Inca, Manco Capac founded the city around AD 1200 as the capital of his empire. He named it Cusco (*Q'osq'o* or *Qusco* in Quechua) the "Navel of the World," because it represented the intersection of both the main axes of the Inca empire. Cusco, however, could also mean "stone of conquest."

Perhaps Manco Capac had the shape of a puma in mind while designing the city – Sacsayhuamán forming the head, Cusco the body and the Huatanay River the tail of the big cat. Since the time of the Incas, the city has had two distinctly separated parts: the upper and the lower city. The Incan nobility lived in the north and workers, servants, farmers and migrants lived in the lower city to the south. Cusco

85

was given a totally new face in the middle of the 15th century. The Inca, Pachacutec Yupanqui (1438-1471), who was responsible for the immense expansion of the Inca Empire, completely razed the city after he successfully repulsed the siege of Cusco by the militant Chanca Indians. It was rebuilt, using 50,000 slaves, to symbolize the strength of the Incas, at the center of the new Inca Empire. Cusco now received an ingenious water-supply system, paved streets and imposing stone houses in place of the old straw huts. The farmers irrigated the fertile valley below the city and planted potatoes, beans, corn and *quinua* – a native cereal.

The Spanish conquerors, led by Francisco Pizzaro, reached Cusco in 1533. They proceeded to plunder the city – which was rich in gold and silver ornamentation – destroying the buildings

Above: At the time of the Incas, Cusco was considered to be the "Navel of the World." Right: Quechua Indians in front of the cathedral (Plaza de Armas).

and banishing or murdering the 15,000 inhabitants.

In 1536, there was a bloody revolt led by Manco Inca. Thousands of Indians laid siege to the city for a month and set it on fire time and again with fire-tipped arrows; a large part of Cusco was consumed by the flames. During reconstruction of the city, the Spaniards left most of the massive Inca foundations as they were and placed smaller blocks of stone from Inca temples and ramparts on them, to form the external walls for various buildings, which they later decorated with artistic façades. Once again, as had been the case during Incan times, this attracted the best craftsmen and artists in Peru to the "Navel of the World" – who created magnificent churches and colonial palaces. The Cusco Style of painting, architecture and sculpture evolved, which soon became renowned throughout South America and Spain.

The new splendor did not last for long however, as over 80 percent of the structures erected by the Spaniards collapsed

like houses of cards in the earthquake of 1650. Unlike the Incas, they had not built earthquake-proof structures. In 1950 another severe earthquake shook the city. Into the 1960's, Cusco remained a quiet, almost sleepy, Andean city. Only the discovery of the nearby Machu Picchu brought vitality and life back to the old alleys.

Plaza de Armas

Before starting a tour of the city, one should buy a *Boleto Turístico General* (BTG). This season ticket, valid for five days, provides access to 16 of the most important sights in and around Cusco, and is available at the OFEC in the Av. Sol 103, as well as other places.

The wide **Plaza de Armas**, the parade square of Cuscos, was called *Huacaypata* (place of moaning) in Incan times. Even then, it formed the center of the city and, from here, four major roads led into the four regions of the Tahuantinsuyo empire. According to Spanish chroniclers,

when the *conquistadors* arrived, the square, surrounded by temples and palaces, was apparently covered by half a meter of earth, which travelers had brought to the "Navel of the World" from all parts of the land as a symbol of their subjugation.

The huge cathedral, with the two churches Triunfo and Jesús María y José, is at the upper edge of the square, diagonally opposite the Iglesia La Compañía. The numerous colonial arcades, parks and small alleys branching off it, give the square charm and a pleasant flair. During the day, the square teems with people – shoeshine boys and Quechua-speaking Indian women and girls, who try to sell lottery tickets, *pulseras* (woolen bracelets), alpaca sweaters, and caps to visitors to the city. The benches in the center of the square provide a peaceful spot from which to observe the colorful comings and goings. Admire too the house-high statue of Christ (near the Temple of Sacsayhuamán), which resembles that on the Corcovado in Rio de

87

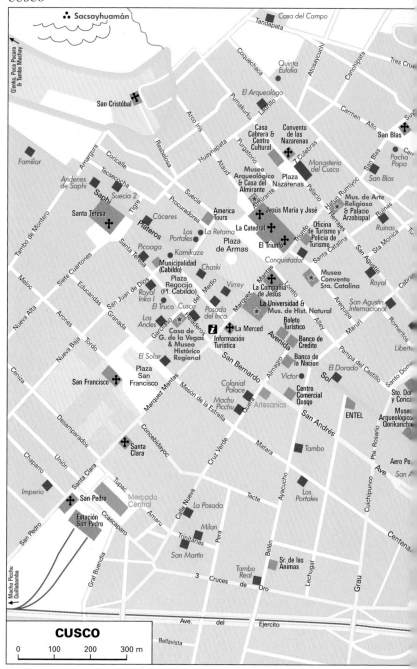

CUSCO

0   100   200   300 m

Janeiro. In the buildings around the square there are cozy cafés, travel agencies, exchange bureaus, and souvenir shops. The Peruvian national flag and the rainbow flag of Tahuantinsuyo, which symbolizes the four regions of the Inca Empire, flutter atop a high flagpole. Both these flags are hoisted every Sunday and for specific festivities such as the Labor Day parade, and before the procession of Corpus Christi.

The **Catedral** (cathedral), which is one of Cusco's most significant attractions, is actually a complex including two other churches. The main portal of the cathedral is only open during mass, so access for tourists to all three buildings is via the **Iglesia El Triunfo** to the right. The **Iglesia de Jesús María y José** – the Church of the Holy Family (1733), is located to the left of the entrance. A major renovation of this church was completed in 1998, so that it is now radiates with renewed splendor.

The **Iglesia El Triunfo** was the first Christian church to be built in Cusco. It was constructed by the Spanish, using hard gray andesite stone, in thanksgiving for and commemoration of their successful defeat of the Indian uprising of 1536. At this place the blazing arrows of the 200,000 attackers under the leadership of Manco Inca struck the roof of an arsenal, but as if by a miracle were extinguished, and the Spaniards gathered there did not come to any harm.

The construction of the cathedral started in 1559, and took over 100 years to complete, entailing a great sacrifice by the local population. Stones from the old Incan palace were broken off, stone blocks were dragged from Sacsayhuamán, and moved down to Cusco, where they were placed on the pre-existing foundations of the Huiracocha temple. The architects decided on a combination of the Spanish Renaissance style and Incan stone masonry, and did not spare any expense.

A bell, named *María Angola* – at six tonnes, the largest on the continent – tolled every six hours from the left of the two 33-meter-high towers and it is said that it could be heard at a distance of 40 kilometers.

There is a burial chamber opposite the entrance containing the remains of the famous Incan historian Garcilaso de la Vega, who was born in Cusco in 1539 as the son of an Inca princess. From here, you enter the main church and then the sacristy. Its high walls are hung with large paintings of the bishops of Cusco. Starting with Padre Vicente de Valverde, who incited Pizzaro to murder Atahualpa, the chronicle includes Manuel de Mollinedo (1673-1699), an important supporter of the Cusco School, right up to the present bishop of the diocese.

Above: Many of Cusco's houses and chur-ches are built on the foundations of ancient Incan buildings. Right: On the Monday of the Holy Week, the "Lord of the Earthquakes" is carried through Cusco in a procession.

The cathedral of Cusco is not merely an enormous church (85 x 45 meters), but also a true treasure of colonial architec-ture and art. Several hundred of paintings adorn the walls, including many from the famous Cusco School. This style com-bines European painting styles of the 16th and 17th century with the imagina-tive style of the Indian artist – Indian faces, symbols or objects often appear in Biblical scenes.

Renowned artists contributed to the historical art treasures of this church. The scene of the crucifixion at the back of the sacristy is a copy, made in Cusco, of a painting by Van Boost, from the school of Rubens. In the front right corner of the cathedral, between the sacristy and the high altar, hangs Marcos Zapatas' giant painting entitled *The Last Supper*, a typi-cal example of the style of the Cusco school. The Apostles, some of them with distinct Indian facial features, surround Jesus Christ, who is not breaking bread, but offering his followers Peruvian *cuy* – or guinea pig.

The neo-classical silver altar is to the left of *The Last Supper*. Church dignitaries had it made, believe it or not, from a whole tonne of silver. From the silver altar, one can look up the steps to the high altar, to the left of which hangs a large painting that has become blackened by the smoke from the countless votive candles lit there. It depicts the huge earthquake of 1650 but, even in the dim light of the cathedral, one can immediately recognize present-day Cusco. A procession carrying a large crucifix is entering the Plaza de Armas, fervently praying for the end of the earthquake. According to legend the earthquake did stop at that moment, thus saving Cusco from total destruction. The Cuzqueños call the crucifix depicted in the painting, originally a gift from Emperor Charles V (also the King of Spain), *El Señor de los Temblores* (the Lord of Earthquakes) and carry it through the streets of the city every year on Easter Monday, as a precaution.

The attention of visitors will also be drawn to the extremely fine carvings on the choir stalls – masterpieces from the 17th century – which are opposite the silver altar. Forty life-size figures of saints are carved on them and small half reliefs of polished, bare-bosomed Indian women in the stalls served generations of priests as hand rests. Extensive renovations are currently under way in the cathedral, and are expected to be ctake until 2005.

In the cathedral one will always find people at prayer, particularly women. They pray in front of the Madonna of the Immaculate Conception, lovingly called *La Linda* (the Beautiful One), to be blessed with many children (or for successful birth control). The cathedral is well worth the visit, but visitors should be sure to respect the worshipers at all times.

To many visitors to Peru, the Jesuit-built church **La Compañía de Jesús**

seems even more magnificent than the cathedral. It is situated on the southwest side of the Plaza de Armas. When the original construction began in 1571, stones from the palace of Inca Huayna Capac, the 11th ruler of the Inca Empire, and possibly even blocks from the Incan school *Amarucancha*, were used for the foundation. When this church collapsed in the earthquake of 1650, the Jesuits began to erect, at that same location, by far the most splendid church in the city. It was intended to surpass even the magnificence of the cathedral. The bishop was, however, far from pleased with this competing church and tried to prevent the construction. The argument was carried to Rome, and Pope Paul III eventually decided in favor of the cathedral. However by the time the Pope's decision reached Cusco, the Jesuit church, with its splendid Baroque façade, was already complete.

The interior of La Compañía is also richly decorated: magnificent paintings, altars carved from the finest cedar, and

91

statues of the saints attest to the wealth of the Jesuits. Nevertheless, the treasures collected here convey only a fraction of the original grandeur, for after the expulsion of the Jesuits from Peru in 1767, a large portion of the church treasures was auctioned off. Two large paintings at the main entrance to the church depict two wedding celebrations of noble Cuzqueños in the early days of the Spanish era in Cusco. The detailed representation provides an excellent impression of the clothing and the festive customs of that time.

To the right of the church is the university, **La Universidad**, founded by the Jesuit order in 1622. In its decorative façade, Indian influences can clearly be seen.

The natural history museum, **Museo de Historia Natural**, which has exhibits of the fauna and natural history of the

Andean highlands, is situated in the university. Beside the entrance to the museum, a narrow staircase leads to the roof. From here there is a marvelous view across the Plaza and a large section of the city.

To the south of the cathedral, at the Calle Arequipa, is the monastery **Convento Santa Catalina**. Until 1533 this was the location of an Incan shrine, which housed 3000 chosen women, who were dedicated to the sun god Inti. **The** *mamaconas* (priestesses) instructed the *acllaconas* (virgins) in prayer, sewing, weaving, and in the preparation of *chicha*, a corn beer required for religious purposes. Today, the beautiful building serves as a museum for colonial and religious art.

Up the hill to the right of the cathedral, one comes to the Calle Hatunrumiyoc, the "Street of the Great Stone." One of the most magnificent colonial constructions in Cusco was erected here on the foundations of the residence of Inca Roca. First aristocratic families lived in

Above: The restored altar of San Antonio de Abad – shining in new brilliance. Right: Llamas strolling through town.

this house and later the Archbishop of cusco Today the Bishop's Residence or or **Palacio Arzobispal** accommodates Cusco's museum of religious art, the **Museo de Arte Religioso**. Furniture, as well as valuable paintings of the Cusco school, can be seen here. A portion of the foundations of the former Inca palace includes a giant twelve-sided rock, weighing a several tonnes, which was fitted into the wall with unbelievable precision, and without the use of mortar.

The church, **Iglesia San Blas,** lies at the heart of the city quarter of **San Blas**, further to the east. This simple adobe church has one of the most beautiful Baroque wood pulpits in the country, supposedly carved by an Indian out of a single piece of cedar. He had survived an epidemic and therefore dedicated his life to the glory of God. According to legend, he had his own skull placed at its top after completing the masterpiece (and after his death). San Blas is also the artists' quarter of Cusco – a stroll through its narrow streets leads past numerous shops selling hand crafted items, galleries and artists' studios.

On the Incan walls on both sides of the **Callejón de Siete Culebras**, the "Alley of the Seven Snakes," these reptiles coil up and down as fine half reliefs. The Incas once trained their warriors at the place where the colonial monastery **Convento de las Nazarenas** is situated today (at the corner of Callejón de Siete Culebras and Calle Pumakurku). The monastery, now housing offices, has a beautiful portal in the Incan-Colonial style. The **Casa Cabrera**, also from the colonial era, diagonally opposite the Plaza Nazarenas, houses the *Centro Cultural*, where various art exhibitions are held.

The beautifully restored monastery of **San Antonio de Abad**, also located in the Plaza Nazarenas, now houses the luxury hotel **Monasterio del Cusco**, which pampers its guests within the historical walls. Apart from magnificent rooms and a fine restaurant, the complex includes a splendid chapel and a well-maintained garden.

93

The **Museo Arqueológico**, with interesting exhibits of the Inca culture and the pre-Incan civilizations, is itself located in a historical building, namely the **Casa del Almirante**, which was built on old Incan foundations. This 17th-century palace with its large inner courtyard was totally renovated after the earthquake of 1950.

The **Iglesia San Cristóbal** church, to the north of the Plaza de Armas, also has a close link to Incan history – built in front of the ruins of the palace attributed to the legendary Manco Capac.

In the historical center of Cusco, yet not directly in the vicinity of the Plaza de Armas, there is further evidence of the city's past. The convent church **Santo Domingo** (south of the Plaza, on a street of the same name) was built on the walls of the wonderful Incan temple **Coricancha**, dedicated to the Sun God Inti. After

Above: The Inca temple Coricancha formed the foundations of Santo Domingo. Right: The Iglesia La Merced is worth a visit.

the conquistadors had plundered and – as far as possible – razed this structure, Juan Pizarro took possession of the temple. The Spaniard bequeathed it to the Dominicans, who immediately began to build a church on the Incan foundations. The church of Santo Domingo collapsed in the earthquake of 1650, was reconstructed, but collapsed again in 1950. This time the earthquake had caused so much damage, that in some places the Incan foundation walls reappeared. It was then decided to excavate the Incan shrine and to preserve the remains. Black and white photographs, displayed at the entrance to the church, show the extent of the destruction of the 1950 earthquake, during which the old Incan foundations and structures unexpectedly came to light.

In its time, the Coricancha temple was decorated with gold, silver, jewels, and precious stones, but today only the bare walls remain – the conquerors having melted down all the precious metal and burnt everything that was heathen.

The Quechua word *coricancha* means "Golden Court" and the whole structure was indeed coated with gold. Some 700 gold plates, each weighing two kilograms, corn cobs of gold and silver, which were ritually planted by the priests during ceremonies, golden altars, llamas, children, and even a golden sun shone in the radiant light of the highlands. Even the temples of the moon, the stars, the weather gods, thunder, and the rainbow as well as the sacrificial hall (*Sala del Sacrificio* or *Masma*) were extensively coated with gold. Figures of gods once stood in the many niches and fine curtains covered the artistically built doorways. The mummies of the Incas were preserved at Coricancha and, covered with rich fabric and heaped with jewelry they were displayed in public processions. The Coricancha temple was also a center for religious ceremonies and served as an observatory for the astrologers of the Incas. One example of the astonishing architecture of the Incas is a round, perfectly designed six-meter-high wall, which has survived all earthquakes unscathed.

The "Golden Court" was completely restored in 1995. During the restoration work, ancient wells, previously unknown, came to light.

A visit to the small **Museo Arqueológico Qorikancha** on the Av. Sol is also worthwhile. It houses exhibits of ceramics, historical photographs, and a model of the whole temple complex.

The **Iglesia La Merced**, to the west of the Plaza de Armas on the Avenida Marquez Mantas, is one of the most beautiful churches in Cusco. It was built in 1654 and has a magnificent main altar and masterfully crafted choir-stall of cedar, which, alone, would make a visit worthwhile. A door to the left of the entrance leads to the monastery and to a small museum. A famous monstrance from the year 1720 can be admired here. It is made of pure gold, is 1.3 meters high, and is studded with 615 pearls and 1518 diamonds. In the large cloister, paintings show scenes from the life of the Spanish

95

founder of the order – San Pedro Nolasco (1189-1258). An underground monk's cell, which a hermit completely covered in frescoes in the 18th century, is presently being restored.

Diagonally opposite the town hall and the Hotel Cusco, on the Plaza del Cabildo, is the house which is the **birthplace of Garcilaso de la Vega**, the first native historian and author of "*Comentarios Reales de los Incas*" (Royal Commentaries of the Incas). The son of a Spanish aristocrat and an Incan princess, de la Vega traveled to Spain at the age of 21 and there, many decades later, related tales, sometimes richly embellished by his own imagination, of the glory of the Inca Empire and the victories of the Spanish conquistadors. His remains rest in an urn in the cathedral of Cusco. The

Above: The "Virgen del Rosario" (Madonna of the Rosary) – a masterpiece from the Cusco school, in the Convento Santa Catalina. Right: A condor, revered by the Incas as holy, watches over Cusco.

birth house of de la Vega today houses the **Museo Histórico Regional**, which provides information about the history of the Cusco region.

The **Iglesia de San Francisco** (in a square of the same name) is a Franciscan church with a monastery, dating from the 17th century. It has (besides its fine choir of cedar) numerous paintings from the colonial period, including of the life of St. Francis of Assissi. On the Plaza in front of the church is the historical coat-of-arms of Cusco, a castle surrounded by eight condors.

Following the Calle Santa Clara from the San Francisco monastery, one comes to the **mercado** (market) opposite the **train station of San Pedro**. It is from the station that the early morning train to Machu Picchu departs. The well-stocked market hall offers a great variety: snack bars, hand crafted items, household goods, vegetables, fruit, fresh bread, and cakes as well as wrist watches and – be careful! – clever pickpockets.

The Cuzqueños are masters of the art of celebration – especially on the most important festive day of the year: **Inti Raymi**. The sun festival was one of the most important festivals of Cusco even before the arrival of the Spaniards. The Incas congregated with their entire court in the large square early on the morning of the day of the winter solstice, to greet the sun and show off their finest and most valuable ornaments.

The Solstice festival continues to be celebrated every year on June 23 and 24. Thousands of *campesinos* from the entire region dress up for this festive occasion and sing and dance in groups, as they move through the streets. The big Inti Raymi play is also performed in Sacsayhuamán at that time. After the end of the official festivities, masses of people throng to the valley of Cusco and celebrate all night long. Cusco begins to burst at the seams two weeks before the beginning of the festival itself.

AROUND CUSCO

Acclimatized trekkers can reach the villages and ruins in the immediate vicinity of Cusco on foot without any problem, but taxis can also be rented. Some of the locations listed below can be visited on the way to the Sacred Valley of the Incas. The sunlight falls most photogenically on the small villages and old Inca walls in the late afternoon, at which time they appear almost mystical in the beautiful mountainous landscape.

Sacsayhuamán

The footpath from Cusco to **Sacsayhuamán** ("Falcon's Nest") begins at the Plaza de las Nazarenas. On the way up, during one of the many absolutely essential pauses for breath, take a good look at the roofs. There, clay bulls and condors symbolize the eternal struggle for supremacy between the cultures of the Spaniards and the Incas; small crucifixes or painted miniature clay churches are sup-

posed to bring luck to the inhabitants. The walk along the old Incan road takes about 45 minutes. When you arive at the top you will be greeted by llamas, whose heads are decorated with red bands in honor of the *Pachamama* or "Earth Mother."

Only a quarter of the original structure of Sacsayhuamán, which the English speaking guides like to pronounce as "sexy woman," remains standing today. The Spaniards broke off smaller stone blocks from the walls to build churches and palaces in Cusco. During this process they also destroyed the head of the puma, whose teeth were formed by 22 zigzag lines. A few archaeologists think that the walls represented a gigantic sundial. The massive walls of Sacsayhuamán are generally interpreted as having been part of a fortress, but it is more probable that the place had some religious significance.

In the fortress, square stone blocks, weighing more than 100 tonnes each, form invincible ramparts. One block, with dimensions of 5 x 5 x 2.5 meters,

**CUSCO AND THE
SACRED VALLEY OF THE INCAS**

0   10   20   30 km

weighs a full 160 tonnes (more than a Boeing 707) and, according to the reports of the chronicler Garcilaso de la Vega, was apparently heaved up the mountain by 20,000 Indians using long ropes. According to estimates by historians, tens of thousands of Indians worked on the construction of the place for seven decades, using only primitive stone tools.

Before the arrival of the Spaniards, there were three towers on the ramparts. The tower named **Muyuc Marca**, whose foundation can still be seen, was an astonishing 22 meters in diameter and was used as a water tank. This was storage for their drinking water, which the Incas, according to de la Vega, brought to Cusco via underground canals. Food for

the thousands of warriors, who were evidently stationed here, was stored in the other structures. Some historians maintain that a labyrinthine system of tunnels led from Sacsayhuamán to the temple of Coricancha in Cusco, three kilometers distant, which the Inca could use to retreat. Three years after the original capture of Cusco, Sacsayhuamán became the staging ground for a siege of the city by a rebel army led by Manco Inca. With a force of just 50 Spanish mounted soldiers, Juan Pizzaro was supposedly able to put several thousand footsoldiers to flight. The bodies of the countless dead attracted swarms of scavenging condors. Condors are depicted on the coat of arms of Cusco as a reminder of this bloody

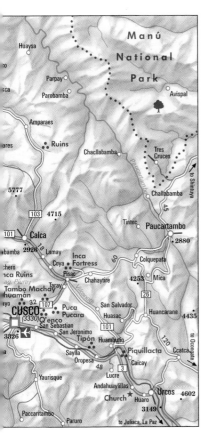

sion, resemble an exposed brain. The site was possibly a place of sacrifice during the Chavin culture. The five-meter high chalk cliff, in which one's imagination may be able to make out the form of a puma, is covered with carved symbols. The dark tunnels, with niches in which the mummies were probably seated during ancestral rituals, give the place a mysterious air. Two 20-centimeter high rock cones could perhaps have served as sighting stones for astrological observations.

Puca Pucara and Tambo Machay

Puca Pucara (the red fortress), located at a height of 3650 meters, and seldom visited, is also on the way to Pisac. It probably served as a strategic checkpoint for the entrance to the Incan capital of Cusco and to the holy springs of **Tambo Machay** (Place of Happiness), which can be reached by a gravel path up the valley some 300 meters from the main road. Tambo Machay is often called **El Baño del Inca** – the bath of the Incas. It was, though, less of a bath and more of a spring, surrounded by carved stone blocks, from which the Incas retrieved their sacred water. Natives consider this water to be the milk of *Pachamama*, the Mother Earth, and swear that whoever drinks from the stream is granted eternal youth, everlasting beauty and everlasting fertility. In the large niches on the upper terraces, Incan nobility waited for the sun to rise, then carried out ritual water ceremonies. Historians surmise that Tambo Machay may also have served as a hunting lodge for the Inca Yupanqui.

Chinchero

Chinchero, the "city of the rainbow," does not lie in the valley of the Incas, but rather at a height of 3760 meters, on the road through the pass from Cusco to Urubamba. Magnificent views of snow-

slaughter. Since 1944, Sacsayhuamán has been the scene of the solstice festival of *Inti Raymi*.

Q'enco

The Q'enco shrine (meaning: winding or snaking) on the road to Pisac, derives its name from the snake-like grooves that were carved into the cliff by Inca stone masons, for sacrificial purposes. Possibly the Inca priests poured *chicha* (corn beer), blood or consecrated water into these grooves. This religious site, located four kilometers above Cusco, with its striking stone formations may also have been used as a kind of open-air theater. The unique rock forms, caused by ero-

covered mountain ranges make this route as delightful as the route via Pisac. The peaks of the mountains Veronica (5750 meters), Chicón (5500 meters) and Salcantay (6271 meters) can be seen especially clearly early in the morning and in the late afternoon. The heavenly view was perhaps the reason many Incas had their summer residence in Chinchero. This Andean village is the oldest and most typical of the region, with its centuries-old houses, historical **church,** and traditionally attired inhabitants. The nearby Inca excavations, with their numerous terraces, are yet another example of the absolutely superb work of the Inca stonemasons – some of the rocks have even been carved into the shapes of chairs and steps. The village square still has a thick Incan wall with ten trapezoidal niches, and the village church, with

Above: Huge blocks of stone, perfectly dovetailed with each other – Sacsayhuamán is a masterpiece of stonemasonry. Right: At the Sunday market in Chinchero.

its beautiful wall paintings, was built on old Inca foundations.

A small **museum** in the church square displays paintings from the Cusco school. The colorful and lively Sunday market of Chinchero is less touristy than the one in Pisac. It takes about three hours to descend along a wonderful hiking trail the church down to Huayllabamba in the Urubamba valley.

Piquillacta and Andahuaylillas

Thirty-two kilometers from Cusco, along the route to Lake Titicaca, and one kilometer to the left off the main road, is the ruined city of **Piquillacta**. This Huari settlement (AD 800-1200), is about 50 hectares in area and is surrounded by massive walls, which were originally 10 meters high. It was presumably used by the Incas as a large store for food, arms and clothing. It is possible that long before the Incas, the city was occupied by Aymara Indians, who were in contact with Tiahuanaco (in present day Bolivia).

Another worthwhile stop is 10 kilometers further along, at **Andahuaylillas**, which lies amidst lush green pastures, grain fields, and eucalyptus forests. The adobe church in the square of this small village, with its matte red roofs, is considered to be the most beautiful in the Andean highlands. If an employee of the adjacent presbytery can be found, who will open the church on request, one is astonished at the stately Baroque interior, with a richly ornamented gold-plated altar, and large paintings in splendid frames. Such richness is scarcely to be expected in this idyllic, rural setting. If you look up, the Moorish-style ceiling, painted in glowing colors is just as much of a surprise as the fine organ, featuring angel figurines, making music on Baroque instruments.

Quillabamba

The bus trip from Cusco to the tropical **Quillabamba** (which used to be the last station on the Machu Picchu railway line) in the jungle to the north of Cusco, requires more than just one day. The 35,000 inhabitants of the city, situated at an altitude of 1000 meters, live mainly by growing and trading fruit and vegetables; papaya, mangoes, bananas, oranges and lemons thrive here, as do coffee, tea, cocoa and coca. Quillabamba has no specific worthy sights – apart from its large **market hall** and the **Plaza de Armas –** which is lined with restaurants, but the city serves as the starting point for trips into the mountains (Huancacalle/Vilcabamba) and the jungle, as well as being the end-point of rafting trips on the Urubamba. The hospitable, mid-range Hotel *Quillabamba*, with a pool and mini zoo, is ideal for relaxation.

THE SACRED VALLEY OF THE INCAS

According to the Spanish chroniclers, the Incas considered the Urubamba Valley between Pisac and Ollantaytambo sacred because it had the best soil in the

101

Empire, an excellent climate, a sufficient water supply, and was situated near the capital city of Cusco.

A visit to this valley is one of the high points of every visit to Peru. In this area, 30 kilometers to the north of Cusco and 600 meters lower in elevation, the valley is wide and fertile but, after Ollantaytambo, it narrows and then tapers to a deep ravine with tropical vegetation. The **Río Urubamba** is actually called the Vilcanota further upstream and the Ucayali downstream. Since the temperatures in the valley are much higher than in Cusco, especially at night, the Incas selected this area as their agricultural center. They sent seeds from the plants they cultivated here to all the other regions of their realm.

There is no shortage of things to see and do in the **Sacred Valley of the Incas** (*Valle Sagrado*). The ruins, situated

Above: The view into the "Sacred Valley of the Incas." Right: In Pisac the old Inca terraces are still used for agriculture.

among the magnificent scenery, small villages, haciendas, colorful Indian markets, and the peach blossom festivals in the early part of the year, can all be seen in the course of a stay of one or two days. This can be combined with treks along the mountain slopes.

In the villages of the valley one can find mid-range hotels and simple, friendly lodgings, often in beautiful locations and offering comfortable rooms.

River rafting on the Río Urubamba, in inflatable boats, is a particularly entertaining and wet manner of seeing the valley. The half-day or full-day tour begins in Huambutio and the price includes the necessary equipment and food. It can be booked at all the major travel agencies.

The boat trip leads past several exciting rapids in which you will undoubtedly receive a few splashes of cool mountain water, and ends at San Salvador. A second route leads from Ollantaytambo to Huaraqpunko. The section between Pisac and Ollantaytambo is not navigable due to a dangerous whirlpool near Huarán.

Pisac

The pretty village of **Pisac** lies 32 kilometers northeast of Cusco in the *Valle Sagrado*, and can be reached over a steep, winding pass. High above the village, are the ruins of an Incan fortress, which are well worth a visit.

It is idyllically peaceful in the village for four days of the week, but on Tuesdays, Thursdays and Sundays the big **mercado** on the Plaza, and in the side streets around it, attracts visitors and traders from near and far. Indian women and *campesinos* offer fruit, onions, leeks, corn, *quinua*, sweet potatoes, tropical fruits, fashion jewelry, leather goods, alpaca sweaters, watercolor paintings, hats, and a lot more.

If one follows the narrow, paved lane leaving the upper right corner of the Plaza and after some 50 meters turns to the left, one comes to a large inner courtyard. The local people run a bakery here and prepare typical specialties of Peru in an old clay oven. The warm onion bread is one of the tastiest delicacies of the region. Countless huts and houses hang a little red flag from their doors on market days, thus signaling that they have freshly made *chicha* (traditional corn beer) for sale.

Every Sunday, after High Mass in the church on the Plaza de Armas, a small, solemn procession moves through the market. At the front are the venerable mayors (*varayoc*) of the surrounding villages, proudly carrying their official insignia – a long cane decorated with silver (*vara*). Dressed in their traditional clothing, they march towards the presbytery, accompanied by their assistants.

While roaming through the market, the beautiful, small restaurants along the sides of the Plaza provide a great opportunity to relax for a while. Subtropical flowers and trees are planted in their inner courtyards, which makes a very inviting setting for a cup of coffee. Salmon trout is a culinary specialty of Pisac, prepared particularly well at the *Samana Wasi* restaurant.

Refreshed, one can then tackle the steep steps leading from the village square to the **Ruins of Pisac**, 400 meters higher up.

The ruins can also be reached by car by the approximately 10 kilometer long and winding road, passing through the Chongo Valley. If possible, one should be dropped at the upper parking lot near Quanchisraqay, and then slowly climb down through the ruins on the, at times, dizzying path. The view of the Sacred Valley of the Incas will leave you breathless! Condors circle high over the Urubamba, and the bustle in the village far village below looks like the activity of an anthill.

The ruins are located on a narrow rock spur, surrounded by numerous agricultural terraces with an ingeniously designed irrigation system. Here too, the stones in the walls of the most important buildings

Above: View from the ruins of Pisac into the Urubamba valley. Right: Women in Pisac wearing typical headgear.

and temples are carefully polished and precisely matched, often with projecting stone studs as leverage points. The houses that are still standing were probably inhabited by servants or astronomer-priests. As at Machu Picchu, the Incan astronomers erected a sun shrine, **Intihuatana**, in Pisac as well. Literally translated, *inti* means sun, *huata* means year and *huatana* means observation, on which the description "Hitching Post of the Sun" is based. In every large center of the Incas, such an Intihuatana formed the heart of the site, with a large **sundial**, temples and palaces. A round pole, carved from the surrounding rock, stands on a semi-circular structure, and served as part of the observatory for measuring the path of the sun or to check the solar calendar.

On the steep wall on the other side of the valley, to the south of the ruins, one can see countless holes in the cliffs. The Incas dug about 2000 graves there, to bury their mummies – making this area one of the largest Inca cemeteries in Peru.

If you look down towards the river, one can see the many terraces that the Incas used for defense and agricultural purposes.

Twenty kilometers farther along the Río Urubamba brings one to Calca – the largest town in the valley – but it is not particularly interesting for tourists. Another 20 kilometers beyond Calca is the long drawn out village of **Yucay** with the most luxurious hotel in the valley, the **Posada del Inca**. The former hacienda has a pretty inner courtyard with a garden, a comfortable restaurant, and even a bar with a fireplace and a piano.

Ollantaytambo

Four kilometers past Yucay, the road to Chinchero and Cusco branches off. Here, at an altitude of 2880 meters, lies the somewhat larger town of **Urubamba**. Five kilometers further west, at Tarabamba, a bridge across the river provides access to the **salt terraces**, which are three kilometers up the hill toward **Maras**. From here, an unpaved road leads to **Moray**, where the Incas created terraced fields in perfectly regular circles, the purpose of which mystifies researchers to this day.

Returning to the Sacred Valley of the Incas: the asphalt road ends 18 kilometers past Urubamba at **Ollantaytambo** (2750 meters). A route for buses and trucks, the railroad, and foot-paths leads further down into the jungle. The small town, situated below the ruins, with its romantic old narrow streets, small shops, and homes selling *chicha*, is divided into rectangular *cancha* or enclosures, each of which is centered on an inner courtyard – all in all, a vivid example of the town planning of the Incas.

Manco Inca retreated to Ollantaytambo after his defeat at Sacsayhuamán. In the year 1536, Hernando Pizarro tried to capture the Inca, with the assistance of 50 mounted soldiers and hundreds of Indian and Spanish foot soldiers. The effort was in vain: stones and arrows rained on

the attackers, and when Manco's men flooded the low ground in front of the fortress with water, they caused the soldiers and horses of the Spaniards serious difficulties. The conquistadors retreated and were pursued by Manco's warriors, as they tried to escape. A little later, the Spaniards attacked again, this time reinforced with troops from Chile, and were more successful. Manco fled, but was eventually massacred by Spanish assassins.

You will require a visitor's ticket (BTG) for the visit to the **Ruins of Ollantaytambo** (see picture on page 18). The Incas used the impressive fortress to defend the Urubamba Valley from the wild jungle tribes towards the north. It was also an Incan shrine, with a temple located on the highest of the many terraces, where the Incas buried the hearts of their princes. The fortress is named after the

Above: A village saloon in Ollantaytambo.
Right: Built with adobe bricks: a farm in the Andes highlands.

famous General *Ollantay*, from the time of Inca Pachacutec Yupanqui; the word *tambo* meaning "station" or "store." The general led most of the very successful campaigns of conquest in the regions of present-day Chile, Argentina, Bolivia, and Ecuador. In gratitude to the general, the Incas offered to fulfill any request. Ollantay asked for the hand of the Inca's daughter, Kusi Qoyllur – who returned his love – but the Incas could not allow this wish to be fulfilled, because of their rigid class society. The two men fought over the matter, and Pachacutec Yupanqui sent the general into exile. Kusi Qoyllur steadfastly refused to marry any other man, and therefore was designated to be the chosen virgin, whose life was dedicated to the Sun God. However, the tragic story does have a happy ending: many years later, after the death of Yupanqui, the couple was finally reunited. The Incas made the dramatic story of General Ollantay into a play, which is still regularly performed on the stages of Cusco and Lima.

If one climbs to the highest point of the ruin, one can see the quarry on the other side of the Río Urubamba from which the huge blocks of rock came. They were transported for a distance of five kilometers from the quarries at Cachicata, over the river Urubamba, to the fortress. A long ramp was used for transporting these blocks, but a few large porphyry blocks never made it to their destination. They lie along the path, near the site of the temple, and were given the name "tired stones." Massive blocks, ingeniously clamped together with metal brackets, can also be seen here.

High above the terraces of Ollantaytambo, beside the **temple**, which is revered by New Age believers as a "place of energy," with its well preserved monolithic walls, one can see the so-called **Inca throne**, a chair-shaped niche chiseled out of the rock. An easy 10-minute walk on a very beautiful path along a steep cliff leads to the Intihuatana (sun stone) and, later, down through terraces back to the village. At the bottom of the valley, is a smooth slanted rock slab, which the children of the village now use as a slide. It probably once served as a run-off surface for prophecies determined using liquids; in this ritual, the direction of flow showed the meaning of the prophecy.

In a garden that is a part of the ruin, opposite the parking lot, is the **Baño de la Ñusta –** the bath of the princess – a block of rock decorated with geometric figures, into which a stream of water splashes.

Pumamarca

Anyone who has a full day for a visit to Ollantaytambo can hike from there to **Pumamarca**, a military outpost of the Ollantay fortress, which was meant to guard two Inca passes over the Cordillera Urubamba. A good trail, starting from the souvenir market place, follows along the river upstream – a trip requiring about four hours. The way leads past a village with small water mills and homes offer-

ing *chicha*, and then enters a narrow gorge. Soon a steep slope appears, which the master builders of the Inca period completely covered with terraces for growing corn, thus turning the landscape into a genuine work of art.

Further upstream the valley widens, allowing for fertile fields, and then divides at a large village. Here the route crosses two bridges to the other bank, and then becomes a narrow trail that climbs steeply towards the east and Pummarca. A few houses and a large section of the defensive wall of the Inca bastion, have been preserved on this site, which also offers marvellous views.

EL CAMINO INCA –
THE INCA TRAIL

For anyone who has become sufficiently acclimatized to the 3000 to 4000

Above: Along the Inca Trail. Right: There are hundreds of different types of orchids around Machu Picchu.

meter elevations, is interested in Incan culture and nature, and likes to hike, the three to five days of trekking on the Inca trail can be an incomparable experience. This route, north of Cusco was used by Incan relay runners at least 500 years ago. One can discover things that could never be seen elsewhere in such variety. For example, one may see different kinds of stone creations of the Incas (house walls, tunnels, stairs), as well as ruins such as Runkuracay, Sayacmarca, Phuyupatamarca, and Huiñay Huayna, which are accessible only on foot. The trail traverses high passes and thundering rivers, and leads through untouched cloud forests and dense jungle. However, the **Camino Inca** tends to be somewhat overrun during the main tourist season, between June and August.

The trek can also be arranged from Lima or Cusco as an organized and guided tour, complete with porters.

It is important to make careful preparations for the trek and to be sure to have the necessary equipment: sturdy hiking-boots, poncho, warm jacket, waterproof trousers, sunscreen and sunglasses, a tent, camping stove, and sufficient provisions. Sterilizing tablets for the water from brooks and rivers are important, as is mosquito repellent, a camera, and the latest detailed map, which can be obtained from the tourist office in Cusco. Good physical condition, lots of energy, and a love of trekking – quite simply "wanderlust" – are other obvious requirements.

The journey to the point of departure at "Kilometer 88," begins early in the morning from the San Pedro train station in Cusco. An alternative is to travel by minibus to the busy train station of Ollantaytambo. From there, it is a half-hour's train ride (three stops) to **Kilometer 88**. A word of caution: not all trains stop there, so make inquiries first, and if possible purchase the tickets a day in advance.

The trail starts by crossing the roaring **Río Urubamba**. Until a few years ago, it was necessary to sit on a small wooden platform and pull oneself over the river along a steel cable. Now, if one is not susceptible to vertigo, one can more comfortably balance across a high suspension bridge, and then climb up a steep mountainside, not very far from the ruins of *Tarapata*, *Machu Qente* and *Huayna Qente*. One can then hike through picturesque eucalyptus forests to the ruins of **Llactapata**, which are surrounded by terraced fields. Soon afterwards, one crosses the **Río Cusichac**a, and follows it upstream to the only village on the Camino Inca: **Huayllabamba** (2270 meters). Camping is possible in the village, or farther uphill.

Now, the Inca trail turns from the Río Cusichaca towards the **Valle Llullucha,** situated to the northwest. It continues farther through moss-covered forests, steeply upwards to the large clearing of **Llullucha Pampa** (3380 meters) – an ideal place to set up camp. After breakfast, the first and highest pass of the trail, the **Abra de Huarmihuañusca** (4200 meters) requires a huge effort from the trekker – two to three hours of sweat and toil. The steep and strenuous descent leads to the **Río Pacamayo**, on whose banks one can camp. Numerous waterfalls cascade from the steep mountainsides into the valley.

After crossing the river, the trail leads upwards for an hour to the ruins at **Ruinas Runkuracay**, followed by the challenge of the second pass**,** the **Abra de Runkuracay** (approximately 3900 meters). On the way down, one passes three small lakes, climbs over stone steps neatly chiseled in the rock, and hikes along irrigation channels, still in use, to the ruins at **Ruinas Sayacmarca**.

A two-hour ascent through cloud forest with marshy ground, leads to a stone tunnel made by the Incas and then to a point from which one can look down

a sheer drop of 1000 meters to the Urubamba. Soon, the next campsite, at the **Ruinas Phuyupatamarca** (3680 meters) is reached.

Four hours later one reaches the ruins of **Huiñya Huayna**, only discovered in 1941, after which the trail slopes gently down through wide mountain meadows, again providing fantastic views deep down into the steep valley of the Urubamba. The Inca trail now leads up and down, through dense forest, through the first Inca gate, then further to **Intipuncu**, the second Inca gate. From here, one gets the best view of Machu Picchu in the morning, in the soft light of the rising sun and with no people in sight – a privilege reserved exclusively for trekkers. The end of the Inca trail, Machu Picchu, is not just a site of ruins steeped in legend, but also a paradise for plant-lovers: a hundred species of orchids alone have been counted there. After visiting the site, the trail descends the direct but steep steps to the train station of **Puente Ruinas.** Anyone who has energy left over can con-

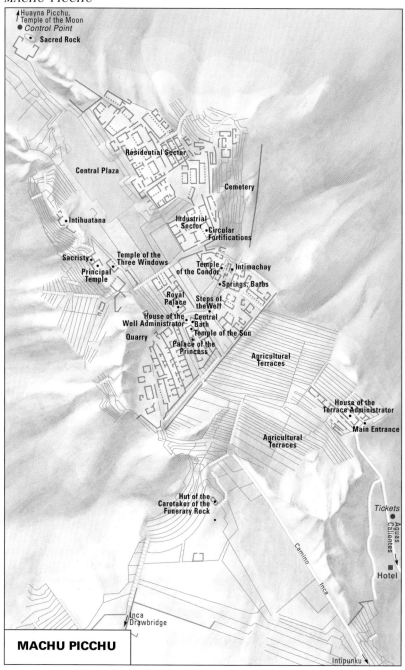

Huayna Picchu,
Temple of the Moon
● Control Point
● Sacred Rock

Residential Sector

Central Plaza

Cemetery

● Intihuatana

Industrial
Sector
● Circular
Fortifications

Sacristy ●
Temple of the
Three Windows
Temple ● Intimachay
of the Condor
● Principal
Temple
● Springs; Baths

Royal
Palace
Steps of
the Well

House of the
Well Administrator
Central
Bath
● Temple of the Sun

Quarry

Palace of the
Princess

Agricultural
Terraces

House of the
Terrace Administrator
●
● Main Entrance

Agricultural
Terraces

Hut of the
Caretaker of the
Funerary Rock

Tickets
● *Aguas
Calientes*

Camino
Inca

■ Hotel

Inca
Drawbridge

MACHU PICCHU

Intipunku ◄

tinue to hike to the next station in the small village of **Aguas Calientes** (which is also known as **Machu Picchu Pueblo**), to relax in the hot springs, or to eat pizza in one of the restaurants on the platform. There are also some nice, economical hotels, right beside this train station.

For trekkers with less stamina, there is a shorter alternative to the Inca trail. One can either follow along the river from Kilometer 88 to Kilometer 107, or simply get off the train at Kilometer 107. There a steep path leads uphill from the station directly to the ruins of Huiñya Huayna and continues via Intipuncu to Machu Picchu. This trek takes about seven hours in all.

MACHU PICCHU

This most mysterious of all the Inca ruins is often referred to as the "Lost City of the Incas." It can be reached in only two possible ways: either via a three to five day trek on foot along the *Camino Inca*, as described above, or by train from Cusco. Many tour organizers however also arrange a timesaving bus trip from Cusco to Ollantaytambo, where one can then join the train. The spectacular train ride winds along the valley of the increasingly wild Río Urubamba, past Kilometer 88 – where the trekkers disembark – and then continues to **Aguas Calientes**, a village with hot springs, and some hotels and restaurants.

Arriving at half past ten, the passengers push out through the train station in droves and climb into one of the tourist buses. These buses take the visitors 400 meters higher, a journey of 20 minutes along some eight kilometers of hairpin bends, to the ruins of Machu Picchu (old mountain) and Huayna Picchu (young mountain), at an altitude of 2360 meters. The route was personally opened to the public by Hiram Bingham in 1948. Before heading towards the main plaza with your ticket, it is a good idea to check

everything that you will not require during the visit in the baggage room near the entrance. Be sure to take along something to drink. A comprehensive visit to the site takes several hours.

The Discovery of Machu Picchu

A number of Spanish chroniclers had reported the existence of a mysterious city by the name of "Vilcabamba" in the jungle to the north of Cusco, which – undiscovered by the conquistadors – had been abandoned at some unknown time. **Hiram Bingham**, who studied at prestigious Yale University in the US, traveled through Peru in the year 1909, following the trail of Simón Bolívar. In 1911 he returned with a Yale University expedition, and, in July of that year, explored the ravine of the Urubamba. Searching for Vilcabamba, he questioned many locals in the villages along the river. The *campesino* boy, Melchor Arteaga, who had chanced upon some remains of Incan ruins during his wanderings, guided Bingham through impenetrable jungle to the location, which even today, decades after its discovery, raises many puzzling questions and is considered to be one of the greatest mysteries of archeology in the world.

Bingham assumed at first that he had at last found Vilcabamba, the last retreat of the Incas, and stayed at this mountain crest for four years in order to lead the excavation work. During this same period, he also excavated some other ruins in the vicinity. In the 1940's, a Peruvian expedition discovered another important Incan site, **Huiñay Huayna,** nearby on the Inca trail.

To this day, a number of questions remain unanswered: Why did the Spaniards never find Machu Picchu? Did renegades live there, whose presence later was to be carefully concealed? Was this the country seat of the Inca, Pachacutec, which was completely abandoned after his death? The beginning of construction around 1440 and the style of construction speak in favor of this theory, but also the fact that the inhabitants abandoned Machu Picchu (which Bingham called the "City in the Clouds") apparently around the time of the arrival of the Spaniards.

Did an epidemic wipe out the flourishing city? Or did wild jungle tribes overpower Machu Picchu? Was the site perhaps, as a few archaeologists believe, the central area for the cultivation of coca leaves for the nobility of Cusco? According to the most recent research, Machu Picchu was a religious and astronomical center, built from 1420 onwards and abandoned around 1520. It was inhabited by approximately 1500 people in 200 dwellings, would have had an adequate water supply for occasional increases in the population.

Walking Tour

The weather in the mountains around **Machu Picchu** is unpredictable. Therefore, to undertake an extended tour of the extensive ruins, which can take several hours, one should be equipped with protection against rain and sun, and wear sturdy shoes. The names of the individual structures on the site are derived primarily from Hiram Bingham. These designations, at times rather imaginative, often say nothing about the actual function of the structure.

From the main entrance, a slightly zigzagged path leads uphill through the agricultural terraces to the Inca trail. Here, at the highest observation point, just below the **Hut of the Caretaker of the Funerary Rock**, one has a sweeping view over Machu Picchu, can enjoy the landscape, and get one's bearings. This observation

Right: Trapezoidal windows: a characteristic feature of Incan architecture (Temple of the Three Windows in Machu Picchu).

point gives those visitors not yet acclimatized to the altitude a chance to take a deep breath and relax. Often, the clouds in the Urubamba valley float past just below the mountain peaks. One thousand meters below, the Río Urubamba winds through its narrow valley. The small train station at Aguas Calientes, the train station for Machu Picchu, and a part of the serpentine road are visible from here.

In the center of the large terraced areas for agricultural production, which the Incas fertilized with guano from the coast, stands the **House of the Terrace Administrator**. He was responsible for the ingenious irrigation and drainage system (similar to that installed at many other settlements), and supervised the cultivation of corn, grains, and different types of sweet potatoes.

A few steps farther north, towards the main plaza, one crosses the **Steps of the Well**, surrounded by small waterfalls in artificially created basins of various shapes. Hiram Bingham assumed that Machu Picchu was abandoned because the water from these springs, the site of numerous religious ceremonies for worshipping water, dried up one day.

From the well one comes to one of the landmarks of Machu Picchu – the **Temple of the Sun**, a round tower, and therefore also known as **El Torreón**. Its walls, built almost without joints, have a large number of niches that accommodated sacrificial offerings and idols. There are recesses, carved into the doorposts, into which the priests could probably hang an entrance door or curtains. At the base of the rocky outcrop, there is a pit, often explained as the "grave of the kings," although no bones were found there.

Was perhaps El Torreón a part of an observatory, a watchtower, or a grain storehouse? Or did the Incas really breed snakes here, as Bingham thought? The tower definitely had a place in the calendar system of the Incas, because in June,

on the day of the winter solstice, the light of the rising sun falls exactly through a window onto a long straight line, engraved in the center of the tower.

Next to the Torreón is the "Palace of the Princess," **El Palacio de la Ñusta**, which once had two stories. Because of its lavish construction, Bingham named it "Residence of the High Priest." Simple structures, which were probably grain stores, surround the palace.

In the immediate vicinity, above the main well, stands the **House of the Administrator of the Well**. This unusual three-walled building, the thatched roof of which has been renovated, was open on one side and was therefore probably not used as a dwelling house. The thick stone wedges that served to fix the wooden roof trusses to the stone wall can still be recognized at the upper end of the wall.

In the **quarry** at the top end of the Steps of the Well, lie a few incomplete blocks carved out of the rock – the so-called "tired stones."

The **Royal Palace**, opposite the Temple of the Sun, and on the other side of the steps, is made up of a number of structures and has enormous door lintels, weighing up to three tonnes. Together with the elegant trapezoidal door, this points to the presence of noble inhabitants.

On the side of the **Temple of the Three Windows** that opens onto the courtyard, two strong pillars were apparently meant to carry the door lintel, which was never apparently erected. Through the three trapezoidal windows at the back, one can look down from a great height over the large square. According to one of the legends regarding its origin, four Inca sibling-pairs are supposed to have set forth from here in their search for land. However, only Manco Capac reached the destination of Cusco with his sister-consort, after having first disposed of their other siblings.

The **Main Temple** of Machu Picchu has a large altar-shaped stone slab in the middle – the only Inca temple to have this

feature. The large stone blocks, with which the lower part of the wall is constructed, are truly impressive. The stones of its three walls become narrower towards the top, making the structure look higher than it is. The square stone blocks of the main temple were carved, polished and fitted together with absolute precision. It is easy to imagine that this was once, in the heyday of the city, a grand and richly furnished structure. As the only temple at Machu Picchu, it has a side temple, or **sacristy**, next to it. The door posts are flanked by artistically carved stones.

A flight of steps leads to the **Intihuatana** (Hitching Post of the Sun) at the top of a hill behind the main temple. This 1.8 meter high stone, carved out of the rock, was apparently the most important shrine in the city. There were also shrines for

Above: The Intihuatana, "The Hitching Post of the Sun," was the most important shrine in Machu Picchu. Right: El Palacio de la Ñusta, the "Palace of the Princess."

sun worship in other places, such as Pisac (see Ruins of Pisac, p. 104). As a center for astronomical observations, for calculation and review of the calendar, it played an important role in determining the rainy season and sowing time. The Hitching Post of the Sun, a magnificent sculpture, made it possible for the priests to predict the solstice, thanks to the correspondingly oriented longitudinal sides and an east-west diagonal. The Intihuatana of Machu Picchu is the only sun stone not destroyed by the Spaniards.

One can now cross the large **Main Plaza**, on which one will usually see tame llamas grazing, and below the plaza, come to a large **dwelling area** with simple structures. Two shallow pits with a diameter of half a meter have been carved in the stone floor in one of the buildings. Bingham interpreted these completely smooth, shallow pits with the flat edges as mortars for corn, especially since he also found a number of pestles in the same house, but this explanation has not yet been totally accepted.

114

There are differing opinions among experts on the possible number of inhabitants of this place of cult worship. With about 200 dwellings in Machu Picchu, the present estimates of the archaeologists are that about 400 inhabitants lived in the *City in the Clouds.* Some estimates suggest 10 to 20 times this number, primarily based on the fact that the agricultural terraces could have supported a considerably larger population.

In the **Artisans' Quarter,** situated farther to the south, Hiram Bingham found stone tools, bronze objects and tools for weaving and sewing. From here, a steep staircase leads down to the **Temple of the Condor**, a deep underground room with niches, which probably was once used as a temple. The name for the structure comes from a wide, flat stone on the floor in which the form of a condor is carved – the head is particularly easy to recognize.

Bingham's imagination really ran wild here: in his opinion, he had found the prison of Machu Picchu. The underground vault appeared to be the perfect location for a dungeon. What Bingham had not understood however was that the Incas did not have prisons in our sense of the word. Rather, they meted out physical punishment, loss of class privileges, or the death penalty, by being thrown into a pit with wild animals or into a nest of snakes.

Intimachay is the name of the small cave above the Temple of the Condor, an observatory for monitoring the summer solstice in December. On the front wall of the cave, one can make out a window that has been carved out of a single stone. In the ten days around the solstice, the light of the rising sun enters through this window and falls precisely onto the back wall of the cave.

The recommended tour around the center of Machu Picchu ends here. One can walk back to the hotel or restaurant from Intimachay.

One destination for an interesting walk is the **cemetery** above the terraces. Around the huts that stand alone here

115

Bingham found 144 skeletons, individual bones and entire mummies. The very ambitious and rudimentary evaluations that were possible at that time concluded that 80 to 90 percent of the bones were from female skeletons – which triggered all kinds of fanciful speculations.

After enjoying the exhilarating view down into the Urubamba valley, one can continue towards **Intipuncu**, the sun gate on the Inca trail. There is an even more enchanting view of the ruins from this point. The full hour required for the return trip is definitely worthwhile. On certain days, the inhabitants of the buildings high up in the western part of Machu Picchu could have seen the sunrise through this gate.

The **Holy Rock** (also called the Temple of *Pachamama*, the goddess of the earth) at the northernmost point of the

Above: The Machu Picchu train station in the Urubamba valley is the needle's eye, through which most tourists reach the Inca ruins.

site consists of one huge block of rock. The outline of the flat stone is identical to that of the mountain silhouette in the background.

The path to **Huayna Picchu**, the granite peak rising to 2700 meters above sea level and 700 meters above the Río Urubamba, and which was devastated by a forest fire in 1997, begins 100 meters north of the Central Plaza. Before starting up the steep mountain peak, one must sign the register at the checkpoint – for safety's sake. Ascents are not allowed after 1 p.m. One should count on an hour and a half for the journey there and back. One has to overcome dizzying and slippery sections, and at some places fight through dense tropical vegetation. Having reached the top, one is rewarded with a magnificent view, as from an eagle's perch, be able to look down at the terraces, which wind around the granite mountain. These terraces were probably used more as ornamental gardens, than for agricultural purposes.

In 1936 archaeologists discovered the underground **Temple of the Moon** (*Templo de la Luna*) on the northern slope of Huayna Picchu, surrounded by an impressive wall and secured by a gate. The path up to it is very strenuous.

Most visitors to Machu Picchu only come once in their lifetime to this unique "city in the clouds." Therefore, take sufficient time for the tour through the ruins, and pause, now and then, to admire the deep Urubamba valley or the dark green mountaintops on the other side of the river, and to enjoy the unique ambience of Machu Picchu. This is best possible outside of the peak visiting hours; most tourists come to the area between 10 a.m. and 2 p.m. The self-serve restaurant of the Ruinas Hotel, opposite the main entrance, is totally lacking in style and the prices are exorbitant. Cheaper – and sometimes better – food is available in one of the small restaurants in the village of Aguas Calientes.

CUSCO (Area Code 084)
Accommodation

LUXURY: **Monasterio del Cusco**, Plaza Nazarenas, tel: 241777, fax: 237111, formerly the San Antonio de Abad Seminary. **Libertador**, Plazoleta Sto. Domingo 259, tel: 231961, fax: 233152, successful combination of Inca and colonial architecture with a modern hotel. Good restaurant.

MODERATE: **Incatambo**, tel: 222045, fax: 223073, San Cristóbal, hacienda-hotel next to Sacsayhuamán, pretty, quiet. **Posada del Inca**, Portal Espinar 142, tel/fax: 233091/227061, near the plaza, small rooms. **Ruinas**, C. Ruinas 472, tel: 260644, fax: 236391, new, tasteful décor. **Hotel Tambo**, Ayacucho 235, tel: 223221, fax: 236788.

BUDGET: **Casa de Campo**, San Blas, Tanapata 296, tel: 244404, fax: 241422, quiet hillside location, great view of old city. **Andenes de Saphi**, C. Saphi 848, tel: 227561, fax: 235588, individual, well-lit rooms. **Hostal Pascana**, C. Ahuacpinta 539, tel/fax: 225771, for small budgets, nice rooms.

Restaurants

La Retama, Portal de Panes 123, tel/fax: 226372, incredible view of the plaza, local specialties. **El Patio**, Portal de Carnes 236, new, tables in the courtyard. **Trattoria Adriano**, C. Mantas 105, tel: 233965, best Italian food in Cusco. **Pacha Papa**, Plaza San Blas 120, tel: 241318, local menu, pretty courtyard. **El Meson de los Espaderos**, corner of Plaza/C. Espaderos, grilled specialties. **Café Ayllu**, corner of Plaza/C. Almirante, good for snacks.

Discos / Peñas

Las Queñas, Hotel Savoy, Av. Sol 954. **Centro Qosqo de Arte Nativo**, Av. Sol 604, folklore daily at 6:50 pm. **Cross Keys Pub**, Plaza de Armas, where globetrotters gather. **El Muki**, Sta. Catalina, "in disco." **Uptown**, Plaza/corner C. Suecia.

Tourist Information

Tourist-Hotline, 24-hour, tel: 252974. The BTG Ticket is on sale at: **Información Turística**, opposite Iglesia La Merced, Mon-Fri 8 am - 6 pm, Sat 8 am - 2 pm., tel 263176; and **OFEC**, Av. Sol 103/INC, C. Garcilaso, Mon-Fri 7 am - 6 pm, Sat 8:30 am - 12:30 pm, tel. 226919.

Sights / Museums

La Catedral and **San Blas**: Mon-Wed, Fri & Sat, 10-11:30 am, Mon-Sat 2-5:30 pm. **Museo de Arte Religioso**, Mon-Sat 8-11:30 am, 3-5:30 pm. **Convento de Sta. Catalina**, Mon-Thu & Sat 9 am-5:30 pm, Fri 9 am-3 pm. **Museo Histórico Regional**, Mon-Fri 8 am-5:30 pm. **Museo Arqueológico de Qorikancha**, daily 9:30 am-6 pm. **Archäologische Stätten**, daily 7 am-5:30 pm. The BTG mulit-ticket – approx. US $10 (US $5 with student ID) – is valid for all of the museums above. Extra charge for: **Coricancha**, Mon-Sat 8 am-5 pm, Sun 2-4 pm.

Museo Arqueológico, Mon-Fri 9 am-5 pm, Sat 9 am-2 pm.

Airlines

The Velasco Astete Airport is 10 min. south of the Plaza de Armas, taxis cost max. US \$5. **Aero Continente**, Portal de Carnes 254, tel: 235686, fax: 235660. **TANS**, new airline, info at the airport. **Aero Condor**, airport, tel/fax: 252774, on Mon, Wed & Fri flies over the Nazca line drawings. **Globos de los Andes**, a new attraction in Peru, hot-air balloons! An exclusive adventure for US \$300 per hour and person. Info: tel/fax: 201116; Pilot Jeff (US American) tel: 201143.

Buses

No central bus station; the bus companies **Cruz del Sur**, **Sur Oriente** and **Señor de las Animas** cover routes in all directions.

Trains

Terminal Huanchac, Av. Pachacutec, trains to Juliaca, Puno and Arequipa; Cusco-Puno, Mon, Wed, Fri & Sat 8 am. **Terminal San Pedro**, C. Cascaparo/San Pedro, tel: 238722, trains to Machu Picchu daily 6, 6:25 and 7 am.

THE VALLEY OF THE INCAS
Accommodation

PISAC: *MODERATE:* **Royal Inka Pisac**, Carretera Pisac Ruinas, tel: 203064, new, superb location. **YUCAY**: *MODERATE:* **Posada del Inka**, Plaza Manco II 123, tel: 201346, fax: 201345, hacienda with large garden and great view. *BUDGET:* **La Posada del Libertador**, Plaza Manco II 104, tel: 201115, fax: 201116, charming house.

URUBAMBA: *BUDGET:* **Antigua Misión San José de la Recoleta**, Jr. La Recoleta, tel/fax: 201-004, former colonial monastery. **Hostal Hammer**, Urb. La Cantuta G-8, tel: 201194, pretty garden.

OLLANTAYTAMBO: *BUDGET:* **El Albergue**, at the train station, tel: 204014, has a sauna.

AGUAS CALIENTES: *MODERATE:* **Machu Picchu Pueblo**, tel: 211032, fax: 223769, comfortable cabins in a beautiful location, over-priced. **Machu Picchu Inn**, tel: 211056, on road to the hot springs, former youth hostel, renovated, impersonal.

MACHU PICCHU: *MODERATE:* **Machu Picchu Ruinas**, tel: 211038, fax: (01) 4406197, the only hotel directly beside the ruins.

Restaurants

URUBAMBA: **El Maizal**, Cabo Conchatupa, tel: 201054, rustic, pretty garden. **AGUAS CALIENTES**: **Indio Feliz**, C. Lloque Yupanqui 4, tel: 211090, fine French-Peruvian food.

Trains

Tourist trains to Machu Picchu leave Ollantaytambo daily at 7:45, 8:15 and 8:45 am.

AT LAKE TITICACA

LAKE TITICACA
PUNO
SILLUSTANI
ISLANDS OF LAKE TITICACA
THE SOUTHERN SHORE OF
LAKE TITICACA

The *puna* (high plateau) with its extremely thin air is also called the **altiplano** in Peru. Endless, wide spaces contrast with the majestic mountain ranges of the **Cordillera Real** with their eternal snow – a paradise indeed for mountaineers, vicuñas, alpacas and llamas, but less so for the many generations of inhabitants of these highlands, who had to and still have to eke out a basic existence.

The Departamento of Puno, with an area of 72,000 square kilometers, has a population of about one million, who live at altitudes of between 2800 and 4500 meters above sea level. The *campesinos* of the *puna* live mainly in poor conditions here in villages and small towns. They live in brown adobe huts with roofs of straw or corrugated material, between sparse green meadows and fields of alfalfa and fodder barley. Their work in the traditional agricultural *comunidades* barely provides them sufficient nourishment. The infant mortality rate is 30 percent, with more than 70 percent of the small children being undernourished. In the last 10 years, the life expectancy has dropped below the Peruvian average of 65 years.

Previous Pages: Fish is an important food around Lake Titicaca (market in Puno). Left: An Uros Indian in his boat made of rushes.

Even though the thin air of the altiplano forces visitors to take an involuntary rest sometimes, to catch their breath, the region surrounding Lake Titicaca is without rival anywhere in the world. It boasts a uniquely spectacular railway route; the "folklore capital," Puno; a rich Indian cultural heritage and interesting archaeological sites. There are few cars on the gravel roads, a multitude of waterbirds at the lake, people who live on the floating islands; and the brilliant light of the altiplano.

LAKE TITICACA

The core of the altiplano is the **Lago Titicaca** (Lake Titicaca), which, at 3822 meters above sea level, is described by almost all travel guides as the highest navigable lake in the world. That is not quite correct as the Lago de Junín in the Peruvian Central Andes is located at 4000 meters above sea level and is also navigable! Nonetheless, Lake Titicaca can lay claim to two superlatives. With a surface area of 8300 square kilometers, it is both the largest lake in the world above 2000 meters above sea level and the largest in South America. At its longest point it measures 194 kilometers, at its widest, 65 kilometers and at its deepest, 300 meters. Actually, one should speak

121

LAKE TITICACA

0   25   50 km

of two lakes. The smaller Lake Huiñai-marca has 11 islands and is separated by the road from Tiquina from the six times larger Lake Chucuito, with 25 islands,

The approximately 160 million cubic meters of slightly salty water maintain a temperature of 10-13°C the whole year, but at that height, the lake still functions as a heat sink. Lake Titicaca, part of which belongs to Bolivia, had an abundance of fish (today: salmon trout, *suche, pejerrey*, and *carachi*) which provided several ancient cultures with a secure means of existence. It also has sufficient water and heat for the cultivation of *maís* (corn), *quinua* (a highland cereal), barley, *frijoles* (beans) and many different types of potatoes.

It was a holy lake for the Incas. According to local tradition, the legendary first Inca, Manco Capac and his sister-wife, Mama Ocllo descended around AD 1200 to found the Inca Empire of Ta-

huantinsuyo. Today, Peru and Bolivia share Lake Titicaca – *titi* belongs to the Peruvians, *caca* to the Bolivians – or the other way round, as the local tourist guides are often fond of joking. Actually, *titi* means puma and *kak* means rock, and when the Sun God, Inti, left the earth to ascend to heaven, he is said to have left a footprint on the Sun Island in the lake. That is why the Isla del Sol was first called Titicaca, and later, so was the lake.

JULIACA

Although **Juliaca** is not located right on the lakeshore, the city is the largest in the Departamento Puno. Its population of 195,000 is almost exclusively indigenous. An airport at 3825 meters above sea level, with connections to Lima, Cusco and Arequipa, a few good hotels, and only a few worthwhile sights, make the city a connection center rather than a city that people travel to for a vacation. The prices of woolen articles at the large Monday market, as well as at the

Right: Farmers near Lake Titicaca, winnowing their harvest.

daily market along the railway tracks, are relatively attractive, but the goods offered are not as varied as those, for instance, in Pisac. Apart from the Plaza de Armas with the large city church, the only other point of interest is the office of the state-owned railways ENAFER Peru (Av. San Martín) which is important for booking the train to Cusco or Arequipa. In comparison, there is more to see in Juliaca's neighboring city, Puno.

PUNO

Puno, capital of the Peruvian province of the same name, at an altitude of 3828 meters, has a population of about 100,000. It has the biggest harbor on Lake Titicaca. Founded in 1668 at a silver mine called *Laykakota*, it drew more than 10,000 people here in its time. The "golden" days of Puno are long past, but in the early days of the city, the upper classes had plenty of money, which is evidenced in buildings such as the cathedral, the Palace of Justice, the Pinoteca

art gallery and other buildings of the colonial period.

La Catedral, the cathedral, located on the Plaza de Armas was completed in 1755. Its façade demonstrates the strong influence of local traditions on the art of the conquerors. In the room behind this lavish *Mestizo* façade, only the valuable silver altar could be considered of great interest. The nearby **Museo Municipal Carlos Dreyer**, named after a previous owner, is at the corner of the Calles Conde de Lemos and Deustua. It contains a private collection of historic Peruvian art, textiles and ceramics of the region.

Eight thousand young Peruvians attend university in Puno today at the **Universidad Nacional del Altiplano**. Founded in 1825 as a primary school by the Latin American freedom fighter Simón Bolívar, it also served for some time as a military academy. Some of the students play in the city's soccer team. The team wins almost every championship game against the Peruvian teams from the lowlands, which are held in the large **stadium** near

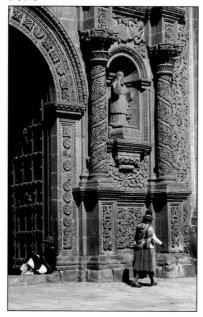

the railway tracks. This is simply because at this height, the opposing players very soon literally run out of breath.

A walk to the **Huajsapata Park**, a quarter of an hour from the Plaza de Armas, is worthwhile. The park has a larger than life-sized statue of the first legendary Inca, Manco Capac. It commemorates his "birth place" according to local legend. There is also a wonderful view of Lake Titicaca and the city of Puno from the statue.

The **Arco Deustua**, a memorial in the Calle Independencia, serves as a memorial to the Peruvians who lost their lives in the battles of Junín and Ayacucho, during the struggle for Peruvian independence.

The **mercado** (daily market) in the Calle Ugarte, near the railway tracks, sells quality woolen items at reasonable prices. Keep an eye out for *chullus* (hand-

Above: The cathedral of Puno is famous for its richly decorated façade. Right: Rushes grow around the shores of LakeTiticaca.

knit woolen caps with close-fitting ear-flaps) which are very useful here, as well as vegetables, fruit, and all sorts of household goods.

The excursion boats that cast off for Taquile, Amantani, and the floating islands of the Uros, anchor at the quay at the end of the long Avenida del Puerto.

In the cheaper hotels in Puno, and most of them are that, one should make sure to have adequate covers on the bed during the cold nights. Because of the proximity to the lake, the nights can be damp too. There are frequent frosts between June and August. The wet season lasts from October to April (it is especially wet from December to March). There can, nevertheless, be many sunny and warm days in these months. The extremely strong sun and intensive UV radiation make it essential to have good protection for the skin, lips and eyes. Thus prepared, you can take a better look at the sights of Puno.

Puno, The "Folklore Capital"

The **fiestas** and **folklore** in the Departamento Puno are famous throughout Peru. More than 300 different Indian folk dances, some with Spanish influence, have survived the Inca and colonial times. Although many of the dances are of pre-Columbian origin, they are often performed on Catholic holidays such as Epiphany, Candlemas (*Fiesta de la Virgen de la Candelaria*, February 2) and St. John the Baptist's Day (June 24). They are often performed at Christian wedding celebrations (favourite month: August), and during the one-week-long town festival of Puno (early November) in memory of the legendary arrival of Manco Capacs and Mama Ocllos on the Island of the Sun. For some years now, the voyage of the founders of the Inca dynasty across the lake, has been reenacted by the locals, dressed in magnificent costumes. The journey from the Bolivian side of the lake

to Puno, in a boat made of reeds, takes several days.

Today, the events still reflect their origins in the traditional agricultural calendar. The participants wear festival clothes that have been stitched and embroidered with much love and care and include layered skirts (*polleras*), animal costumes, and colorful or hideous face-masks. All the dances, even those that seem to the observer to be quite wild, have structure and underlying meaning. They are mostly tales of the past, for example, of the suppression of the Incas by the tribute collectors, Spaniards, silver-mine operators, and big landowners.

The ancient Devil's dance (*diablada*), which is presented during Candlemas on February 2, probably originated before the Incan period. In the Diablada, it appears as though the dancers, in their grotesque masks and colorful costumes, actually fight, but the dance ends without any apparent casualties or dead.

Music groups accompany these dances with traditional musical instruments.

Here too, the inhabitants of the altiplano have, understandably, adopted modern developments and stimulae from abroad. Along with several types of bells and rattles, the participants beat large drums (*wankaras*) and tambourines (*tinyas*) and play bamboo flutes (*flautas*) and pipes (*quenas*).

SILLUSTANI

About an hour by car along a good asphalt road from Puno is the archaeological zone of **Sillustani,** located at about 4000 meters above sea level. En route, one travels past intensely cultivated, partly irrigated land, on which *quinua* and potatoes are grown. From the small, poorly maintained museum in the valley, one can stroll up about 150 meters, to the high burial towers of the Colla Indians. These form a landmark which is visible from a great distance. The southern quarter of the Inca Empire, Tahuantinsuyo, was called *Collasuyo* after the tribe living there. The Collas, together with their

rival tribe, the *Lupaca*, controlled the area around Lake Titicaca. The Inca Empire more or less absorbed both peoples. The people of the Colla tribe spoke the Aymara language, were inclined to be warlike, and attached a great deal of importance to lavish burials of their dead noblemen in so-called *chullpas* (Aymara word for "walled burial towers"). Some of these *chullpas* have survived in several places in the Puno region.

The **Chullpas of Sillustani** are those in the vicinity of Lake Titicaca that are most worth seeing, because of their well-preserved condition and size. Here, on an idyllically situated peninsula in lake Umayo, the Collas selected a particularly impressive burial ground. Archaeologists consider that most of the *chullpas* predate the Inca period. These burial towers, usually round, reach a stately height of up to 12 meters and have a diameter of five

meters. They contained mummies of individual noblemen or entire noble families in squatting positions. In the largest tower, the Chullpa del Lagarto, the dead were stacked one on top of the other five storys high.

The dead were buried with food and drink. After the burial, the tiny doorway, usually facing the east (towards the rising sun) was sealed at the ground with stones. In those times, the death of a nobleman meant death for his entire family. Spanish chroniclers have reported that something like 20 llamas were cremated at the burial of a nobleman, and the women, children and servants of the deceased were all killed.

The outer walls of the towers were made of superbly carved blocks of basalt and trachyte, similar to the Inca style of construction, and at least as complex and lavish. Not all the towers were completed, however, and at some individual *chullpas*, one can still see the construction ramps and the filler material that was poured into the hollow towers from the

Above: A herd of llamas in the thin air of the altiplano. Right: The chullpas (grave towers) of Sillustani are part of the Colla heritage.

top. Some of the outer stones are decorated with chiselled figures, e.g., a beautiful lizard and a long snake.

Generations of grave-robbers cleaned out the chullpas long ago and destroyed important clues about the culture of the Collas forever. One treasure did, however, escape the attentions of these *huaqueros*. In 1971, Peruvian archaeologists discovered treasure from the Incan period, near the **Chullpa del Lagarto** at a depth of just one meter. It included numerous small pieces of jewelry and almost four kilograms of gold.

Is there some deeper meaning to this extremely time-consuming and expensive burial tradition of the Collas? According to the theories of German-Peruvian anthropologist Frederico Kauffmann-Doig, there could be a connection with fertility cults in honor of *Pachamama*, or Mother Earth. The grave towers, which in some cases clearly assume the form of a powerful, erect phallus, symbolize the life-force, creation, and re-birth.

THE ISLANDS OF LAKE TITICACA

A few of the islands in the lake have developed into tourist attractions in the past few decades and can be visited by motor-boat.

The "Floating Islands" of the Uros

The **Islas Flotantes** (floating islands) in the Bay of Puno, which are inhabited by the Uros tribe, are the main tourist attraction in the Puno region, and understandably so. Where else in the world will you find an Indian tribe that spends its entire life on floating islands, and that in such unique surroundings as Lake Titicaca, with the mountains of the snow-covered Cordillera Real as a backdrop?

The Uros originally had their own language but now, due frequent intermarriage with Aymara-speaking Indians, they speak in the Aymara language. The last pureblooded *kotsuns* (lake people) died in the 1950's. They claimed to have

127

black blood, which, according to their legend, made it possible for them to survive the cold nights on the lake without problem. According to other sources, they fled nearly 800 years ago to the hidden reed islands to escape the Incan demand for tributes. About 250 Uros still live on about 80 islands, of which the Islas Santa Maria, Toranipata, and Huaca Huacani are the largest. Not all the floating islands are permanently inhabited today.

The floating islands consist of meter-thick layers of reeds (*Scirpus tatora*), which must be replenished again and again, because the lowest layer eventually loses its ability to float in the cold water and slowly, but surely, rots away. Therefore, as a visitor, it is advisable to step around particularly soft, dark places in the ground, so that one doesn't sink in. Otherwise there is a danger of quickly

becoming a popular, if unwilling subject of camera-happy tourists. The photogenic *balsas*, boats shaped like canoes, are made of the same reeds and generally don't last for more than six to twelve months.

The Uros, who made a living exclusively by trapping birds and catching fish and consuming fresh *totora* stalks until just a few decades ago, now sell hand crafted items, such as small boats and dolls made of reeds. The women weave and elaborately embroider blankets, wall hangings, and shawls. They usually demand money if you want to take photographs of them and make their skimpily-clad, wonderfully runny-nosed children beg a *sol* from the tourists who pass through here.

Young Uros offer tourists on boat tours through the island world of Lake Titicaca on one of their *totora* boats. Doing this, one can get some idea of how the Norwegian adventurer and anthropologist, Thor Heyerdahl, must have felt in 1947 while making his 4300-mile cross-

Above: Uros Indians in front of their house of rushes. Right: The floating islands of the Uros have become a tourist attraction.

ing of the Pacific in his reed boat, the Kon-Tiki.

On one of the floating islands, there is even a small "hotel" with three rooms. An overnight stay in the reeds must certainly be an unforgettable experience. But the effects of the relentless tourist traffic are already visible, even though most of the islands are closed to tourists. This means that all the more tourists, from all over the world, are welcomed on three or four of the islands. A few years ago, the business-minded Uros built an observation tower on the largest one. Tourists can climb the tower for a small charge. Indefatigable missionaries from the Adventist church in the USA have also discovered the Uros and made them targets of their conversion activities. A few decades ago, they started by building small churches and schools with corrugated metal roofs. Using donations from abroad, they distribute money among the Uros and thus hope for permanent conversion of the Uros to the Adventist Church.

And yet the Uros already have enough problems surviving in this inhospitable terrain. Chronic rheumatism, chronic influenza, and frequent colds result in their having a much shorter life expectancy than that of the other inhabitants of the altiplano. Unbalanced nutrition and the increasing alcohol consumption of the men and women do the rest. In addition, there are problems from outside. The water is increasingly polluted because the Puno municipal drains empty into Lake Titicaca and because of the ever-increasing seasonal variations in the water level (more than four meters). The lake water will soon become unpotable and the fish will disappear. The reeds, which are absorbing increasing amounts of toxins, will eventually carry these toxins to humans through the food chain. Nevertheless, most Uros want to continue to live without any official personal papers. They reject attempts to integrate them into Peruvian society and do not consider themselves to be citizens of the Andean state.

Isla Taquile

The crossing from Puno to the idyllic **Isla Taquile** takes about three hours. The island, which is six kilometers long and a kilometer and a half wide, can be seen from a considerable distance because of its many hills. There are still some isolated ruins at the top of these natural peaks. The practiced eye can make out the Incan terraces on the slopes. These terraces, some of which are still in use today, are gradually falling into disrepair.

In contrast to the floating islands of the Uros, Taquile is a natural island. Its approximately 1000 inhabitants speak Quechua and marry almost exclusively among themselves. They wear lovingly woven shawls, skirts, and capes, whose designs contain cryptic information about the social status of their wearers. On Taquile, there is no electricity, there

Above: On Isla Taquile, it Is the men who do the knitting! Right: The design on the cap indicates the social status of its wearer.

are no roads or cars, not even bicycles, and, strangely, there are also no dogs.

Since the Taquileños own the boats that take tourists from Puno to the Isla Taquile, they can decide for themselves how many visitors they wish to permit on their island every day. Nonetheless, insider tips have made this a very popular tourist destination. Three restaurants in the Plaza Central serve fresh fish from the lake. They all serve salmon trout, which can weigh up to 14 kilograms. So far there are no hotels; visitors wanting lodging can stay privately with local families.

If there is time before the boat has to return to Puno, one should take a walk on the deep, reddish and very fertile ground to the red-and-white painted lighthouse at the southern end of the island.

Once a year, the otherwise sleepy town of Taquile experiences hustle and bustle as, on July 25, the feast day of Saint James, the Taquileños celebrate their biggest festival. Until the beginning of August, there's dancing, singing, and drinking. At the end of August, sacrifices are made to Mother Earth *Pachamama* in the hope of a fruitful harvest.

Isla Amantaní

An excursion to the **Isla Amantaní** is rewarding, if only if only for the reason that it is farther from Puno and is thus less frequently visited and quieter than Taquile. The men of Amantaní wear traditional woolen clothing and the women, as is often the case at these altitudes, wrap themselves in several layers of skirts and shawls. All the inhabitants of Amantaní live from the sale of their woven work, from harvesting grain, and from breeding trout. Here too, on Amantaní, accommodation is available for visitors with the local families. The accomodation is very simple, but gives one a memorable insight into the daily life of the locals.

THE SOUTHERN SHORE OF LAKE TITICACA

The towns along the Peruvian southern shore of Lake Titicaca can be reached easily by bus or minibus in one day. This is also on the road to La Paz (Bolivia), should you be planning to travel there.

The village of **Chimu** is eight kilometers from Puno, on the shore of Lake Titicaca. One can reach it on foot, which at this height, will reveal how fit you are. Apart from agriculture, the inhabitants of Chimu mainly live from the manufacture of *totora* products (canoes, hats, baskets, purses, etc.). During the day, one can watch the craftsmen as they cut the reeds to size, lay the bundles out in the sun to dry, make them elastic, and then fashion them into boats or roofs.

In the village of **Chucuito**, 18 kilometers east of Puno, one can see two beautiful, colonial churches: La Asunción and Santo Domingo. Opposite the village church, is a rectangular area surrounded by typical Inca walls. It contains an oversized stone phallus, surrounded by many smaller ones, that probably was part of the fertility temple of **Inka Uyu**. Four kilometers before Juli, on the right-hand side of the road, is a huge stone gate, **Aramo Muro,** dating from the Tiahuanaco culture. The villagers call it the *Puerto del Diablo*, the Devil's Door, and tell blood-curdling stories about it.

Juli is located 78 kilometers southeast of Puno, on the highway to Bolivia. It is worth a visit because of its proximity to Lake Titicaca and its colorful Thursday market. The residents of Juli, approximately 2000 in number, are justifiably proud of their four large colonial churches: San Juan Bautista; La Asunción (recently damaged by a storm); San Pedro (restored); and Santa Cruz (with a large image of the sun, the symbol of the Inca's sun-god on the façade).

The **Iglesia San Juan Bautista**, the oldest church in Juli, has large, lavishly framed paintings from the life of John the Baptist and of St. Theresa serving as a reminder of the times when the town was

much wealthier than it is now. The high-quality wood of the pulpit, the altar, the pews, and the gallery as well as the gold and precious stones set into the altars give some impression of the former prosperity of the Departamento Puno. San Juan Bautista is filled with Indian-style elements in the paintings, the stonemasonry, and the wall paintings, and is now a religious museum. It is usually open in the morning.

One should also have a quick look at the **Iglesia de la Asunción.** It was built at the beginning of the 17th century and needs renovation. From the beautiful square in front, there is a great view of the permanently snow-covered Illampu massif (6550 meters). All four churches in Juli seem to be one size too large for the town, which was the mission base of the Jesuits in the 17th century. After the end of the colonial period, the villagers did not have the finances to keep these

Above: The market in Juli – silversmithing has a long tradition here.

richly decorated churches in a reasonable state of repair.

Twenty five kilometers farther south (hence about 106 kilometers south-east of Puno) is the village of **Pomata**. The Iglesia Santiago, which was built around 1700, stands on the village hill. It has masterfully worked stone reliefs in which Baroque and Andean-Mestizo elements have been fascinatingly combined. Several alabaster windows are a special feature. This translucent material transforms the intense highland sunshine into a soft, milky light, which enhances the dancing figures on a frieze in the entrance area in the inside the church.

Worthwhile destinations in nearby Bolivia include: the town of **Copacabana,** superbly located on the lake; the charming **Isla del Sol** with a view of the 6000 meter high peaks of the Cordillera Real; the excavations at **Tiahuanaco** with the famous sun gate; and **La Paz**, with its Indian markets which, at 3300 to 4000 above sea level, is the highest metropolis in the world.

JULIACA
(Area Code 054)
Accommodation

The hotels in Juliaca usually serve tourists who can't get a room in Puno (47 kilometers away), especially during Easter and Christmas, and from July to September. As a result they are rather simple.

MODERATE: **Royal Inn**, San Román 158, tel: 32-1561, fax: 321572, new and clean. **Samarí**, Jr. Noriega 325, tel: 321870, fax: 321852, heat, TV, has its own power supply.

BUDGET: **Don Pedro**, C. Bolognesi 475, tel: 321-442. **San Antonio**, C. San Martín 347, tel: 321701. **Santa María**, C. Cusco/Jr. M. Nuñez 411, tel: 321-427.

Restaurants

Hotel Restaurant Royal Inn, the best in the city. **Restaurant del Altiplano**, simple, typical Peruvian menu, near the train station.

Buses

Several daily connections to all large cities in southern Peru, incl. Lima. Regular shuttle service to Puno. The bus companies are: **SurPeruano**, **Cruz del Sur** and **Transportes 3 de Mayo**.

Trains

Juliaca's train station is the busiest in Peru; this is where the lines to Puno, Arequipa and Cusco cross. It is recommended that you book tickets at least one day in advance. Ticket counters are open 7-10 am, 4-7 pm and 8-10 pm. If you can afford to, buy a first-class ticket – anything else takes a lot of courage. The trains don't travel every direction every day. Schedule changes are a regular occurrence.

Airlines

Aero Continente connects Juliaca with Arequipa and Lima, C. San Román 152, tel: 321522, fax: 322-978.

PUNO
(Area Code 054)
Accommodation

LUXURY: **Libertador Isla Estevés**, 5 km southeast of Puno on the Estevés Peninsula, directly on Lake Titicaca, tel: 367780, fax: 367879, nice, quiet location, all rooms have a view of the lake, heat, minibar and a room safe.

MODERATE: **Sillustani**, Jr. Lambayeque 195, tel: 351881, fax: 352641, can be a bit cold and noisy. **Ferrocarril**, opposite the train station, supposedly Peru's oldest hotel and worth a visit just to see its old furniture, noisy. **Colón Inn**, C. Tacna 290, tel/fax: 351432, Belgian owner, small, clean rooms, nice ambience. **Hacienda**, Jr. Deustua 297, tel: 356109, near Plaza de Armas, well equipped. **Los Portales**, Jr. Cajamarca 152, tel/fax: 353384, restaurant with a panoramic view.

BUDGET: **Tumi**, Jr. Cajamarca 243, tel: 353270. **El Lago**, Av. El Sol 865, tel: 352286, fax: 352625. **Cofre Andino**, Jr. Bolognesi 154, tel: 351973, small, intimate.

Restaurants

Restaurant La Casona, Jr. Conde de Lemus 128, tel: 351108, excellent regional menu in a colonial atmosphere. **Hilda's House**, Jr. Moquegua 189, tel: 351293, pasta and Chinese. **Café Internacional**, Jr. Libertad 161, tel: 352109, Peruvian and international menu, nothing earth shaking, but reliable. **Wiñay Wasi**, Jr. Grau 298, tel: 352015, typical Peruvian menu. **Rico Pez**, Conde de Lemus 231, tel: 354466, fish specialties.

Trains

The train to Cusco leaves Mon, Wed, Thu and Sun at 7:25 am, travel time is ca. 12 hours – an absolutely unforgettable journey that is among the most beautiful in South America! The train to Arequipa leaves daily at 7:45 pm. Ticket counters are open from 6:30 am-8 pm, with occasional short breaks. Be extra aware of pickpockets throughout the entire train station! If you can afford a first-class ticket to Cusco you can enjoy lunch and the train hostess service. In the afternoon you cross the 4319-meter-high La Raya Pass, after which it is all downhill! There is plenty of time to buy woolen articles from locals on the platforms during the regular stops (ca. 1 hour in Juliaca to change locomotives). Bring plenty of your favorite motion-sickness medicine if you tend to get sick easily!

Buses

Regular minibus shuttles to Juliaca and Juli. Daily buses to Arequipa, Cusco and La Paz (Bolivia). Trips to Sillustani are organized by the plentiful travel agents. It is essential to shop around for trips to Bolivia, as prices vary greatly.

Tourist Information

The Tourist Information Office is located at Calle Arequipa 314, tel: 351449 and 353804.

Boats

To the islands of Taquile and Amantaní, and the floating islands of the Uros: several boats, whose owners ask every passer-by if they want to go to one of the islands in Lake Titicaca, wait at the wharf (*embacadero*) every morning after 7:00. The prices are low and mostly the same, but not all of the boats inspire confidence (even with a life jacket it is too cold to swim...).

CHUCUITO (Area Code 054)
Accommodation

Hotel Chucuito, Carretera Panamericana 17/5, tel: 622208, fax: 352108, quiet, views of the lake. **Las Cabañas**, Jr. Tarapaca 153, tel: 351276, cabins and camping.

THE WEALTHY SOUTHERN COAST

AREQUIPA

SOUTH OF AREQUIPA

NAZCA

ICA

PARACAS

FROM PISCO TO PACHACAMAC

At first sight, the southern tip of Peru, which faces the Pacific Ocean, does not seem at all attractive. It consists of endless desert with minimal precipitation, a dreary coastal strip, only a few villages and towns, and wide, uninhabited stretches of land. Looking more closely, however, one discovers captivating oases, with Arequipa, one of the most beautiful cities in Peru; the fascinating archaeology of the Inca culture and the mysterious Nazca Lines; the Islas Ballestas with interesting sea fauna; the beach resort of Pisco; irrigated meadows and fields along the Panamericana highway; giant poultry farms and fishmeal factories along the coast; and the biggest wine-growing area in Peru. And if you venture farther into the hinterland, you can see the Cañón de Colca, the "deepest gorge in the world," and volcanoes that are snow-covered all year round.

AREQUIPA

Located in a semi-desert area, 2380 meters above sea level, the river oasis of Arequipa survives on the precipitation and snow melt of its mountainous sur-

Previous Pages: A colony of sea-lions on the Islas Ballestas. Left: The gorge of the Río Colca, Peru's "Grand Canyon."

roundings. These include: the volcanic cone El Misti (5822 meters); the imposing 6075 meter Chachani massif; and the 5669 meter high Pichu Pichu. With a population of 900,000, this sun-drenched capital of the Departmento of Arequipa is one of the largest cities in Peru. It shares its name with the department and is one of the Peruvian cities that is most worth visiting. This is true, at least, of the colonial city center. The slums, however, which are inhabited by migrants from the countryside on its fringes, are at least as miserable as those of Lima, Arequipa's eternal rival.

The white tuff (*sillar*) that the three huge volcanoes have tossed into the valley over thousands of years was for a long time used as the construction material for the grand palaces, monasteries and the modest-looking but equally impressive houses in the city. Arequipa is known in Peru as *La Ciudad Blanca*, the "White City," a reference to Merida, the "White City" of Mexico.

Arequipa was founded in 1540 on the Feast of the Assumption of the Virgin Mary (August 15) which the city still celebrates with a week-long festival that includes a firework display. Arequipa does not have any modern skyscrapers, but, despite numerous earthquakes in the past, it does have a very harmonious cityscape

137

and travellers appreciate the many magnificent churches and generously laid-out monasteries.

The **Plaza de Armas** of Arequipa is said to be the most beautiful in Peru. The cathedral, several venerable old colonial hotels and some charming cafés and restaurants, surrounded by blooming jacaranda trees and high palms that sway in the warm desert wind, are situated here. Old gas lanterns, two-story arcades, a lovely white tuff well in the middle of the plaza, and decorative flowers give the plaza the ambience of a large open-air living room. The plaza also provides a view of the snow-covered volcano, the Nevado Chachani. Very often, one can see typists, equipped with typewriters, waiting in the plaza in the hope of finding work. The comfortable, ornate cast-iron park benches invite locals and visitors to pass some time relaxing. It only becomes

Above: Arequipa is surrounded by desert.
Right: The inner courtyard of the Jesuit church Iglesia La Compañía.

really quiet in the heart of Arequipa after midnight, when the nocturnal revelers have left the streets for one of the numerous *peñas* or nightclubs.

The **cathedral** is located on the northern side of the Plaza de Armas. The massive, formidable neo-classical façade seems to have been built to last forever. In the interior, the altar of Carrara marble and the oversized chandeliers attract one's attention as one enters. In addition, the artistically carved pulpit and an organ imported from Belgium, said to be the largest in the subcontinent, also catch the eye. The pulpit was donated by the daughter of an aristocrat from the city, in the hope of securing her place in heaven.

Opposite the cathedral is the town hall, where one will also find the tourist information office.

If one goes down the street to the right of the town hall and crosses the street, one comes to a showpiece of Arequipa's colonial period, the **Palacio Goyoneche** (Banco de Reserva). Large verandahs, several patios and a well of black stone in

the main courtyard, a rarity for the white city of Arequipa, give the impression that time has come to a standstill here. The interior of the carefully renovated building is open to visitors in the mornings.

The Jesuit church of **Iglesia La Compañía**, one block to the southeast of the Plaza de Armas, is a very special gem of art history. On the main façade, which dates from 1698, some of the angels' faces have unmistakably Indian features – one angel even has Indian feathers on its head. In 1960, an earthquake shook the building, but the main structure remained undamaged. Some good did come out of this, as the earthquake brought the old sacristy with its unique, multi-colored dome of the chapel of San Ignacio, to light. The most beautiful decorations in the church are the colorful frescoes, which are accentuated by wood carvings in glittering gold, rich green and vivid red.

In the same street as La Compañía (Av. San Francisco), one block northeast of the Plaza, is the impressive relief portal of the **Casa Rickett** (Casa Ugarteche) dating from the colonial period. The building first served as a theological seminary, afterwards a local patrician family bought it. A few decades ago, the Banco Continental bought the house and lot, and had the house restored at great expense for use as a museum and art gallery.

The **Iglesia San Francisco** was built in the 16th century. The **Silver Altar** and the **Chapel of the Madonna of Tears** are worth seeing. Every year on the Festival of the Immaculate Conception, December 8, pilgrims carry this figure of the Virgin Mary, with huge quantities of floral arrangements and candles, in procession through the city.

The **Museo Histórico Municipal**, opposite the church, has a collection of Peruvian paintings, historic papers, photographs, maps and other evidence of the history of the city of Arequipa.

The road on the left of the museum ends, after just a few steps, in front of the massive walls of the **Monasterio de Santa Catalina**. Resembling a medieval

139

city, the picturesque convent is hidden behind the walls, and is one of the most important sights in Arequipa. The convent, founded in 1580, was extended in the 17th century to its present size. At that time up to 450 nuns and 500 servants lived here, in complete isolation from the rest of the world.

Santa Catalina had very strict selection criteria: only novices of Spanish descent, with an immaculate past, and the substantial deposit of 1000 gold pesos could be admitted. On entering the convent they were required, furthermore, to take a vow of silence.

Tourists visiting the site alone are advised to join one of the guided tours (available in many languages). If one tries to go around the Santa Catalina alone, one could easily get lost in the la-

byrinth of alleys, small inner courtyards, named after Spanish cities, chapels, kitchens, laundries, assembly rooms, penance cells and huge Araukari trees. The guided tour takes one hour, and the young female tour guides (mostly students from the nearby university) tell – with a pleasant dose of sarcasm and irreverence – delightful anecdotes about the long-dead nuns, priests, and bishops of the city. The compound has been fully restored and one can see exhibits with valuable paintings of the Cusco school, as well as beautiful old furniture. Furthermore the nuns have also set up a small cafeteria, to care for the "bodily" needs of their visitors.

On the occasion of his visit to Arequipa in 1985, Pope John Paul II beatified the former prioress of Santa Catalina, Sister Ana de los Ángeles Monteagud y León, who was born in 1602. And many Arequipeños are extremely proud of that fact. That surely includes the sisters from the convent, approximately 25 in number, who today keep it

Above Left: The main portal of the Iglesia La Compañía is decorated with angels who have Indian features. Above Right: The carvings in red and gold are La Compañía's main attraction.

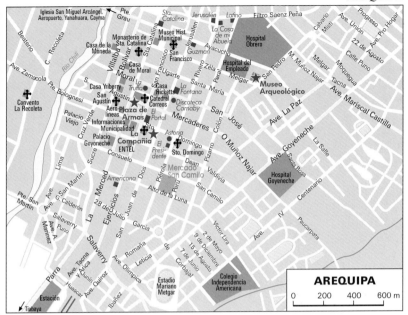

operating today, around the northern quarter of the complex.

Diagonally opposite the entrance to the Santa Catalina convent, is the museum of the Catholic University, the **Museo Santuario Andino.** It has a special treasure in its keeping: the frozen mummy of a young girl from Inca times, who was sacrificed to the gods and who was probably buried alive in the glacier on the volcano Ambato. The discovery of *Juanita*, as the unfortunate girl has been named, is regarded as one of the most significant archaeological finds in recent years in Peru. This Andean mummy, which is astonishingly well preserved, is dispayed in a glass showcase and preserved at a temperature of minus 20°C.

If you turn right on leaving the monastery and turn right at the next intersection, one comes to the **Casa de la Moneda** (at the corner of Av. Ugarte and Villalba). The Royal Mint was once situated here, before the Quiróz family bought the house in 1738 and had the not very modest inscription, *Después de*

Dios, Quiróz (after God, the Quiróz), above the gate.

A magnificent mulberry tree (*moral*) in the idyllic patio gave the **Casa de Moral** in the street of the same name (corner of Bolívar) its name. Take a look at the stone reliefs above the portal: vigorous pumas with frightening snakes crawling out of their mouths, at one time symbolized the power of the royal administration. Today, the museum belongs to the Banco Industrial, which maintains a small museum depicting the history of the house.

Round the corner is the **Casa Yriberry,** which was built in 1793 as an aristocratic colonial residence with tasteful inner courtyards. Today, the house is a part of the university.

Just one block away there is a church, **Iglesia San Agustín**, whose splendid stonemasonry can compete with that of La Compañía. An earthquake destroyed the once-wealthy monastery, leaving only the façade, a masterpiece of Mestizo architecture, standing.

141

Other churches worth seeing are located somewhat distant from the city center and are best reached by taxi. On the other side of the gorge, through which the Río Chili flows, is the Franciscan monastery, the **Convento La Recoleta,** which was built in the 17th century. It has a phenomenal library, with some items dating to the 15th century, and a museum with several sections (e.g. religious art, fauna, the peoples of the Amazon basin, a pre-Columbian collection).

To the north of the Avenida Ejército is the suburb of **Yanahuara**. The church of San Juan Bautista (1750) is located here and from the square in front of it, there is a good view of the city center of Arequipa. The Avenida Ejército meets the Avenida Cayma farther to the west. The 18th century church, **Iglesia San Miguel Arcángel** is in the suburb of **Cayma**. It

Above: In the Convento de Santa Catalina.
Right: The volcano El Misti dominates the skyline of Arequipa (seen here from Santa Catalina).

was consecrated to the Archangel Michael. An impressve, exceedingly ornate portal, with double columns on both sides, is located between the simple church towers. There is a good view of the city from the high church towers.

The suburb of **Tingo**, to the south of the city center is a popular excursion destination for the city folk, with a lake, swimming pools, and typical Peruvian restaurants.

The old **Molino de Sabandía**, eight kilometers to the north of Arequipa, is also worth a visit. A bank in the city had this large, abandoned, decaying water mill, with granary, restored to its original 18th century state. This was done by the architect Luis Felipe Calle, a renowned restorer of colonial buildings. The building, idyllically situated beside a small stream, houses a museum with historic paintings and a cafeteria. One can sit and enjoy a rich black espresso, and hear the water splashing on the mill wheel in the background or the large bell at the entrance, ringing to announce new visitors.

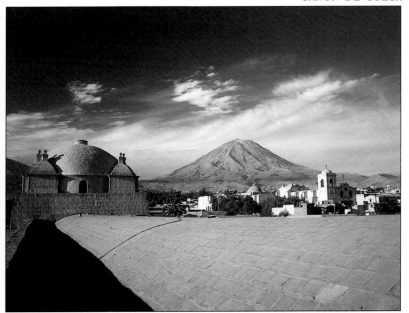

Excursions from Arequipa

For many visitors an excursion lasting several days to the **Cañón de Colca** is an obligatory part of their itinerary, as is an adventurous, wet, white-water ride in the cold and very windy valley basin. That the gorge is the deepest canyon in the world, can be confidently considered to be nothing more than advertising hype of the tour managers. Despite the long and wearing drive, the tour of the Cañón de Colca is an unforgettable experience of nature.

One leaves the city to the north, crosses a long stretch of uninhabited desert, and passes the nature reserve of Pampas de Cañahuas. The reserve is 3850 meters above sea level and is home to vicuñas and rare, shy guanacos. After the village of Viscachani (4150 meters), one reaches the 4800 meter high pass, and from here, one catches a view of the peak Ampato (6288 meters). Then there is a steep drop towards **Chivay**, where hot springs wait to refresh travelers. One

can then follow the southern edge of the Cañón de Colca and see the many agricultural terraces, dating from the times before the Inca dominion. After the village Yanque, near Achoma, is the **Cruz del Cóndor**, the best vantage-point for seeing the gorge.

To reach the deepest point in the canyon, however, one would have to trek on for another few hours. The **Río Colca** flows 1200 meters below and there are plans to some day use the water that this huge gorge carries for the irrigation of agricultural plantations. In the early morning hours, the condors glide majestically, high above the gorge. In clear weather one can see, on the other side of the gap, the snow-covered, cone-shaped peak of the El Mismi volcano (5597) which rises more than 3000 meters above the Cañón de Colca.

Many terraced fields in the canyon now lie fallow. When the Spaniards began transporting silver ore from the mines of the highlands through the gorge, to the coastal ports, they enslaved the

143

farmers living there and made them work as miners. As a result, only a few of the terraces are in use today, and those mainly grow barley for the large brewery in Arequipa.

Another interesting destination for an excursion is the archaeological site of **Toro Muerto** (Dead Bull), not far from the village of Corire. It consists of many carved rock blocks, which are scattered over several kilometers in this hot and extremely dry mountain desert. Archaeologists consider that artists or shamans of the Huari culture created these petroglyphs around AD 700. One can only speculate about the meaning of the warriors, priests, dancers, pumas, condors, llamas and guanacos depicted in them.

At first, the **Valle de los Volcanes** looks more like a lunar landscape than a "valley of volcanoes," but when one looks more closely, one can see

Above: Cañón de Colca with old terraced fields. Right: Peru" "easiest" six-thousander – the Chachani (El Misti in the background).

numerous small volcanic cones. The 70 kilometer-long valley, which can be reached from the village of Andagua, via Corire, stretches across up to the foot of the **Pico Coropuna**. At 6425 meters above sea level, it is one of the highest mountains in Peru. Since visiting the Valle des los Volcanos involves a rather long trek, there are not many people to be seen here. To that extent, the comparison with a lunar landscape is rather apt.

One can start the ascent of the **Volcán El Misti** (5822 meters) only after registering at the police station near the dam. After a day's brisk walking, one reaches the high-altitude camp (4800 meters). On the following day, one should reach the summit as early as possible to be able to enjoy the view of Arequipa, the endless desert, and perhaps even the Pacific. With ice picks and climbing irons, the route to the summit of the El Misti is not considered technically difficult, but one needs to be very fit and sufficiently acclimatized. In addition, the weather here is a completely unpredictable factor.

The sprawling extinct volcano **Nevado Chachani** (6075 meters), which towers over Arequipa, is the easiest six-thousand-meter mountain in the Andes to reach and to conquer – if no snow has fallen recently. One can drive up to 4800 meters in an off-road vehicle. From the end of the track at the northeastern wall, the climb and descent take about 12 hours; or if one is satisfied with the ancillary Fatima peak (6010 meters), about 10 hours (crampons, ice picks and elevation-acclimatization necessary). Crampons are required for crossing a steep, ice-covered slope at 5400 meters.

Most of the travel agencies organize tours to El Misti (e.g., in the Calle Jerusalén). Mario Mazuelos Quevedo, Tel. 270519, is an experienced Chachani mountain guide with a Swiss diploma.

After a mountaineering expedition, anyone, who has the time and the inclination to relax in a hot bath in unique surroundings, can visit the **thermal springs of Jesús** (10 kilometers from Arequipa) and **Yura** (30 kilometers). Both springs, with sulfurous, hot water can be easily reached by bus from the city center.

SOUTH OF AREQUIPA

The places in the southwestern tip of Peru are mainly of interest to those on their way to Chile, because here, apart from an endless, dreary desert, there are only a few oases and two beach resorts.

After travelling 42 kilometers from Arequipa, past beautifully formed sand dunes, one comes to the **Panamericana highway**. In Repartición turn off to the left towards **Mollendo**, a port city with about 20,000 inhabitants. The beach resort, frequented by the Arequipeños between January and March has three beautiful, wide, sandy beaches with pleasant water temperatures in mid-summer. The city also serves as a starting point for visiting the nature reserve of Mejía. Its days as a port city, however, seem to be numbered. Nowdays, most of the larger ships tend to anchor at Matarani, 15 kilometers north.

145

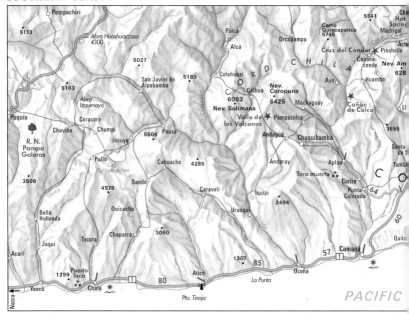

Mejía is also only lively in summer when the Arequipeños stay there in vacation homes and eat in the restaurants. There are no hotels. Six kilometers to the southeast of Mejía is the **Reserva de Lagunas de Mejía**. The 700-hectare coastal lagoon is home to crakes, herons, gulls and gannets.

The *Panamericana Sur* goes further into the interior and crosses the artificial oasis of **La Joya**, which is irrigated at great effort and expense. It continues across the valley of the Río Tambo and after a long, lonely stretch of desert, reaches the turn-off to the city of **Moquegua.** This city of 13,000 inhabitants is the capital of the Departamento of Moquegua. Located 1400 meters above sea level, on the **Río Osmore**, the river here makes it possible to cultivate grapes and avocados. In this region, 220 kilometers to the south-east of Arequipa, it almost never rains, and therefore many houses have rooftops made of sun-dried clay bricks that are held up by sugarcane rods. Moquegua is the point in the Peruvian

desert with the lowest average precipitation. The desert continues southwards, as the Atacama desert of Northern Chile, the driest desert in the world. The wide streets in Moquegua are paved with cobblestones, as are the narrow alleys, which are lined by numerous colonial houses. In the shady **Plaza de Armas**, which has a pretty cast-iron well, is the church **Iglesia Santo Domingo**, whose treasures consist of a beautiful Baroque altar and the mortal remains of St. Fortunata. Also worth seeing are the ruins of the **Iglesia Matriz de Moquegua**. This ruins of this church, which collapsed in 1868 after seven severe earthquakes, are a reminder of those troubled times.

Fifty-four kilometers farther on, a spectacular road turns off the Panamericana highway to **Ilo**. An overseas port, located in the middle of inhospitable desert, it is used as a free-trade zone by Bolivia. From here, Peru ships copper from the Toquepala mine, which geologists estimate to contain about 500 million tonnes of copper. Sugarcane, avocados,

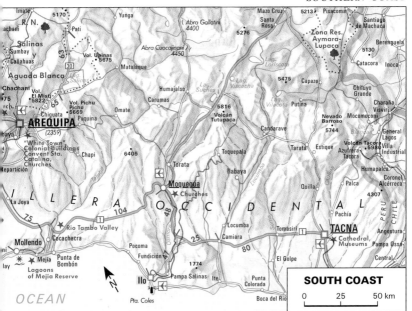

SOUTH COAST
0   25   50 km

olives, wheat, corn, grapes and cotton are also exported from Ilo to Japan, the USA and Europe.

The last large Peruvian city before the border with Chile is **Tacna**; it is situated 565 meters above sea level, a good 1300 kilometers to the south of Lima along the Panamericana highway. It is the capital city of the Departmento of Tacna, and has a population of 55,000. After the War of the Pacific, Tacna belonged to Chile from 1880 to 1929, when its inhabitants voted in a referendum to return to Peru. The tastefully designed and well-maintained city center stands out from the other, rather shabby border towns in Latin America. In the long drawn out **Plaza de Armas,** there are two bronze statues in honor of the Peruvian generals Bolognesi and Grau. The French architect, Gustav Eiffel, famous for his steel Tower in Paris, has also become immortalized here. He designed not only the Neo-Renaissance cathedral, **La Catedral**, begun in 1872, but also the six-meter tall **bronze fountain** in the Plaza,

which is similar to the fountain in the Place de la Concorde in Paris. Next to the Casa de Cultura, and worth visiting, is the **Museo Ferroviario Nacional** (national railway museum), which contains locomotives from the late 19th and early 20th century. Both Bolivia and Chile have a consulate in Tacna, just a half-hour drive from the border. The city – probably because it is a military base – is known, not only for its good, state-subsidized schools, sports facilities and hospitals, but also for its particularly skilled pickpockets who prey on tourists travelling through.

FROM AREQUIPA TO NAZCA

Several important Peruvian cultures have left behind their traces in the desertlike coastal strip to the north of Arequipa. Oases and irrigated fields appear only rarely when traveling along the very twisty, mostly well maintained Panamericana highway, which winds its way through the hilly desert landscape. None-

147

theless, this region of Peru has its very own character, and there are some places worth visiting here.

Having reached the Pacific coast from Arequipa via Repartición, one encounters **Camaná.** This summer beach resort for the Arequipeños is near the estuary of the Río Camaná. It has several wide beaches, but only a few hotels. The locals spend their holidays in their private holiday homes. A state-run, irrigation project was started recently and is facilitating rice cultivation in extensive fields.

Chala is the name of the next fishing port to the north, a welcome stop for those travelling by bus to Lima. The *chasquis*, Incan relay runners, used to take fresh fish from Chala to the Inca court at Cusco, achieving this distance with two days of continuous running. The only question is, how fresh was the fish really?

Above: Fiesta de los Reyes Magos (Arequipa region). Right: Coastal desert along the Panamericana highway.

NAZCA

The city of Nazca, located a short distance away from the usual tourist routes, and its numerous archaeological sites, should not be missed during a visit to Peru. The valley oasis of Nazca played an important role in the early history of Peru. Because of the very favorable conditions for preservation in the dry desert sand, we know quite a bit today about the pre-Columbian cultures of the region. The city of **Nazca** is situated at 600 meters above sea level, 447 kilometers to the south of Lima. Nazca now has a population of 38,000. In the middle of an almost endless sand desert, the city is a fertile oasis in which many people make their living from the cultivation of cotton and farming on smallholdings. Nazca has a small municipal museum in the Plaza de Armas and a few large hotels that attract visitors from all over the world.

The desert sands had literally covered the history of the Nazca culture until the beginning of this century. The German-

American archaeologist Max Uhle (originally a beer brewer in California) discovered through his excavations from 1901 onwards traces of a culture that was clearly different from the other coastal cultures in Peru. Unfortunately, Uhle's success had another undesired effect. Dozens of *huaqueros* (grave robbers) started searching the desert for burial relics, stole these valuable burial relics, and as a result caused a huge amount of damage.

With the decline of the Paracas culture around AD 200 the Nazca culture began to develop, but shortly after its heyday, it almost literally disappeared under the sand around AD 800. Based on the differences in the pottery, it can be roughly divided into three phases. The people built their temples and houses from the hard wood of the *algarrobo* (St. John's bread or carob) tree, irrigated their fields with a magnificent system of canals and developed a distinctive religion. The **ceramics** of the Nazca culture – clay bowls as well as jugs and figures – show many

details of the peoples' daily life. These ceramics enable conclusions to be drawn about: the food; the gods and the religious cults of the people; their musical instruments; their rites; domestic animals; and crops. The Nazcas attached a great deal of importance to the manufacture of water jugs with seemingly playful functions – often with two openings and a bridge-like handle, so that a whistling noise would sound when water was poured out. While the depictions on the pottery were quite realistic at first, they later became more abstract. Their colors, mostly painted on the objects immediately after firing, always remained vivid and rich in contrast.

The Nazca Lines

The most puzzling inheritances of the Nazca culture are doubtless their **ground drawings**, which have been the cause, at times, of exaggerated speculation. In 1939, the American Paul Kosok discovered the first figure, a bird, from an

149

aircraft. Kosok called the figures in a 50 by 20 kilometer strip in the Pampa Colorada (between Nazca and Palpa) the "biggest astronomy book in the world." Maria Reiche, a mathematician who had emigrated from Germany, heard of the drawings, set off for Nazca and made a life-long study of the furrows in the desert sand. The furrows are often just 20 centimeters wide and finger-deep.

The Nazca artists transferred a small original drawing onto the ground, on such a large scale that the resulting pictures can only be seen from the air. (A plan for such a drawing on a piece of cloth was found only recently in the sand.) They used stakes and ropes to mark, for example, astonishingly accurate circles and spirals in the ground.

By these simple means, they drew about 1300-1700 years ago, a 188-meter-

Above: Mysterious lines in the desert sand (here, the "hummingbird") – heritage of the Nazca culture. Right: Mummy from Cahuachi, at one time the Nazcas' capital city.

long lizard (whose tail is intersected by the Panamericana highway) and a condor with a majestic wingspan measuring 180 meters. If one makes a round trip by plane, one can recognize a hummingbird, a dog with its tail in the air, several triangles and trapezoids, a whale, a tree with spreading branches, and an 89 meter long monkey. Depictions which can also be seen clearly include: human hands, a llama, an iguana, a spider, and last, but not least, the "space traveler," a drawing, of which the outline is reminiscent of an astronaut.

In all likelihood, this really is a gigantic astronomical calendar, comparable to the Intihuatana of the Incas and the stela arrangements of the Mayas. On December 21, the summer solstice, for example, the sun sets exactly where an extrapolated line of one of the figures would meet the horizon. But not only the sun lines, also the moon and star lines were supposed to help the people to know the correct time to sow their crops in the fields. Important religious holidays could also be observed accurately. Parts of the animal figures form such astronomical lines. For instance, the beak of a bird points to the rising sun on the day of the summer solstice. The desert figures are also thought to mean something else. According to one theory, they could be proof that people knew how to fly, using kites or hang gliders, long before the arrival of the Europeans. Other propositions say that the lines were for running races or for performing rain dances.

From where were the Nazca people themselves able to recognize these huge pictures? It is scarcely possible from the hills of the desert, because at that kind of distance, the lines become completely indistinct in the hazy air. From a hot-air balloon, maybe? The American anthropologist Jim Woodman has carried out experiments and shown this solution to be at least within the realms of possibility.

From an **observation tower** on the road towards Ica, erected with a donation from Maria Reich, just a few kilometers outside of Nazca, one can admire some of the lines. The drawings can however be seen vto much greater advantage by taking a **round trip flight** in a small plane (ideally in the morning, about US $50). If you want to save yourself the long trip to Nazca, you can also do this flight, starting from Ica.

In recent times, the survival of the Nazca lines has been jeopardized – footprints and car tracks of tourists and the air pollution, caused by the industrialization of Nazca, have done more damage to the drawings in the desert sand than was once believed possible. Therefore, entering the area is now strictly forbidden. The title "UNESCO World Cultural Heritage" alone is not enough to preserve the pictures.

Maria Reiche, the "keeper" of the drawings, died in 1998. A small museum was opened in her honor, 30 kilometers to the north of Nazca, in Ingenio.

Around Nazca

Some 28 kilometers from the city of Nazca is a graveyard called the **Cementerio de Chauchilla**. At first sight, it is difficult to believe one's eyes: bones one thousand years old, skulls, and even entire mummies, cloths and fragments of clothing, as well as shards of ceramic urns, lie around, openly scattered in the desert sand. The *huaqueros* (grave robbers) long ago removed all the valuable burial relics and only because of their irreverent and criminal search for gold and jewelry did the body parts from the graves come to light. The peace of the dead has been disturbed forever and, according to the beliefs of the early Nazcas, the reincarnation of the dead hindered as well. That could only take place if the entire body was preserved. In addition, a priest had to take out the innards, mummify the body, and also place valuable cloths and jewelry (for example, little pieces of silver leaf in the mouth) in the grave with the dead body.

A few kilometers to the northwest of the city, across the Arica bridge over the Río Seco (a riverbed that is usually dry), are the **Ruinas Paradones**, with the remains of an Incan settlement. Of even more interest are the neighboring underground irrigation channels, which were built by the Incas and still function. The **Aqueducto Cantallo** supplies water to the nearby fields even today.

Just a few kilometers to the west of the Nazca Lines are the remains of the city of **Cahuachi**, once the capital of the Nazca culture. As is the case with Chauchilla and Paredones, there are many travel agents in Nazca who organize excursions to the pyramids of Cahuachi, where entire rows of tree-trunks lie half-buried in the desert sand. Nobody is able to say what the significance was of this remarkable arrangement of wood, which is so rare here.

Above: A sixth century fan, which was found in a Nazca grave. Right: Sunset in the Pampas Galeras.

A visit to the **Santuario de Vicuñas** in the **Pampas Galeras** requires a longer excursion by jeep or minibus. One hundred kilometers to the east of Nazca, in the mountains, large herds of the shy vicuñas live in the cold and windy landscape of the high steppes.

ICA

After driving for several hours from Nazca, large billboards suddenly begin to appear in the lonely desert – one is nearing a large city. And sure enough: **Ica**, founded in 1563 by Jerónimo Luis de Cabrera, is today home to 175,000 inhabitants. The desert metropolis is about 400 meters above sea level and is therefore spared the coastal fog, *garúa*. On the contrary, the climate in Ica is pleasant: always dry and sunny, never too hot, and there is usually a mild sea breeze blowing. Even though it is an hour's drive from the Pacific, giant sand dunes surround the city. Here, agriculture would not have been possible without water

from the **Río Ica** which has been diverted into numerous canals. Grapes, alfalfa, cotton and tropical fruits flourish around the city. Many vineyards and distilleries for the notorious Pisco, an ingredient of the Peruvian national cocktail, Pisco Sour, provide employment for many inhabitants of Ica. The best time to visit the wine cellars and distilleries, here called **bodegas**, is during the grape harvest from February to April. The Bodegas Tacama, Ocucaje, and Vista Alegre as well as Peña, Lovera, and El Carmel in the city district of Guadalupe are among those most worth seeing.

One should visit the **Museo Regional** on the outskirts of Ica before, and not after, a round of wine tasting. Located in a simple concrete structure, it's not the most modern museum from a pedagogical standpoint, but it has a clear layout and is very informative. The Regional Museum exhibits artifacts from the Paracas, Nazca, and Inca cultures. These include: trepined skulls; captured trophy heads; ceramic figures; large clay vases;

mummies; beautiful examples of the weaving skills of the Paracas; feather coats from later periods; and even the fascinating *quipus*, the encoded knotted cords of the Incas. Outside, in the museum's courtyard, one can see from a viewing platform a small-scale reproduction of the Nazca Lines, giving a good first overview.

The **Museo Cabrera** in the Plaza de Armas is devoted to a completely different theme. It has a display of 10,000 stones and blocks of rock with engravings, some with depictions of adventurous pre-Columbian head surgery and scenes from daily life from more than 1000 years ago. The operator of the museum asserts the authenticity of all his exhibits though there is room for doubt in some cases.

Just five kilometers to the west of Ica, between high sand dunes, is the incredibly beautiful **Huacachina Oasis**. In this endless desert, it has the effect of a Fata Morgana from A Thousand and One Nights. A lake, surrounded by large

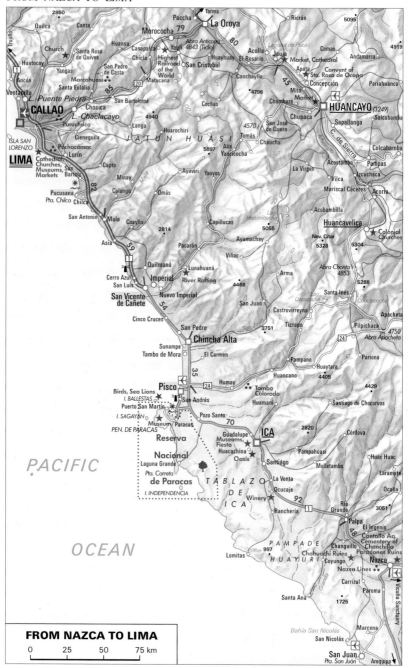

FROM NAZCA TO LIMA

0   25   50   75 km

palms and colorful bushes of decorative flowers, invites one to go paddle boating or even for a swim. Many locals do, in fact, swim in it, but probably so do all species of bacteria in the world. Huacachina is the ideal place for a midday stop between Ica and Paracas, because there are two good, venerable old hotels here. The Mossone (medium category, renovated) and the Gran Hotel Salvatierra (budget class) invite the traveler to come and relax for a few hours or even days, and furthermore they both serve tasty meals.

The days of the Huacachina oasis also appear to be numbered. Since the farmers began to drill new and deeper wells a few years ago in the Ica valley, the water level in the lake of the oasis has been falling alarmingly.

PARACAS

The **early history** of the **Paracas culture** has been known only since 1925. In that year, the Peruvian archaeologist Julio Tello and his colleague Samuel Lothrop, from the United States, discovered underground of this culture, which had its heyday from 1300 BC to AD 200 on what is today an arid peninsula. Because of the excellent condition in the dry desert sand, the researchers were able to recover more than 400 mummies, which were covered in the finest woven cloths. According to Tello, the findings made it possible to distinguish two periods in the Paracas culture: the Cavernas period (500-300 BC) and the Necropolis period (300 BC - AD 200).

In the Cavernas period, the people built bottle-shaped family crypts up to seven meters below the ground and walled them up. The mummies were placed in a squatting position, wrapped in cotton cloths, in narrow baskets of bast. They were surrounded by musical instruments, decorated gourds, clay bowls, figures of gods, and jugs. The jaguar cult must have played a significant role in the religion of the Cavernas period. A jaguar is often depicted on ceramics and textiles.

In the Necropolis period, people seem to have placed even more value on the burial of their dead. They built underground burial cities with wooden roofs and decorated their mummies with strings of pearls, placed gold leaf in their mouths and eyes, and covered them in artistically woven clothes that were full of mythological symbols. The cloths for the mummies' shrouds, woven with unimaginable patience, measured up to 20 x 4 meters, and are unequalled anywhere in the world. Archaeologists have been able to distinguish more than 22 colors and almost 200 different nuances in the depictions of fish, sea birds, geometric figures, half-humans, and demons. One sensational discovery was that of skulls that were apparently opened surgically and then closed up again with gold plates. This means that the Peruvians had managed complicated surgical operations even before the Incas.

The anthropologists of Peru are still not sure why the dominance of the Paracas culture, which lasted almost 1500 years, was replaced (by the Nazca culture, and that in turn by the Huari culture, and then by the Ica culture). This question will probably remain unanswered forever. On the other hand, it is certain that it did not take the Incas too long to integrate this historical region into their giant empire.

The Paracas Peninsula and the Ballestas Islands are important nature reserves on the coast of Peru. The **Península de Paracas**, a few square kilometers in size, is nothing but a treeless sandy desert. Today, there is nothing to remind one of the great Paracas culture, and only the bays with their clear, cool Pacific waters attract swimmers and sunbathers. Swimming, however, is not such a good idea on all the beaches, because at some there are sea urchins and jellyfish.

From the wooden dock projecting far out into the Pacific in the small beach village of Paracas, motor boats leave from early morning till late in the day for the two- to three-hour cruise to the bird and sealion colonies of the islands, **Islas Ballestas**. From the fast-moving boats, one can see the wrecks of several old Russian ships and, on the coast of the Paraca Peninsula, catch a glimpse of the 50 meter long **Candelabro** (candlestick), an over-sized trident, dug in the sandy ground. Is it related to the Nazca lines, or, as Erich von Däniken has speculated, possibly a landing sign for extra-terrestrials?

One would normally associate the fauna that is found on the Islas Ballestas with much colder regions, nearer to the poles. The icy water from the ocean depths that is driven to the surface along the Peruvian coast, the Humboldt current – named after the German naturalist and

Above: The oasis of Huacachina invites you to relax on the way to Paracas. Right: Inca terns on the Islas Ballestas.

geographer – permits this phenomenon a mere 1500 kilometers south of the equator. Out of the pale sunlight, the islands appear, with pelicans hovering majestically and gannets diving in swarms from the sky. The air is full of screaming gulls, Inca terns with their black and red colors, and black-and-white feathered cormorants. Curious seals accompany the boat, as it chugs along. The acoustics of the natural amphitheater of rock walls magnify the roaring of the sea lions. Peruvian Humboldt penguins waddle, clumsily rather than elegantly, over the rocks. Mussels, crustaceans, and sea urchins have made the rough rock walls into their permanent anchorage.

On one of the small islands, which is uninhabited because it is a nature reserve, one can see a guano factory, with loading ramps and conveyor belts. Every year Peru exports 20,000 tonnes of fertilizer, made from bird droppings, collected from the island cliffs of the Pacific. Once again, this proves that it is indeed, true, that where there's muck, there's brass!

FROM PISCO TO PACHACAMAC

A quarter of an hour's drive to the north of Paracas is the city of **Pisco.** This city is 240 kilometers to the south of Lima and has a population of 90,000. Pisco is also the name that has been given to the grapes that are made into the famous Pisco brandy. The main reason for a stay in Pisco is usually to make an excursion to the Península de Paracas or the Islas Ballestas in the Pacific. Since there are too few hotels in the beach resort of Paracas, 15 kilometers to the south, many travelers tend to stay in Pisco.

Worthwhile sights in Pisco include: the charming **town hall**, the façade of which has some Moorish style ornamentation; and the church of **La Compañía**, with its gold-covered altars, which is now a museum. Less impressive, but unfortunately, hard to ignore, are the fishmeal factories around Pisco. On many days, their pungent, penetrating odor is blown by the sea breezes into the outer suburbs of the city.

Anyone wishing to see the ruins of **Tambo Colorado** should do so from Pisco by taxi or bus (going towards Huancavelica). These ruins derive their name from the yellow, white and red walls of a crumbled palace. The **sun temple** with its trapezoidal niches and doors seems to indicate an Incan heritage, but the shrine to the right of the street, seems to have been the work of master builders from before the Incan era. Anthropologists are not yet unanimous about whether or not Tambo Colorado was a military fortress to secure a conquest. Visiting the ruins requires idealism and energy. The bus takes almost two hours to cover the 50 kilometers from Pisco, over bumpy gravel roads. There is neither a restaurant nor a drink stand there. In addition, the polychromatic decoration of Tambo Colorado seem to be fading visibly.

The next large city between Pisco and Lima is called **Chincha Alta**, and is home to 40,000 inhabitants. In the 13th century, it was a small principality until it

157

was conquered by the Incas around 1390 and forced into submission. However, in the Inca Empire, the prince of Chincha still had some influence and he usually lived at the court in Cusco or Cajamarca. Only the ruins of **Tambo de Mora,** with their temple, *La Centinela*, 10 kilometers southwest of the city on the Pacific, remain today as a witness of the Chincha culture. However almost nothing remains of them, except a stepped pyramid with chambers built of clay bricks.

If one travels further along the Panamericana highway, one reaches the small town of **San Vincente de Cañete**, an oasis with cotton fields. It is 145 kilometers south of Lima. Cañete was settled even before the Incan period, but became modestly important only because of the Spaniards. To the south of the village, in the cotton fields, there is a small pa-

Above: This artistically woven cloth from the Paracas culture is more than 2000 years old! Right: A tame Humboldt penguin along the southern Panamericana highway.

lace, which was at one time the country seat of a Spanish viceroy. The building is suposed to be turned into a museum in the next few years. Anyone who likes white-water rafting or kayaking can do so between December and March on the **Río Cañete**, starting from Cañete or Lunahuaná.

Seventy kilometers to the south of Lima, located in a picturesque bay, is the fishing village of **Pucusana**. The city-dwellers come here to swim, take boat tours or to feast in one of the fish restaurants. One special attraction is the "**Devil's Jaws**" (Boca del Diablo), a rocky abyss through which the breakers roar with a thundering sound.

Pachacamac

It is well worth seeing the site of the ruins of **Pachamac,** which is just an hour's drive south of Lima. A shrine, constructed here in the sixth century, was dedicated to the creator and preserver of the universe, Pachacamac (*pacha* = earth, *camay* = to create). It is modeled after the "Weeping God," Huiracocha, which had been worshipped in Tiahuanaco (Bolivia) for a long time. Pachacamac, with an area of six square kilometers, was huge – the biggest pre-Columbian settlement along the Pacific coast and, as a shrine, was probably the best-known pilgrimage site.

The entire site of Pachacamac is comparable with that of Teotihuacan in Mexico: there are wide ceremonial streets, large buildings, artificial hills and sacrificial altars at which the priests made offerings of plants, animals and human blood to the gods. It is quite possible that here even human beings were sacrificed to the gods.

The walls of this center of cult worship were painted with depictions from nature – particularly of animals – which, in this dismal, gray-brown coastal desert, must have made a strong impression on the pilgrims. The ninth Inca ruler, Pachacutec

Yupanqui, known as the *Shaker of the Earth* because of his expansionist tendencies, conquered Pachacamac around 1470, but did not destroy the shrine. Instead, he converted it to suit his own purposes. He did not destroy the magnificent pictures either, but started the construction of a large pyramid for his most important god, the sun-god, Inti. Even the **Casa de las Mamaconas** complex, the house of the chosen women (or sun virgins), which has been carefully excavated, was built on the initiative of the Incan ruler. Its massively walled foundation and the large niches carved out of the adobe proclaim the typical Incan construction style.

The cult of the god Pachacamac was a common popular topic of discussion even at the beginning of the 16th century in the Inca Empire. The conquistadors soon heard of it. In 1533, Hernando Pizarro conquered Pachacamac and he had all the priests executed, the centuries-old paintings destroyed, considering them to be idols, and the treasure-chambers opened, in order to get at the gold and silver hidden in them as soon as possible. At the Casa de las Mamaconas, the state of Peruhas placed a memorial to its most famous archaeologist, Julio C. Tello. The German anthropologist Max Uhle has also been immortalized with a bust and a plaque. He interpreted the main temple as a shrine of the moon god during his many years of excavation work in Pachacamac.

In the **Templo de Pachacamac** (Sun Temple), located on a rise, a few frescos that escaped the destructive frenzy of the Spanish conquistadors can be seen today. From here, one can see the restless Pacific breakers exploding on the long beaches beyond the Panamericana highway.

The **Museum** at the entrance exhibits the results of the excavations of Uhle and Tello: textile work; numerous ceramic urns; and a wooden ceremonial baton of the god Pachacamac, which is more than two meters high. The recesses, empty today, probably held gold, silver, and jewelry with precious stones.

AREQUIPA (Area Code 054)
Accommodation

LUXURY: **Libertador**, Selva Alegre, Plaza Bolivar, tel: 215110, fax: 241933, spacious park, pool, sauna, room safes, very good service. *MODERATE*: **La Maison d'Elise**, Av. Bolognesi 104, tel: 256185, fax: 271935, pool, nice rooms. **La Fontana**, C. Jerusalén 202, tel: 234161, fax: 234171, good value for your money. **Villa Baden Baden**, M. Ugarteche 401, well cared-for, friendly. **La Posada del Puente**, Puente Grau/Av. Bolognesi 101, tel: 253132, fax: 253576, pretty riverside location, good restaurant, garage, room safes. **La Posada del Monasterio**, C. Sta. Catalina 300, tel/fax: 215705, central location, quiet, colonial charm, but modern fittings. *BUDGET*: **La Casa de mi Abuela**, C. Jerusalén 606, tel: 241206, fax: 242761, good location, nice pool, garden with mountain view. **La Casa del Melgar**, C. Melgar 108, tel: 222459. **Hotel Jerusalén**, C. Jerusalén 601, tel: 244441, fax: 243472, rooms with bathtubs, TV, terrace and sauna. **Hotel Santa Catalina**, C. Sta. Catalina 500, tel: 243705, popular with backpackers, friendly. **Albergue Juvenil** (youth hostel), Ronda Recoleta 104, tel: 257085, former Franciscan monastery.

Restaurants

Astoria, C. Sto. Domingo 130, simple and inexpensive. **Sol de Mayo**, Yanahuara, C. Jerusalén 207, tel: 225546, excellent local specialties. **Restaurant Cosqo**, Plaza de Armas, Portal Sn. Agustín 133, good Cusco-style menu, terrace with a view of the plaza. **La Truffa**, Paseo La Catedral 111, delicious pasta. **La Posada del Puente**, Av. Bolognesi 101, tel: 253132, elegant and expensive. **El Camaroncito**, San Francisco 303, tel: 202080, large selection of seafood and pasta.

Entertainment

Las Queñas, C. Sta. Catalina 302, tel: 215468, live music, folklore. **La Italiana**, San Francisco 303, tel: 202080, dinner, folk music, dancing.

Sights / Museums

Monasterio Santa Catalina, C. Sta. Catalina 301, tel: 229798, daily 9 am-5 pm, only with guided tour (English, French, German or Spanish), telephone registration requested. **Iglesia La Compañía**, C. Sto. Domingo, Mon-Sat 9:30 am-1 pm, 4-6 pm. **Convento y Museo de la Recoleta**, C. Recoleta 117, tel: 270966, Mon-Sat 9 am-12 noon, 3-5 pm. **Convento San Francisco**, Plaza San Francisco, Mon-Sat 9 am-12:30 pm, 3-6:30 pm. **Museo Santuarios de Altura** ("Juanita"), C. Sta. Catalina, opposite the San Francisco Monastery, Mon-Sat 9 am-5:45 pm. **Museo Histórico Municipal**, Plaza San Francisco, Mon-Fri 8 am-6 pm.

Transportation

BUSES: The bus companies are on Calle San Juan de Diós. Buses to all large cities several times daily. All travel agencies/hotels offer inclusive (strenuous) tours lasting several days to the **Colca Canyon**.
AIRLINES: **Aero Continente**, Portal San Agustín 113, tel: 237334/219914, fax: 219788, 1-2 daily flights to Juliaca. **TANS**, Portal San Agustín 117. **Lan Peru**, several daily flights to Lima, Cusco and Tacna. The Rodriguez Ballon Airport is just 5 kilometers from Plaza de Armas.
TRAINS: The ticket counter at the Estación Ferrocarril del Sur del Peru, Jr. Tacna y Arica 200 for trains to Puno and Cusco opens only from 3-5 pm and the lines can be very long. Night trains leave Arequipa at 9 pm and arrive in Puno at 8 am.

Tourist Information

Plaza de Armas, Portal Municipalidad 112, tel: 211-021, Mon-Fri 8 am-noon, 2-5 pm, Sat 8 am - noon.

SOUTH AND NORTH OF AREQUIPA
(Area Code 054)
Accommodation

CAÑÓN DEL COLCA: *BUDGET:* **Hotel Rumi Llacta**, Chivay, tel: 521020, fax: 521098, rustic, but comfortable, rooms and bungalows. **El Parador del Colca**, Parque Curiña, Yanque, reservations in Areq: tel: 288440, fax: 218608.

MOLLENDO: *BUDGET:* **Hostal La Cabaña**, Av. Comercio/Plaza de Armas, tel: 533833. **Mollendo Hotel**, Av. Arequipa 100 (corner of Plaza Grau), tel: 533104.

MOQUEGUA: *MODERATE:* **El Mirador**, Alto de la Villa, tel: 761765, fax: 761895. **Los Limoneros**, C. Lima 441, tel: 761649.

ILO: *MODERATE:* **Karina**, Abtao 780, tel/fax: 781397, terrace with view of the ocean. **Paraíso**, C. Zepita 751, tel: 781432, fax: 782926.

TACNA: *MODERATE:* **Camino Real**, Av. San Martín 857, tel: 721891, fax: 726433. **El Meson**, C. Hipólito Unanue 175, tel: 725841, fax: 721832.

CAMANÁ: *MODERATE:* **San Diego**, C. Alfonso Ugarte/28 de Julio, tel/fax: 572854. *BUDGET:* **Las Cabañas**, Panamericana highway, Km 836, tel: 571576, cabins, camping.

CHALA: *BUDGET:* **Hotel de Turistas Chala**, Av. Lima 138, tel: 571608, basic, some roms share bath, beautiful location right on the ocean. **Puerto Inka**, Panamericana highway, Km 603, tel: 237122/281571, directly on the beach.

Restaurants

MOQUEGUA: **A Todo Vapor**, C. Ancash/Plaza de Armas, local menu, good and inexpensive.
TACNA: **El Viejo Almadén**, Av. San Martín/C. Apurimac, Italian, good steaks. **Chifa Say Wa**, Av. San Martín, Chinese.

Buses

TACNA: During the dry season buses drive directly to Lake Titicaca, which takes about 16 hours on mostly gravel roads. Buses to Lima, Camaná, Chala, Ica and Nazca, Moquegua and Arequipa depart from the following bus companies' stations several times daily: **Cruz del Sur**, **Angelitos Negros**, **Ormeño** and **SurPeruano**. **Transportes Peru** offers an hourly service to Arica, Chile. Some buses traveling between Tacna and Arequipa also stop in Mollendo and Moquegua.

NAZCA, ICA AND PARACAS
(Area Code 034)
Accommodation

NAZCA: *LUXURY:* **Nazca Lines**, Av. Bolognesi, tel: 522293, reservations: (01) 4423090, well cared-for facilities, large courtyard, pool, restaurant, bar. *MODERATE:* **Borda**, near the airport, tel: 522576, old hacienda, nice garden, pool. **La Maison Suisse**, tel: 221562, reservations: (01) 4418614, near the airport and Panamericana highway, one-storied buildings, tennis court, pool. **Alegría**, C. Lima, near the Coliseum, tel: 522444. **Las Lineas**, Plaza de Armas, tel: 522488.
BUDGET: **Nazca**, Av. Lima, near the plaza. **El Sol**, Av. Tacna/Plaza de Armas. **Acapulco**, C. Lima, near the plaza.
ICA: *LUXURY:* **Las Dunas**, Panamericana highway, Km 300, tel: 231031, res: (01) 4424180, not in city center, conference hotel, pool, beautiful park. *MODERATE:* **Palace**, Av. Tacna 185.
BUDGET: **Colón**, Plaza de Armas, very modest. **Las Brisas**, C. Castrovirreyna 246. **Sol de Ica**, Av. Lima/2 de Mayo.
PARACAS: *LUXURY:* **Paracas** (resort), directly on the ocean, tel: 221736, fax: 2225379, tennis court, pool, ceramic collection.
BUDGET: **Hostal Mirador**, Tel. 665016.

Restaurants

NAZCA: Restaurants in all good hotels. Also: **La Fontana**, C. Lima, local cuisine. **La Taberna**, C. Lima, good meals with live music on Saturday evenings. **La Cebichería El Tiburón**, Nazca's most famous fish restaurant. **La Casona**, C. Lima, typical and inexpensive menu.
ICA: **El Espía**, Av. Callao, pizza and pasta. **Chifa Hong Kong**, C. Lima, good Chinese.

Buses

NAZCA/ICA: Most bus companies, especially **Ormeño** and **Tepsa**, offer several daily (incl. late evening) services to Lima and Tacna respectively, and stop in all towns along the route.

Tourist Information

ICA: Jr. Cajamarca 179, 7:30 am-3 pm. Also offers info and bookings for the region's *bodegas* (vin-eyards): Vista Alegre, Tacama, Ocucaje, Peña, Lovera, El Carmel.

Literature

"Nazca, Peru: Geheimnis der Wüste / Mystery on the Desert / Secreto de la Pampa," by Maria Reiche. It is filled with illustrations, incl. a comprehensive guide to all of the figures that have been discovered to date. Available at Hotel Nazca Lines in Nazca for US $10.

FROM PISCO TO PACHACAMAC
(Area Code 034)
Accommodation

PISCO: *MODERATE:* **Hostal El Candelabro**, Av. Callao/corner of Pedemonte, tel: 532620, reservations: (01) 4355135, well equipped. **Regency Plaza**, Plaza de Armas, tel: 535919, fax: 535920.
BUDGET: **Hotel Comercio** and **Hotel Embassy**, tel: 532040, both on Av. Comercio.
SAN VINCENTE DE CAÑETE: **Hotel La Casona**, Plaza de Armas. **Hotel Genova**, two blocks from Plaza de Armas.
CHINCHA: **Casa-Hacienda San José**, El Carmen, out in the fields, tel/fax: 221458.
PUCUSANA: **Hotel Bahía** and **Hotel Salón Blanco**, both are on the beach promenade.

Restaurants

PISCO: **Restaurant Candelabrum**, Av. Comercio, near the plaza, large selection, wonderful fresh Pacific seafood dishes. **Restaurant Don Manuelito**, C. Comercio 187, fish, meat, inexpensive.
CHINCHA: **El Palacio de los Mariscos**, directly on the Panamericana highway, fish specialties.
SAN VINCENTE DE CAÑETE: **El Piloto**, on the Panamericana highway, clean bathrooms.

Buses

PISCO: **Ormeño** offers daily services to Lima (4 hours) and to Nazca via Ica, departures one block from Plaza de Armas. **Oropresa** buses leave for Huancavelica daily at 9 am. A colectivo or taxi is recommended for the short drive to Paracas.

PACHACAMAC

ARRIVAL: From Pucusana via the Panamericana highway (40 km), from Lima with a bus or colectivo to Miraflores, further with a taxi (31 km south of Lima's Plaza de Armas).
OPENING HOURS: The area is open daily, except Mondays, 9 am-5 pm. Directly behind the entrance gate and to the right is a small museum with a shady cafeteria.
GUIDED TOURS: Pachacamacs is best visited with a car or a tour group. **Lima Tours**, Calle Belén 1040, offers tours in Spanish and English, daily except Monday. A walking tour of the ruins would take a very long time and be very taxing as it includes difficult desert terrain, despite being near the Pacific.

THE COAST NORTH OF LIMA

FROM LIMA TO CHIMBOTE
TRUJILLO AND CHAN CHAN
CHICLAYO
FROM PIURA TO MÁNCORA
TUMBES

The landscape along the coast of Peru, north of Lima, except for the Tumbes region in the extreme north, is shaped by the cold Humboldt Current. The Humboldt causes minimal precipitation to fall, which results in desert wastes, apart from the oasis-like settlements. The Panamericana highway passes long stretches of desert, oases, and cultivated river valleys with huge sugarcane plantations. Several large cities line the coast, such as Trujillo, with well-preserved colonial buildings and smoking industrial plants. Many large ruins of the Chimú, Mochica, and Lambayeque cultures with pyramids as high as houses, make interesting destinations for excursions. A visit to the almost 1500-kilometer-long northern coast is especially worthwhile for travelers interested in archaeology and culture and for lovers of beaches and water-sports.

FROM LIMA TO CHIMBOTE

Forty kilometers north of Lima lies **Ancón**, a seaside resort of the Limeños. They crowd the curved bay with its light-colored sandy beach, especially on the weekends. The deep blue waters of the Pacific attract swimmers, sailors, sun-bathers, surfers, and water-skiers. The long promenade is reminiscent of the Copacabana of Rio de Janeiro.

After many kilometers of sand dunes, one reaches **Chancay**, a small town with a population of 12,000. Here, the dunes, artistically crafted by the wind, rise to over 100 meters. Bones and ceramic shards indicate the presence of centuries-old graveyards of the Chancay culture.

Farther north, at the mouth of the **Río Huaura**, are the cities of **Huacho** and **Huaura**. The Argentinean General San Martín declared the independence of Peru in Huaura in 1821. The Río Huaura brings Huara water from the mountains of the Cordillera for irrigating the fields. A farther 50 kilometers north, one passes the city of **Barranca**, and a little later (four kilometers beyond Pativilca) the turn-off for the road ending at Huaraz in the Cordillera Blanca.

Expansive sugarcane fields begin after this turn-off. The Panamericana highway then passes by a paper factory, and, level with the village of **Paramonga**, an old, adobe Chimú temple. The Chimú used it either as a fortress or as a sun temple before the Incas captured it.

Now, for a long time, one sees only arid desert from the Panamericana highway. In the harbor city of **Huarmey**, one

Previous Pages: On the way to Trujillo – the Panamericana Norte. Left: In front of the Palacio Yturregui in Trujillo.

165

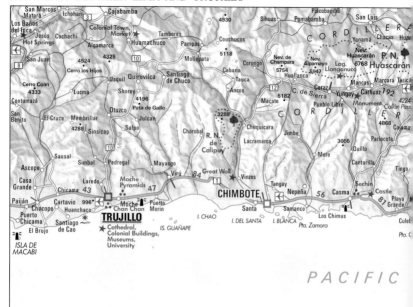

can stay overnight in the formerly state-run Hotel de Turistas. Shortly before the small town **Casma**, another road turns off into the Cordillera Blanca. After about two kilometers, one reaches the **Ruinas de Sechín**, which are very interesting. This excavation site is estimated to be 3200 years old. Adobe houses and temples, massive monoliths with human and animal figures in half relief and skillful frescoes depict the important historical events in Sechín. In a small museum at the entrance to the ruins, photographs of the excavations recall the work of the archaeologist Julio Tello and Max Uhle, an anthropologist of German origin.

Chimbote

Chimbote, population 300,000, is the first large city on the route toward Ecuador and lies 430 kilometers north of Lima. As Peru's largest fishing port and a traditional working-class city, it does have an airport, but no tourist attractions. The factories of the city produce large

quantities of fishmeal, which can also be smelled from a long way away. In the mid-1950's, the government of Peru constructed the only government-run steelworks here. It produces raw steel using hydroelectricity and ore from southern Peru.

TRUJILLO AND CHAN CHAN

Halfway between Lima and Tumbes lies **Trujillo**, one of the largest cities in Peru, with a population of over 550,000. This colonial city was founded in 1534 at the river oasis of the Río Moche. Its ideal temperatures (in winter always above 15°C, in summer around 25°C), sparse rainfall, daily sunshine, and proximity to the Pacific speak for themselves. Trujillo is worth a few days' stay because of its colonial buildings, pre-Spanish ruins and surfing beaches. The city, the seat of a university since 1824, is also well-known in Peru for its numerous galleries, small art museums, and its Fiestas. In the last week of January the Trujilleños celebrate

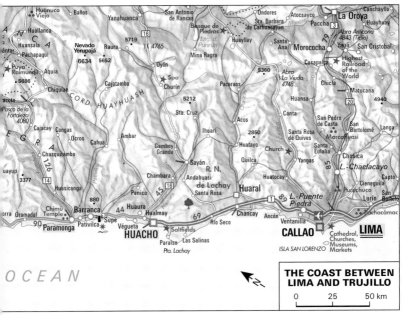

THE COAST BETWEEN
LIMA AND TRUJILLO

0   25   50 km

the *marinera*, the typical folkdance of Peruvian coastal inhabitants. Since 1950, **El Festival Internacional de la Primavera**, the spring festival, is celebrated every year in September, with processions, *marinera* dance evenings, and beauty contests. Performances by the much-loved *caballos de paso* (dressage horses) and night activities in discos, movie theatres, and music bars round off the festival.

A statue in memory of the heroes of Peruvian independence stands in the large **Plaza de Armas**. The Plaza has tall palm trees, floral arrangements, and whitewashed stone benches, which are so typical of Peru. If one tours the square in a clockwise direction, one can see on the right, the **Bishop's Palace** (1616) next to the **cathedral** (1647). Half a block away is one of the most beautiful colonial houses in the city. The **Casa Orbegoso** contains valuable furniture from the colonial period and is the venue of different painting exhibitions. Simón Bolívar is purported to have stayed for a few

months in the **Casa Urquiaga** on the southeastern side of the square around the year 1820. In honor of his Spanish hometown, he named the place, from where he organized the freedom struggle, Trujillo. Beside the house is the **City Hall** with the tourist information center.

From the next corner of the square, if you go down one block and enter the Calle Pizarro, you will see another pretty colonial house, the **Casa Mayorazgo** (today the *Banco Wiese*).

At the southwest corner of the square you will see the striking white towers of the former Jesuit church, **La Compañía** (1634). Among all the structures on this side of the square, only the ochre-colored **Casa Bracamonte** dates from the colonial period. The **Hotel Libertador**, which blends in so harmoniously, was not built until the 20th century.

Trujillo has two interesting museums. The **Museo Cassinelli** is a private collection on the western outskirts of the city and is situated in the basement of a gas station (!). Here, Señor Cassinelli has a

167

lovingly preserved collection of ceramic artifacts from the area around Trujillo. However, due to lack of space, only a small part of the thousands of exhibits can be shown at any one time. The typically Peruvian whistling vessels, are particularly valuable – one is in the shape of a bird. The **Museo de Arqueología** of the university in the Casa Risco (Ca. Junin 682) exhibits ceramics, religious figures, textiles, and finds from the fascinating burial customs of the Mochica people.

The nearby coastal town, **Huanchaco**, is a good alternative to Trujillo for an overnight stay. It has fish restaurants (very tasty: *cebiche* in *El Erizo*), budget hotels (recommended: the *Bracamonte*) and the local fishing boats made of reeds. These *caballitos de totora*, which are suitable for use in the large breakers, can be hired from the fishermen. The season

Above: In the Plaza de Armas in Trujillo, a statue serves as a memorial to the heroes of Peru's independence. Right: Boats made with rushes on the beach of Huanchaco.

for swimming here begins in October and lasts until April; when the ocean reaches temperatures of around 22°C. Hardened surfers, however, romp on the strong breakers throughout the year. Overseas tourists are still a minority here. Large families and young people from Trujillo are the main visitors to this beach, which is several kilometers long.

Huacas del Sol y de la Luna

The fascinating trip to the Huacas del Sol y de la Luna (Temple of the Sun and the Moon) is best undertaken in the morning, as later the sea breezes swirl the sand about a great deal. These two pyramids got their names from their proportions, which, like those at Teotihuacan near Mexico City, are similar to the size of the sun in relation to the moon. The ruined city is nine kilometers south-east of Trujillo, on the southern bank of the Río Moche, and was probably built around AD 500 by the Mochica. The **Huaca del Sol**, which was severely dam-

aged by Spanish treasure-hunters, measures 280 x 136 meters and was originally about 50 meters high. It consists of approximately 50 million clay bricks. The Mochica and Chimú probably buried their dead in or at the 80 x 42 meter wide and 20 meter high **Huaca de la Luna**, which is about 500 meters from the sun pyramid. Impressive colored half-reliefs of clay are proof of the great artistic capabilities that existed long before the Incas.

Chan Chan

Just two kilometers from the Plaza de Armas in Trujillo, on the road to Chan Chan, lies the **Huaca la Esmeralda.** The foundation walls of the "emerald temple" can still be recognized behind a church.

With an area of 20 square kilometers, **Chan Chan** is the largest pre-Columbian city in Peru. With 10,000 dwellings, it was once the largest adobe city in the world. Built by the Chimú as their capital around AD 1200, it had about 60,000 inhabitants, innumerable streets, and 16 large plazas, till it was conquered, but not destroyed, by the Incas around 1470. The Spaniards found Chan Chan, deserted without apparent reason, in 1533. The **Museo de Sitio**, near the turn-off towards Chan Chan, provides a good historical overview.

The **Ciudadela Tschudi**, named after the Swiss archaeologist Johann von Tschudi, is one of the earliest palaces in Chan Chan. It has temple halls, numerous niches, several ceremonial squares, a dungeon, a burial ground, and a number of astonishingly well-preserved and partly restored wall decorations (birds and creatures from fables in half-relief). The complexes of *El Laberinto*, *Uhle*, *Bandelier* and *Velarde*, the *Tumba de la Pirámide* (a grave) and the former living quarters *Gran Chimú* have not been restored.

Well-preserved dragon-reliefs in clay have given the **Huaca el Dragón** (or Arco Iris) its name. This Chimú temple is located on the northwestern outskirts of Trujillo, on the road towards Chiclayo.

CHICLAYO

Along the Panamericana highway, one now passes the towns of Puerto Chicama, Pacasmayo and Guadelupe before coming to the next large city on the northern coast: **Chiclayo**. Settled in 1560 by Spanish missionaries, very few of Chiclayo's historical structures have survived over the centuries. Chiclayo was an unimportant small town until 1900. Thereafter, it quickly grew to its present size due to migration from rural areas and industrial growth. A lively city with 270,000 inhabitants, it is the capital of the Departamento Lambayeque.

The architecture of Chiclayo reflects Indian, Spanish, Creole and European influences. The **cathedral**, for instance, was designed by the English architect Townsend, in the 19th century. On the other hand, the beautiful **Palacio Municipal**, in the Calle Balta, has Spanish characteristics.

At the northern end of the Calle Balta is the busy **Mercado Modelo**, a daily market for vegetables, fruit, meat and fish, small animals, household wares, and hand crafted items. It is also said to be the largest market for nature healers and fortunetellers. *Curanderos* (miracle healers) and *brujos* (sorcerers, magicians) offer their services with herbs, coca leaves, magic bones, magic formulas and exotic mixtures – a treasure trove for fans of traditional Indian medicine!

On weekends, city dwellers stream to the elegant beach resort of **Pimentel** (15 kilometers) or to the more modest neighboring fishing village of **Santa Rosa**.

Sipán

Half an hour (30 kilometers) east of Chiclayo are the twin pyramids of Sipán. Five graves of kings, about 2000 years old, with valuable burial relics, such as

Above: During the 13th century about 60,000 people lived in Chan Chan, the former capital of Chimú. Right: The Mochica grave "El Señor de Sipán."

gold, silver, precious stones, ceramics, and fine textiles, were discovered in the vicinity of these pyramids. The Peruvian archaeologist Walter Alva explored here in the hope of more sensational finds.

The grave of **El Señor de Sipán**, in which Alva found a Mochica priest or prince in a wooden coffin, with gold ear jewelry, a golden breast plate and a number of turquoise stones, was examined and restored by experts in a German laboratory in Mainz. The burial relics form the largest gold treasure ever found in America. Its is estimated to be about 1500 years old. Three adult men, three women, a child, and a dog were buried in the same grave, each in a casket of woven cane. A shaman with a llama and a dog lay in another grave. A small museum building documents the excavation work and the findings of Sipán.

Lambayeque

Eleven kilometers north of Chiclayo, the Panamericana highway comes to the city of **Lambayeque**, with its population of 20,000. The streets of this city wind past well-maintained adobe houses. Several of the churches and chapels of this city, which was founded by General San Martín in 1821, are worth a visit, as is the **Museo Arqueológico Brüning**. Here, the German engineer Hans Heinrich Brüning has put together a collection of gold, silver, copper, remains of clothing, and earthenware figures from the cultures of the Chimú, Lambayeque, Vicus, and Mochica. Findings from Sipán have enhanced this astounding collection.

Túcume, located 40 kilometers to the north of Chiclayo, is considered to have been the former religious and military center of the Lambayeque culture, and continued to develop until the arrival of the Incas. The Norwegian ethnologist Thor Heyerdahl and the Peruvian archaeologist Hugo Navarro discovered about thirty pyramids in an area of three square

kilometers. With a length of 700 meters, a breadth of 240 meters and a height of over 35 meters, the **Huaca Larga** is the largest pyramid at Túcume. A large number of graves, with a total of 20 mummies, and a small museum are also situated in the excavation site.

For those especially interested in archaeology, it is worthwhile making a trip to **Chongoyape**, which is 60 kilometers to the east of Chiclayo. Petroglyphs from the Chavín culture can be seen here on the **Cerro Mulato** (mulatto hill).

The Panamericana highway, running mostly straight as an arrow between Chiclayo and Piura, passes through Peru's widest section of desert, the **Desierto de Sechura**, which is in places 145 kilometers wide. The soil has a high phosphate content and is in general completely lifeless. Once, in 1983, when heavy rainfall for days on end followed a long dry spell, the desert came to life and bloomed. But the roads in the desert, an area of over 100 square kilometers, were covered in mud for months.

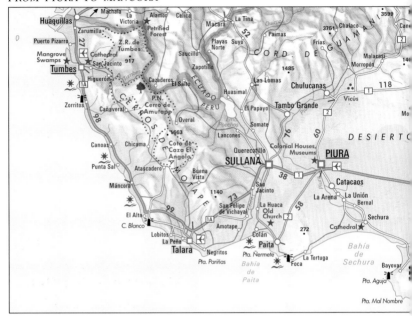

FROM PIURA TO MÁNCORA

The city of **Piura**, with a population of 350,000, is a welcome oasis for travelers in the endless desert. Piura lies 1040 kilometers to the north of the capital Lima and only 160 kilometers to the south of the border with Ecuador. It has a university, and an international airport. Founded in 1531 by Pizzaro as the first Spanish settlement in Peru, today the people depend on the harvests from corn, cotton, rice, and sugarcane fields, and from fruit and tobacco plantations for their livelihood.

The **Plaza de Armas** is adorned by three historical structures: the pretty **Hotel Los Portales**; the **Correo** (the main post office) with an elaborate façade; and the **cathedral** with its golden altar, holy paintings by Ignacio Merino and a pulpit of the best tropical wood, with finely detailed carving. The mayor of Piura declared the independence of his city from Spain on January 4, 1821, in the nearby church, **Iglesia San Francisco** on

the bank of the Rio Piura. Also worth a visit is the **Iglesia Carmen**, (Avenida Libertad), which has a façade and interior in the *Churriguera*-style (rarely found in this region of Peru). In the house where the Peruvian admiral, Miguel Grau was born, the museum, **Museo Grau**, has historical photographs and artifacts which serve as a reminder of the War of the Pacific between 1879 and 1883, which Peru and Bolivia lost to Chile.

Paita, the international port for Piura, was located 50 kilometers north west of the city. In Paita, surrounded by fishmeal factories and a modern whale processing plant, one can swim from the well-maintained beaches, in warm water, a little to the south of the equator. This is a popular leisure activity for people from the city, especially on weekends.

Talara

North of Piura (135 kilometers) the oil city of **Talara**, with a population of 60,000 also lies on the Pacific coast. Its

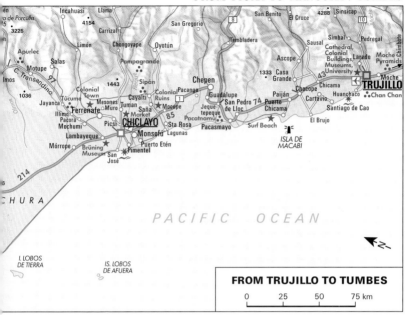

hated odor spreads across many kilometers in all directions. The oil refineries and fertilizer factories spew their waste gases extensively into the fresh sea air without using filters. Before the nationalization of the oil multinationals in Peru in 1969, the American International Petroleum Company had built good housing, schools, a hospital, and even a golf course with artificially watered greens for its employees in Talara.

The beach of **La Peña**, two kilometers north of the city, is worth a detour.

Cabo Blanco

Thirty kilometers north of Talara, a small road branches off toward the remote fishing village of **Cabo Blanco**. Till the 1970's, this village was famous, even beyond the borders of Peru for being home to a deep-sea fishing club. Ernest Hemingway, probably America's most well-known hunter and fisherman was a member of this club and is supposed to have found inspiration here for his world-famous short story, "The Old Man and the Sea," possibly in the bar of the **Fishing Club Lodge** (tel.: (01) 4477283). Due to excessive fishing and the moods of the Humboldt Current, it is now more difficult to catch large marlin.

The Panamericana highway now runs very close to the coast and after about a half hour's drive, it reaches the fishing village of **Máncora**, where the beach, **Playa Máncora**, is famous world-wide for its fantastic surfing conditions. A section of the well-to-do American surfing community also meets here in between November and March in the lukewarm waters of the Pacific. During the beach season (Christmas to May) mid-range beach hotels await vacationers, also in **Punta Sal Grande** (kilometer 1187).

TUMBES

It was on the beautiful beach of **Caleta La Cruz**, 16 kilometers southwest of Tumbes, and thus on Peruvian soil, that the conquistador Pizarro landed on May

173

13, 1531 with his emaciated and disoriented men. This was the beginning of the end of the Inca Empire. With 60,000 inhabitants, **Tumbes** is the northernmost city in Peru, 1320 kilometers north of Lima and 400 kilometers south of the equator. Throughout the year, the Pacific here has a constant "warm bath" temperature of about 30°C, which is also the reason for the mangrove swamps along the coast. A boat excursion to the **Santuario Nacional los Manglares** can be organized from the beach of the nice little fishing village of Puerto Pizzaro.

The city of Tumbes reflects the strong military presence, owing to its proximity to the border with Ecuador. The surroundings of the city are characterized by banana plantations and rice fields. On mild evenings and on weekends, the long promenade **Malecón Benavides** comes to life with strollers and spectators. On

Sunday afternoons, the **Coliseo de Gallos** in the Ave. Mcal. Castilla is filled with the cries of fighting cocks and betting spectators.

The 300-year-old cathedral of Tumbes towers over the **Plaza de Armas**, one block north of the Río Tumbes. Extensively renovated in 1985 after several earthquakes, it is still the emblem of the coastal city. Apart from a few old houses in the Calle Grau, hardly any other historical structure has survived here.

Anyone wanting to travel from Tumbes to Equador can use the border crossing between **Zarumilla** and **Huaquillas** (Aguas Verdes) 30 kilometers further to the northeast. Another option is from Piura, if you travel via Sullana or Tambo Grande inland through Las Lomas to the small border town of **La Tina** on the Río Macará. The peace treaty signed on October 26, 1998 by Peru and Ecuador ended the long border conflict in this region and provided a framework for improved cross-border relations. It also foresees three new border crossings.

Above: Putting out to sea to fish along the coast of Northern Peru.

HUARMEY (Area Code 044)
Accommodation
MODERATE: **Hotel de Turistas**, on the main street, tel: (01) 721928, at present being privatized.

CASMA (Area Code 044)
Accommodation
MODERATE: **Hostal El Farol**, on the main street, south of Plaza de Armas, pretty garden, small café, clean rooms and friendly service.

CHIMBOTE (Area Code 044)
Accommodation
MODERATE: **Hotel Presidente**, Calle Prado, tel: 322411, one block south of Plaza de Armas, pretty rooms, central location. **Hotel San Felipe**, Calle Villavicencio/corner of Plaza de Armas, tel: 323401, well equipped rooms, noisy on weekends.
BUDGET: **Hostal Augusto**, Calle Aguirre/corner of Prado, tel: 323571, popular with backpackers.
Restaurants
Restaurant Gran Hotel Chimú, Calle Galvez/Malecón Miguel Grau (on the beach promenade), good and expensive, pleasant atmosphere. **Restaurant Vicmar**, Malecón Miguel Grau/corner of Calle Palacios, view of the ocean, fish dishes.
Buses
Empresa Transportes Turismo Chimbote has buses to Lima that leave hourly from in front of Hotel Venus (2 blocks south of the plaza). **TEPSA** serves Trujillo, Chiclayo, Piura and Tumbes from Plaza 28 de Julio. **Transportes Soledad** serves Huaraz/Cordillera Blanca, via Casma, from Calle Bolognesi, one block north of Plaza 28 de Julio.

TRUJILLO (Area Code 044)
Accommodation
LUXURY: **Libertador**, C. Independencia 485/Plaza de Armas, tel: 232741, fax: 235641, beautiful location, nice restaurant, pool. **Casino Real**, C. Francisco Pizarro 651, tel: 257034, near Plaza de Armas, well equipped.
MODERATE: **Turismo**, Calle Gamarra 747, nice rooms and friendly service. **Opt Gar**, Calle Grau 595, tel: 242192.
BUDGET: **El Sol**, Calle Los Rubies 516, tel: 231933, modern décor, garden. **Primavera**, Calle Piérola 872, Tel. 231915, restaurant and pool. **Escudos**, Calle Orbegoso 676, good value for money, friendly service.
Restaurants
Restaurant Mochica, C. Bolívar/C. Orbegoso, Creole specialties. **Restaurant Pollos a la Brasa ABC**, C. San Martín 497, chicken served in a variety of ways. **Restaurant Il Valentino**, Calle Orbegoso, tel: 246643, Italian cuisine.

Buses
North- and southbound buses of the larger companies stop hourly along the Panamericana highway.
Airport
Daily flights to Lima and Chiclayo; twice-weekly flights to Cajamarca, Piura and Iquitos from the airport, which is 10 km northwest of Huanchaco.
Sights
Multi-ticket for: **Huaca la Esmeralda**, **Chan Chan** (take bus for Huanchaco) and **Huaca el Dragón** (in the La Esperanza quarter; buses from Av. España/corner of Av. Orbegoso), open 9 am-5 pm. **Huaca de la Luna**, take a taxi.

CHICLAYO, PIURA AND TUMBES
(Area Code 074)
Accommodation
CHICLAYO: *MODERATE:* **América**, Av. Luis Gonzales 943, tel: 229305, fax: 241627, comfortable. **Gran Hotel Chiclayo**, Av. Frederico Villareal 115, tel: 234911, fax: 224031, good restaurant, pool, bar and dance hall. **Tumi de Oro**, Leoncio Prado 1145, tel: 227108, modern decor, reliable.
BUDGET: **Hostal Costa de Oro**, Calle Balta, four blocks south of the plaza, inexpensive, nice rooms. **Hostal Madrid**, Calle Balta, two blocks north of the plaza.
PIURA: *MODERATE:* **Los Portales**, Plaza de Armas, tel: 322952, reasonable prices.
BUDGET: **Hotel Eden**, Calle Arequipa, one block west of the plaza, cheap. **Hostal Palmeras**, Calle Loreto/corner of Calle Ayacucho, clean, friendly service.
TUMBES: *MODERATE:* **Sol de la Costa**, Plaza Bolognesi, tel: 523991, the best hotel in Tumbes, good restaurant, garden, pool. **Hostal Roma**, Plaza de Armas, nicely furnished.
BUDGET: **Hotel César**, Calle Huáscar 333, great location between Plaza Bolognesi and Plaza de Armas. **Hostal Amazonas**, Calle Teniente Vasquez, tel: 520629, near the bus station, clean rooms.
Restaurants
Good restaurants in the better hotels; everything else is simple traditional fare (e.g. at the markets).
Buses
Since all three cities are located along the Panamericana highway, transportation connections are very good; buses head north and south every hour.
Airports
CHICLAYO: **AeroPerú** flies to Lima almost daily. The airport is 2 km southeast of the city.
PIURA: **AeroPerú** flies daily (mostly evenings) to Lima.
TUMBES: Airlines (incl. **Aero Continente**) offer transfers to airports in the north, including Lima, Chiclayo and Talara.

THE CORDILLERA BLANCA

HUARAZ

YUNGAY

HUASCARÁN NATIONAL PARK

CHAVÍN DE HUÁNTAR

CORDILLERA BLANCA

Trekking in the snow and ice-crowned Cordillera Blanca, the "White Mountain Range," is attractive even for visitors without an ice pick. This is because of the encounters with friendly locals, the hospitable small towns, like Huaraz or Yungay, and the ancient ruins of Chavín de Huántar, which are evidence of one of the oldest cultures of South America. The best time for traveling to this Andean region, in which the *Puya Raimondii*, the biggest bromelia in the world, grows, is the dry season from May to September.

For the last 200 million years, global tectonic processes have been pushing the Nazca plate under the South American plate. More than two million years ago, this gave the upward folding of the Andes an intense thrust, and the peaks of the White Cordillera, 13 of them "six thousanders," (in meters) continue to grow several centimeters each year. The Cordillera Blanca is just a small part of the Andes, which stretch almost 8000 kilometers from Venezuela to Cape Horn. The highest tropical mountain in the

Previous Pages: At 6768 meters, Huascarán is Peru's highest mountain. Left: The landscape near Chavín de Huántar – like a patchwork rug.

world, the 6768 meter **Huascarán**, is located here, as are other magnificent peaks such as the **Alpamayo**, renowned as the "most beautiful mountain in the world," the Huandoy and the Chopicalqui.

Mighty glaciers and huge valleys, such as the Río Santa, which drops from an altitude of 4000 meters to 1800 meters are features of this fascinating mountain world. The **Valle del Río Santa** is of singular beauty and should be on the itinerary of any trip to Peru. Also known as *El Callejón de Huaylas* (after the local district Huaylas), it is 160 kilometers long and up to 40 kilometers wide.

HUARAZ

There are three routes from Lima to **Huaraz** in the Cordillera Blanca. The one most used, over the Gonococha Pass (4020 meters) turns off the Panamericana highway in the coastal city of Pativilca. The second, more time-consuming, leads farther north, via Casma through the Cordillera Negra, or Black Cordillera, which is on average 1500 meters lower than the White Cordillera. The third route leaves the Panamericana highway in the coastal city of Chimbote, and reaches Huaraz via Caráz and Yungay.

The capital of the Departamento of Ancash, with a fabulous mountain back-

179

drop, is to be recommended, because of its many hotels, restaurants, bars, and trek organizers (hiring equipment, arranging guides and pack animals) as a sort of base camp in the Cordillera Blanca. It has a population of about 100,000 and is the primary meeting point for climbers in Peru, but is not at all overrun by tourists. At an altitude of 3091 meters, Huaraz has a pleasant, mostly dry climate. In September, the warmest month, the mountain sun can be enjoyed at 15-20°C. In July, the coldest month, the average temperature is still around 12°C.

In Huaraz, the Río Quilcay merges into the Río Santa, and from the bridge, even today, you can see Indian women washing their colorful clothes in the river, and then spreading them on the banks of the river to dry. There are hardly any buildings from the colonial era in Huaraz now. In 1958, a landslide buried a part of the city, and on May 31, 1970, 30,000 lives were lost in an earthquake. Only a fraction of the city was not washed away. The survivors rebuilt Huaraz as a modern town, with wider roads and larger squares; the main business artery of the town is the **Avenida Luzuriaga**.

The **Museo de Arqueología** (Plaza de Armas/ corner of Av. Luzuriaga) is worth a visit. Huaraz was an important node along a north-south axis in the Inca Empire. This is where the relay messengers changed, and the llama caravans halted. In the small exhibition, mummies, cloth decorations, and *kero* or *aryballo* vessel shapes are clues to the earlier presence of the Incas. Individual monoliths and *huacos* (clay temples) are exhibited in the garden. They are thought to belong to the Huari culture, and partly to the local Recuay culture (55 BC- AD 700). The town of Recuay, surprisingly, survived the above-mentioned earthquake. It is located about 30 kilometers from Huaraz.

If one leaves Huaraz, going towards Yungay, and turns right at the northern end of the Avenida Centenario onto a gravel road, after eight kilometers, past the small farming villages of Jinua and Paria one reaches the **Ruins of Wilcahuaín**. This place was presumably an important shrine of the Huari or the Tiahuanaco culture. The ruins are estimated to be more than 900 years old. That is also the age of the only reasonably well preserved structure of Wilcahuaín, a three-story, rectangular temple with 21 rooms.

If one continues 32 kilometers north along the Santa Valley, one reaches the town of **Carhuáz**, located at a height of 2700 meters at the foot of the Hualcán (6125 meters). Every Sunday morning, hundreds of *campesinos* gather at the **market** in the Plaza de Armas. Colorful cut flowers, sacks of mountain wheat and winter barley, alfalfa, golden-yellow corn cobs, hearty vegetables and even *cuys*, the guinea-pigs, which are a favorite Peruvian delicacy change hands here. On the *Fiesta de la Virgen de la Merced*, the festival of the Virgin of Mercy, on September 24, several thousand believers from the Callejón de Huaylas assemble here every year. They carry a statue of the Virgin Mary in a procession through the streets and prayers are offered in the church from dawn to dusk. For the more pugnacious visitors, there are bullfights during the day, and stirring music and dancing in the evening, with the finale consisting of a big firework display with homemade firecrackers.

YUNGAY

The journey from Huaraz down the Santa valley leads past the small town of Carhuáz on to **Yungay**, located 60 kilometers to the north. A statue of Christ marks the location, where a bustling town of 20,000 inhabitants was located, until May 31, 1970. On that disastrous day, a severe earthquake shook the country.

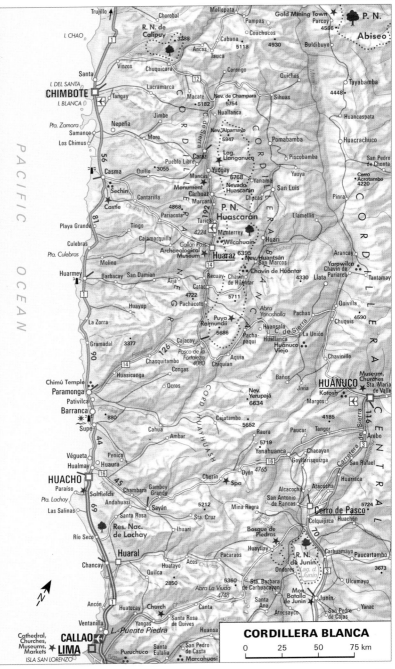

CORDILLERA BLANCA

0   25   50   75 km

Giant masses of ice rolled down from the peak of the Huascarán into a glacial lake, and together with water, boulders and loose earth, formed a deadly avalanche of sludge that raced 4000 meters down a narrow valley, over a 200 meter high hill behind Yungay, and buried houses and people. Only a few people were able to escape in the three minutes between the earthquake and the landslide, by fleeing to the graveyard hill, where the statue of Christ now stands.

Today, between the grass and the undergrowth that has taken root on the piles of rubble, one can see the crosses, erected in memory of the dead, that serve as a reminder of the catastrophe. The tips of three palm trees mark the place where the Plaza and the church of the town were located. The town was rebuilt on a site two kilometers away with donations from all over the world.

Above: Huaraz with the Cordillera Blanca as a backdrop. Right: Hikers camping in the Huascarán National Park, below Hualcán.

Lagunas Llanganuco

The road from the reconstructed Yungay to the 30-kilometer distant lakes, **Lagunas Llanganuco** (3850 meters) opens up a unique experience of the landscape. The view of the highest mountain in Peru, **Huascarán** (6768 meters), is overwhelming. Small queñoa trees with cinnamon-colored trunks surround the bright blue lakes; behind them, black rock walls seem to rise menacingly. A footpath that leads down from the first lake gives access to a unique, tropical, highland vegetation with bromelias, orchids and wild passion-fruit.

Above the lakes, in the dry months from June to August, there are always several groups of tents as mountain climbers and trekkers set up base camp here.

The road that winds its way upwards behind the second lake to the 4700 meter high pass, **Portachuelo de Llanganuco** provides a breathtaking view of the steep, icy flanks of the mountains Huascarán,

Chopicalqui (6400 meters), and **Huandoy** (6395 m).

The **Santa Cruz Trail**, the second-most popular trekking path in Peru, after the Inca Trail near Machu Picchu, also follows this pass. The four to five days require to trek along this route provide pure highland adventure, well away from civilization, and with breathtaking views of the giant glaciers of the Cordillera Blanca. At these great heights, llamas, vicuñas, and alpacas graze, getting their sustenance from the thorny *ichú* grass, condors fly their untiring circles in the sky, and chinchilla rabbits race around restlessly till they suddenly vanish, terrified, into their holes. The trail winds downward to the village of **Colcabamba**. It then leads up again, through the valley of Huaripampa, above which the gigantic needle shaped rock of the Chacraju (6112 meters) towers, to the **Punta Unión Pass** at 4750 meters. After the long descent through the valley of the Río Santa, one reaches **Cashapampa** (2900 meters), which is connected by road to Huaraz.

HUASCARÁN NATIONAL PARK

The **Huascarán National Park**, 180 kilometers long, with an area of 3400 square kilometers of alpine landscape, includes most of the area of the Cordillera Blanca that lies above 4000 meters. The park and its highest mountain are named after the Inca Huáscar.

The internationally renowned Peruvian mountain-climber César Morales Amao had suggested the creation of a nature reserve in the Cordillera Blanca in 1960, and in 1975, the authorities implemented this suggestion in the form of the Huascarán National Park.

If one goes down the Santa valley from Huaraz towards Lima, six kilometers after the town of **Catac**, there is a turn-off from which a dusty road leads to the national park. After another 14 kilometers, you come to a rounded mountain ridge, on which a certain species of plant grows that is amongst the rarest in the world – the **Puya raimondii**. Named after the Italian naturalist Antonio Rai-

mondi, it belongs to the order *Bromelia* (pineapple), but the shape resembles that of the amaryllis and agava plants. It has a very long growth period (about 100 years). The Puya raimondii blooms between May and November, when a slender, lance-shaped blossom grows up to eight meters high, out of a round bush. Like agava plants, the plant flowers just once, for three months, and then dies. In the massive flower, there are up to six million waxy petals, in which humming birds search for nectar.

CHAVÍN DE HUÁNTAR

A full day-trip from Huaraz starts with a four-hour, 110-kilometer drive, over bumpy tracks, to the village of **Chavín de Huántar** and the **Ruins of Chavín**.

Above: The Puya raimondii is said to be one of the oldest flowering plants in the world and is under strict protection by law. Right: A jaguar chiseled into stone – cult animal of the Chavín culture (Chavín de Huántar).

The Chavín culture had a great deal of influence on the religion of the people of ancient Peru. These ruins on the southeastern edge of the Cordillera Blanca are extremely significant, as only a few traces of this culture have been discovered.

The seven hectare site with ruins of the Chavín culture (1200 to 300 BC), is named for the neighboring village and lies at 3200 meters on the banks of the Río Mosna, a tributary of the large Río Marañon which flows into the rain forest. In this region, Peruvian hunters and gatherers probably took the important step of becoming settled farmers. Adequate food supplies, division of labor, and leisure time had a favorable effect on the religious development of the people. They built temples and began the cult of jaguar worship, which was unique to them. The art of stonemasonry also reached a hitherto unknown quality.

In the first millennium BC, Chavín de Huántar was probably the most important pilgrimage destination in Peru, comparable with Jerusalem, Mecca and Rome. The central remains of the site, the Holy Square, and the temple, El Templo, with the two granite stelae, El Lanzón and El Castillo, were excavated by Julio Tello and the German-Peruvian archaeologist, Frederico Kauffmann-Doig. In the year 1945, the "hunt for clues" was set back several years by a landslide.

At the **Holy Square**, in front of the north side of the Castillo, priests and pilgrims assembled for common cult worship practices and rituals. The steps at the side of the square – a sort of spectator grandstand – were often a good nine meters in width. The priests had the granite blocks, weighing several tonnes, dragged from quarries up to 40 kilometers away. The master builders had also taken the rainy season into account. The rain water had to be able to flow through the canals that lead into the Río Mosna, without flooding the Holy

Square. To the right of the entrance, near the Castillo, on one side of the **Plaza Circular,** a circular ceremonial plaza, are the remains of a structure known as **El Templo**. During the cult worship, the priests ascended the stairs to this pyramid and offered sacrifices to the gods, of corn, animals or even blood, on the upper platform, the altar. Inside of the structure, the priests were able to communicate with each other through the extensive, labyrinth-like shafts, which probably also served for drainage and ventilation.

On the inner side of the platform, the priests had erected the four-and-a-half-meter high lance-shaped, granite rock, **El Lanzón**. It was probably the most important, and most revered shrine of the Chavín culture. Its shape is that of a rectangular head with round earrings. The sharp premolar teeth in the hideous open mouth, below the large nostrils, however, seem to indicate that it symbolizes the head of a jaguar. The hair on the head consists of stylized, winding snakes and reinforces the fearsome expression of the

figure, to which the Chavín priests probably offered sacrifices.

Another temple, the 75-meter-long, 72-meter-wide, and 13-meter-high **El Castillo** ("castle") was made up of three platforms, which were originally probably clad with smoothly polished rectangular stone plates. The entrance portal is marked by two round columns with reliefs. These reliefs include: human heads or gargoyles; jaguars; anacondas; eagles; and condors. They show some resemblance to the reliefs on the Sun Gate in Tiahuanaco in present-day Bolivia. The master builders integrated *cabezas clavas* ("nail heads") into the wall with massive pins and, in several places, they chiseled volcanic stone. However, the question about where it came from has remained unanswered to date.

Meanwhile, archaeologists have accommodated two important monoliths of the Chavín culture in the Museo Nacional de Antroplogía y Arqueología in Lima. In 1898, Antonio Raimondi brought the two meter high *Estela Raimondi*, which

185

was named after him and also depicted a jaguar, to Lima, after a villager had used it for a long time as a table top. A few years later, Julio Tello brought an obelisk, later named after him to the Museum of Lima; it probably represents a crocodile that is exhaling birds and jaguars.

From Huaraz to Chimbote

In **Monterrey**, five kilometers to the north of Huaraz, one can relax, after a long trek, in the thermal baths with hot springs that belong to the **Hotel Baños Termales**. Next to the small, really hot pool in the upper area, is a larger pool in the lower part that is ideal for a swim.

The Santa Cruz Trail from the Lagunas Llanganuco ends in **Caráz**, which at 2300 meters, is the lowest town in the Río Santa valley. The city has recovered well from the earthquake but has hardly anything worth seeing. From Caráz, you

Above: One of several scuplted stone heads at Chavín de Huántar.

can visit the **Laguna Parón**, at a height of 4200 meters and 32 kilometers away, by taxi or on foot. On the way to this idyllic mountain lake, at the foot of the 5884 meter high Pico Pirámide, you pass fields of carnations and roses, which were planted on the initiative of a German businessman. Today, the *campesinos* even export flowers, which flourish in the favorable climate, to the United States and Europe.

If one follows the Santa valley northward from Caráz, the road winds its way through a narrow gorge with granite walls that are up to 1000 meters high, and passes through the **Cañón del Pato**. For thousands of years, the water of the Río Santa, mixed with the rubble from the glacier, has been forming this gorge. If one is driving, the road goes through more than 30 tunnels and passes the hydro-electric power station of Huallanca. From here, it is a journey of 150 kilometers by road to the industrial city of **Chimbote**, situated 1400 meters lower on the Pacific coast.

HUARAZ
(Area Code 044)
Accommodation

MODERATE: **Hostal Andino**, Pedro Cochachin 357, tel: 721662, fax: 722830, good restaurant Chalet Suisse (serves fondue!) and a beautiful view of the mountains, climbing equipment rental, mountain-climbing expeditions planned and guided. **Hostal El Patio**, Calle Monterrey, tel: 724965, reservations/fax: (01) 3442701. **Gran Hotel Huascarán**, Avenida Centenario, tel: 721640, on the edge of town, well-equipped, attractive restaurant that serves Peruvian and international dishes. **Hotel Colomba**, Calle Zela 210, tel: 721422, German management, former hacienda. **Edward's Inn**, Calle Bolognesi 121, tel: 722692, fax: 722692, not centrally located, but quiet and cozy, climbing equipment rental. **Hotel Baños Thermales Monterrey**, directly at the thermal springs, tel: 721717, beautiful location, reliable.

BUDGET: **Casa de Guías** (Alpes Andes), Plaza Ginebra 28, tel: 721811, Lima: (01) 4428778, near Plaza de Armas, mountaineer hotel and youth hostel, good restaurant, friendly management. This is where the latest information about hiking and climbing in the Cordillera Blanca is exchanged. Peruvian climbing guides can also be hired and climbing equipment rented. **Hostal Samuel's**, Calle Simón Bolívar 504, tel: 726370, modern, central location.

Restaurants

Chalet Suisse, in Hostal Andino, P. Cochachin 547, the best (Swiss and international) menu in Huaraz, comfortably decorated, friendly service. **Tasco Bar**, Calle Lucar y Torre 560, popular with mountain climbers, Mexican food, one block from Plaza de Armas. **Samuel's**, Calle La Mar/corner of Av. Luzuriaga, affordable Peruvian dishes like *pollos a la brasa* (chicken), and sometimes *cuy* (guinea pig). **Chifa Familiar**, intersection of Av. Raimondi and Av. Luzuriaga, good and inexpensive, typical dishes from the region, such as *lomo saltado* and *pollo con arroz*. **Monte Rosa**, Calle José de la Mar 661, tel: 721447, Italian, Swiss specialties.

Nightlife

Imantata Bar, Avenida Luzuriaga 424/corner of Raimondi, live music in the evenings, very popular. **Discoteca Any**, Avenida Raimondi/corner or Luzuriaga, great disco for dancing. **Peña El Tambo**, Calle La Mar/corner of Bolívar, two blocks from Plaza de Armas, live Peruvian folk music on the weekends, usually crowded.

Transportation

AIRLINES: Huaraz's airport is in Anta, 23 km away. Regular service to Lima was suspended in the 1980s; **Aeor Cóndor** offers charter flights from Lima.

BUSES: Most of the area's bus companies, **Expreso Ancash/Ormeño**, **Transportes Rodriguez**, **Empresa Huaráz**, **Trome** and **Empresa 14**, offer several daily services to and from Lima, which takes about 8 hours. The trip from Chimbote via Caraz also takes 7-8 hours and is offered by the same companies, almost exclusively at night. It takes 10 hours to get to Trujillo. **Transportes Huascarán**, Avenida Raimondo 870, offesr daily services to Chavín de Huántar. The trip takes 5 hours and is hard on your backside. Minibuses leave almost hourly for the thermal springs in Monterrey from Av. Luzuriaga. The pools at Hotel Termas are open from 8 am-5 pm. Buses, minibuses and colectivos to Yungay and the end of the Callejón de Huaylas (Caráz) leave several times daily, but irregularly, from the intersection of Av. Raimondi and Av. Fitzcarrald. The trip to Caráz takes about 90 minutes.

RENTAL CARS: **Empresa de Transporte Turismo Huascarán**, Avenida Raimondi 870, rents cars, VW Beetles built in Mexico and similar small cars.

Tourist Information

The OPTOUR office at Plaza de Armas, Av. Luzuriaga 459, was temporarily closed, but was supposed to reopen in 1998. Mountain guides and information are also available at Casa de Guías, Plaza Ginebra, tel: 721811.

YUNGAY
(Area Code 044)
Accommodation

BUDGET: **Hostal Gledel**, Av. Arias Graziani, north of Plaza de Armas, tel: 793048. **Hotel Yungay**, Plaza de Armas, reliable and clean, no unnecessary comforts. **Hostal Turístico Blanco**, tel: 793115, located outside the city center in an idyllic eucalyptus grove, behind the hospital; simple, but typical of the region; Señor Blanco, an older gentleman, can share fascinating stories about life and climbing in the Cordillera Blanca.

Transportation

BUSES: Colectivos and minibuses depart for the Llanganucos Lagoons several times daily, from Plaza de Armas; off-road vehicles are available if requested.

CHAVÍN DE HUÁNTAR
Accommodation
BUDGET: **Hostal El Inca**, Plaza de Armas.
Arrival
Transportes Huascarán, Avenida Raimondi 870, in Huaraz operates a daily service to the ruins, which takes approximately five hours in each direction. The ruins complex is open from 8 am to 12 noon and from 1 - 4 pm.

CITIES AND CULTURES IN THE NORTHERN ANDES

CAJAMARCA
CHACHAPOYAS
CUÉLAP
MOYOBAMBA

Few travelers to Peru visit the northern Andes and the slopes leading down to the lowlands of the Amazon. The tourist infrastructure here has hardly been developed. It still takes five hours to travel from the coast to Cajamarca – a distance of just 180 kilometers. But there is a lot to discover here: a Peru quite different from that of the highlands; the coast and the lowlands; Cajamarca, the city of destiny of the Incas; and numerous ruins. The ruins include Cuélap, Monte Peruvia, and Yalape, some of which have not been completely excavated and have barely been made accessible. In the coming years, however, they are bound to attract many more visitors. The climate is very pleasant for traveling. The temperatures are sub-tropical even at heights of 2000 to 3000 meters, and the rainfall is scant.

CAJAMARCA

The largest city in this region, **Cajamarca**, is best reached via the Panamericana highway, which runs along the northern coast. Between the two coastal cities of Trujillo and Chiclayo, 15 ki-

Previous Pages: Rice cultivation in the valley of the Río Jequetepeque. Left: The burial niches of Ventanillas de Otuzco, near Cajamarca.

lometers to the north of **Pacasmayo**, a well-constructed road branches off into the long Valle Jequetepeque. One crosses the Río Jequetepeque several times, passes extensive rice fields and climbs gradually. The route goes through the small town of **Chilete**, whose inhabitants mainly work in the mines in nearby mountains, and very soon, a little before Cajamarca, one reaches the **Abra de Gavilán**. At 3190 meters, this pass is the highest point of the trip. The road now quickly descends into the large Valle de Cajamarca. One approaches the city of Cajamarca, passing alder woods, eucalyptus groves and cornfields. This is where Francisco Pizarro gave the signal for the downfall of the Inca Empire.

Turbulent History

Before the Incas captured it in 1470, Cajamarca was, for several centuries, a small, autonomous principality. Atahualpa, the eldest son of the Inca, Huayna Cápac, was staying in Cajamarca, after his victory over his rival half-brother, Huáscar, when the Spanish conquerors found him there and imprisoned him. After Atahualpa was executed by the Spanish method of garroting, and after the destruction of Cusco, the conquistadors expanded Cajamarca and made it

one of their colonial cities. They built a Plaza de Armas with a fountain, paved the main roads, built churches and some *paradores* (inns). In the 17th century, the Spanish-Mestizo *encomenderos* (estate owners) discovered large silver deposits in the nearby Hualgayoc area and started to exploit them. Numerous miners migrated to Cajamarca and the city grew quickly. Alexander von Humboldt visited the city in 1802 as he was interested in the mineral resources and the history of the region. In 1908, the government in Lima made Cajamarca the provincial capital of the Departamento Cajamarca.

Walking Tour of the City

At a height of 2730 meters, the 80,000 inhabitants of Cajamarcas seem to lead a quieter life than those in the large coastal cities. At any time of the day, one can see

Above: The Yanococha gold mine near Cajamarca. Right: In front of the Cathedral of Cajamarca.

clusters of locals in the **Plaza de Armas**, talking to each other or relaxing on the benches. The **cathedral** is situated on the south side of the Plaza. Construction started in 1610 and was finished 350 years later, in 1960. Like many churches in the poorer northern Peru, it does not boast a bell tower. Such a tower would have signified the completion of the church. And that, in turn, would have implied the payment of a "church" tax to the Spanish viceroy. From the inside, the cathedral appears quite simple, but the artistically carved pulpit catches the eye.

The master builders did not scrimp and save, however, on the **Iglesia San Francisco** located on the opposite side of the Plaza. It has high bell towers, a richly ornamented façade, and solid walls. The **Capilla de la Dolorosa** (Chapel of the Suffering Virgin, on the right-hand side of the church), which is worth seeing, is decorated with fine ornamentation and numerous paintings with Biblical themes. In the evenings, the church (and the cathedral) are romantically illuminated.

Near the church, in a simple house, is the so-called ransom room, **Cuarto del Rescate**. Pizarro had promised the Inca subjects that he would liberate their ruler if they were able to fill up this room once with gold and twice with silver. For 34 days, llama caravans hauled gold and silver from all parts of Tahuantinsuyos, but in the end, they had to acknowledge that their labors were fruitless. Pizarro did not keep his word and, on some pretext, had Atahualpa executed, possibly on the large stone in this room.

From the Plaza de Armas, it's just two blocks to the **mercado** on the Avenida Apurimac, at the corner of the Calle Amazonas. Here, in contrast to Cusco, Pisac or Puno, you will see almost no tourists, but mainly *campesinos* and old Indian women who offer pigs, chickens, fighting cocks, iguanas (considered a delicacy in the region), as well as cereal crops and vegetables for sale. Supplied with fresh fruit from the market, one can now undertake the walk to the **Cerro Santa Apolonia**, which, at this height, is literally breathtaking. Apparently, it was from this hill, that Atahualpa watched the parades of his troops. He is supposed to have been seated on a throne of rock. The carved stones that can still be seen here today, however, probably originate from the times of the Chavín culture. Nonetheless, the path to the summit is worthwhile and the view of Cajamarca's red sea of houses is impressive.

From here, you can clearly see the **Iglesia de Belén** (17th century) with its magnificent Baroque façade, which was part of a large monastic complex. There is a hospital (18th century) connected to the colorfully decorated church, in which an art gallery now exhibits the works of local artists. Opposite the church, in a hospital also from the 18th century, the small **Archaeological Museum** displays ceramic articles and local finds.

It is interesting to visit Cajamarcas during the carnival season (with the water and mud fights that are typical of Peru) or during a Fiesta. A festival for tourists is celebrated in the second week

193

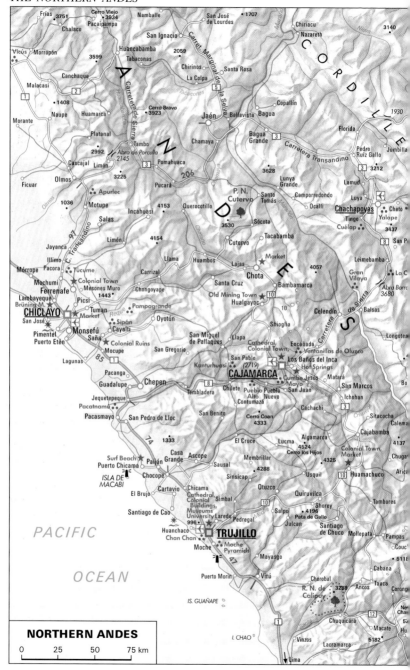

NORTHERN ANDES

0   25   50   75 km

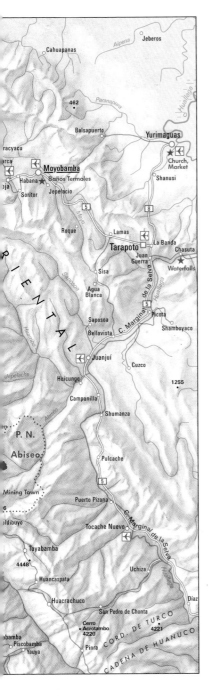

of August, with processions, folklore-shows and dancing competitions, and 10 days after Whitsunday (Pentecost), the festival of *Corpus Christi* is celebrated with processions.

Around Cajamarca

The **Baños del Inca**, the Inca baths, six kilometers east of Cajamarca, have not lost any of their attractiveness since the times of the Spanish conquest. Every year, thousands of locals and foreign visitors come here to bathe in the hot springs, in the same way that Atahualpa is supposed to have done. The hot water runs into walled and roofed bathtubs in which one can, in the company of up to five other persons, get thoroughly warmed up and washed clean. From the canals, constructed by the Incas, the water flows into a larger pool, which is also used by the guests of the neighboring **Hostal Laguna Seca**.

If one is fond of walking or hiking, one can walk, in this glorious scenery, to the **Ventanillas de Otuzco** (which can also be reached by bus). Here hundreds of grave niches have been chiseled out of the rocky outcrop, from the period before the Inca Empire. Unfortunately, the niches are now empty and even the jewelry buried with the bodies has gone. Any paintings that might have been there are no longer recognizable.

For an excursion to the remains of the pre-Incan irrigation system **Cumbe Mayo**, 14 kilometers southwest of Cajamarca, one should allow plenty of time, because here you can see an aqueduct, a shrine, and caves with rock drawings. A badly paved road, in parts very steep and winding, leads to the complex, which, covering 25,000 square meters, is considerably larger than the Inca baths. In the Quechua language, *kumpi mayo* means a "well-made water canal." The Peruvian archaeologist, Julio Tello, examined the 3500-year old, nine-kilometer long canal

and found that four kilometers were laid out as an aqueduct, and 900 meters tediously carved out of the rock. Right angles in the canal system prevented an excessively fast flow, as did the fact that the drop was maintained at exactly 1.5 percent.

At the entrances to the tunnels, one can see make out paintings in the style of the Chavín culture. Even the sacrificial stone and the holy rock in the shape of a human head are clearly recognizable as having beenn made by human hands. Perhaps the Indians of the Chavín culture also used Cumbe Mayo as a burial place for high-ranking public figures.

The trip to the temple site of **Cuntur Huasi** (House of the Condor) takes several hours (more than 100 kilometers) via Chilete, San Pablo and Pueblo Nuevo. If you have enough interest in and energy

for this excursion, you can see the scattered remains of the temple walls above the village at a height of 2100 meters. True, most of the structure has been destroyed, but on individual stone plates in the Chavín style, and on some of the stones, one can see delicately carved reliefs. Archaeologists also found graves with jewelry buried in them. Cuntur Huasi was probably an important religious center of the Chavín culture.

CHACHAPOYAS

If you follow the winding, and barely-paved road that goes northeast into the Amazon jungle, after 115 kilometers (or five hours) you reach the small town of **Celendín**, located at 2700 meters. The weekly Sunday market and the turbulent Fiesta at the end of July every year, in which bullfighters and matadors from all over the world participate, are worth a short visit. The road continues over the main tributary of the Amazon, the **Río Marañon**, which separates the central

Above: In the remote Northern Andes, tourists are still stared at with curiosity. Right: A wall relief in Cuélap, a ruined city where hardly any research has been done so far.

Cordillera from the parallel mountain ranges chain that lie further to the east.

The area around **Chachapoyas** has been a restricted military area for many years, and therefore there are checkpoints along the roads, where all travelers' passports are checked. The city of 30,000 inhabitants is situated at 2240 meters above sea level, which means it has a pleasant climate. Chachapoyas is the capital of the Departamento Amazonas, which has an area of 41,000 square kilometers. The seat of the bishopric, founded in 1538, it has a large Plaza de Armas with trees, bushes, and benches and several churches and monasteries, which date from around 1700, when Chachapoyas was the base for missionaries working in the jungle. The inhabitants of the Departamento cultivate rice, coffee, cocoa, tea, Brazil nuts and cashew nuts as well as coca plants and in addition, earn a livelihood from the export of mahogany trees and holyoke trees from the nearby tropical rain forests. As of a few years ago, Chachapoyas even has an airport with connections to Lima and Chiclayo.

The Tourist Office located at the Jirón Amazonas, just half a block from the Plaza de Armas and near the Instituto Nacional de la Cultura, is very helpful if one wishes to plan a small expedition to the ruins in the nearby jungle. Various *colectivos* (shared taxis) travel any time during the day from the Plaza de Armas to Tingo, Cuélap, and Leimebamba. The staff at the Tourist Office is able to provide information about departure times, routes, and prices.

CUÉLAP

Those interested in archaeology and willing to undergo some further hardship, can set out from Chachapoyas to the fascinating ruins of Cuélap (also written as *Kuélap*). The easiest way to get to Cuélap is by bus from Chachapoyas (about two hours traveling time); there is another

connection from Tingo. **Tingo** is 37 kilometers to the south of Chachapoyas and because of the damage it suffered during the floods of 1993, is not particularly attractive. Apart from a Sunday market and very basic hotels, it has few attractions, and neither electricity nor running water.

After a two-hour drive by pickup truck or a four to five-hour hike on foot from Tingo, one reaches the spectacular fortress city of **Cuélap**, located at a height of 3000 meters, which must have been built long before the Incas. In 1843, the German-Peruvian researcher Ernst Wilhelm Middendorf came upon a round tower, under the jungle-like undergrowth, whose niches and floor were filled with numerous bones and skulls. Did the inhabitants of Cuélap flee here from some advancing army, perhaps that of the Incas? That would also explain the immensely painstaking construction of the massive city wall, which is 18 meters high and several meters thick in some places. Narrow passageways, proper plazas, platforms, numerous dwellings,

Above: The thermal baths in Moyabamba.

and even a large dungeon testify to what life must once have been like in this hidden city. Anthropologists believe that Cuélap was the center and last refuge of the Sachupoya people, who numbered about one million, and had settled in the region to the west of the Río Marañon, and as far as Chachapoyas.

Since the beginning of the 1980's, various teams of archaeologists have been carrying out static improvements in a number of places. At others, even some of the smaller walls and former houses of the Cuélap have been reconstructed. However, so far, the reconstruction has been within sensible limits; it has not distorted the picture, as has been the case at other ruins in South America, but are has stayed true to the original features.

Cuélap is just one of several cities that are in ruins in the Chachapoyas region, that have, as yet, only been explored to a very limited extent. Archaeologists such as Paula and Henri Reichlen (Switzer-

land), Hans Horkheimer (Germany), Gene Savoy (USA), Frederico Kauffmann-Doig and César Torres Rojas (Peru), have tried for many years, to explain the large number of settlements between Chachapoyas, the Río Marañon and Leimebamba, further to the north. Kauffmann-Doig talks of the *Twelve Cities of the Condor*, in which people from the *Chacha* or the *Sachupoya* tribes probably sought refuge from the domination of the Incas. **Cerro Olán** (near San Pedro not far from Tingo), **Yalape** (a complex of several hectares near Levanto, with well preserved dwellings and finely worked stone friezes), **Monte Peruvia** (near Cheto), **Pueblo Alto** (near Pueblo Nuevo, 25 kilometers from Cuélap), and **Gran Vilaya** (65 kilometers to the southwest of Chachapoyas) are just a few examples of fascinating hiding places in the jungles, that hardly anyone has seen so far.

Gene Savoy discovered Gran Vilaya in 1985 and counted 24,000 (!) buildings in a 75-square-kilometer area. Yalape was cleared of bushes and trees and excavated a few years ago under the direction of the amateur archaeologist César Torres Rojas. Rojas, who is technically very competent and lives in nearby Levanto, is the official keeper of the site and can guide interested visitors through the ruins. However, many more years are likely to pass before these mysterious cities are sufficiently excavated and re-searched.

MOYOBAMBA

From Cuélap or from Chachapoyas, via Churuja, Florida and Rioja, one can reach **Moyobamba**, the capital of the Departamento San Martín, with a population of about 20,000. Soon after the conquest of the Inca Empire, the Spaniards founded Moyobamba as the first colonial settlement in the northeastern lowlands of Peru. Here, in the valley 900 meters above sea level, with its delightful landscape, a mosquito net is indispensable at night even in the comfortable Hotel Puerto Mirador. Moyobamba is currently not very tourism-oriented, so that most of the hotels in the blocks to the north of the Plaza de Armas are fitted out only sparingly. The **Instituto Nacional de la Cultura** on the corner of Calle Benavides/Avenida Alvarado, three blocks northeast of the Plaza de Armas, organizes and provides information about cultural events and also has a small exhibition of mounted animals of the region. Those fond of walking can reach the **Baños Termales** near Alto Mayo, not far from the road to Rioja, in a matter of one hour. The hot springs, which are also accessible by car, are enclosed by small swimming pools and bathtubs with hot and cold water.

The "real" tropical rain forest, and thus the Amazon lowlands, is now only about 200 kilometers away, via Tarapoto and Shanusi up to **Yurimaguas** on the Río Huallaga (see page 207).

CAJAMARCA
(Area Code 044)
Accommodation
MODERATE: **Hostal Laguna Seca**, Baños del Inca, Calle Manco Capac 1096, tel: 923915, fax: 923915, beautiful location, very quiet, thermal spa, dreamy cabins. **Casa Blanca**, Plaza de Armas, tel: 922141, colonial building with grandiose, antique wooden furniture and a well cared-for garden.
BUDGET: **Hotel Amazonas**, Jirón Amazonas 637, tel: 922620, modern, acceptable standard, near Plaza de Armas. **Hotel Becerra**, Jirón Arequipa 195, near Plaza de Armas. **Hostal Turismo**, Calle Dos de Mayo 817, tel: 923101

Restaurants
El Real Plaza, Jirón Dos de Mayo 569, good regional dishes. **Salsa**, Plaza de Armas, inexpensive, fast, good. **El Cajamarqués**, Jirón Amazonas 770, tel: 922128, dine on the garden terrace of a swank colonial building, very good.

Entertainment
Hostal Cajamarca, Calle Junín, folk groups perform after 8 pm, good restaurant. **Los Frailones**, Calle Cruz de Piedra/corner of Calle Peru, tel: 924-318.

Transportation
AIRLINES: **Aero Continente**, Jr. 2 de Mayo 574, tel: 923304, flights to/from Lima. Airport, tel: 922-523.
BUSES: **Empresa Díaz**, Calle Ayacucho 758, and **TEPSA** offer daily services to Chiclayo, Trujillo and Lima. **Empresa Díaz** leaves for Celendín daily at 12 noon.

Tourist Information
Dirección de Turismo, Jr. Belén 650, tel: 922-834, Mon-Fri 8 am-1 pm and 2-6:30 pm.

CHACHAPOYAS
(Area Code 074)
Accommodation
MODERATE: **Hotel El Dorado**, Ayacucho 1062, tel: 757047, clean and reliable. **Hotel El Danubio**, Calle Junín 572.
BUDGET: **Hostal Kuélap**, Jirón Chincha Alta, tel: 757136, bathrooms and hot water. **Hostal Johumaji**, Jirón Ayacucho 711, tel: 757138, central location, very cheap, well equipped.

Restaurants
Restaurant Kuélap, Jirón Ayacucho, half a block from Plaza de Armas, good service, inexpensive, well frequented, typical regional dishes, occasionally you can get grilled *cuy* (guinea pig). **Restaurant Chacha**, Plaza de Armas, good steaks, friendly service. **Restaurant Mio Mio**, Jirón Ayacucho, next to the post office, good *pollos* (chicken) and fruit juices.

THE AMAZON LOWLANDS

YURIMAGUAS

IQUITOS

PUCALLPA

POZUZO

PUERTO MALDONADO

MANÙ NATIONAL PARK

Over 60 percent of Peru is covered by tropical forest, but only 10 percent of the population lives in this long (over 1000 kilometer) strip of land in eastern Peru. Yet this comparatively small number of inhabitants has had a massive impact in what was once a stable ecological system. Here, in the *selva baja*, the low-lying tropical rainforest (different from *selva alta*, which is the tropical rainforest of the highlands), it is possible to imagine the catastrophic consequences of the deforestation of the South American rain-forests, which greatly influence the earth's climate.

There are only a handful of cities in Peru's Amazon region that are worth mentioning, however, these cities are enticing destinations that offer richly varied options for excursions into the forest and boat trips on the Amazon and its tributaries. The enormous variety of flora and fauna in the tropical forests is simply overwhelming.

The people who earn their livelihood from rubber-tapping, gold-prospecting, oil production or agriculture, lead an existence full of privation, far from the urban centers on the Peruvian coast. With

Previous Pages: A rainforest village on the Río Ampiyacou, a tributary of the Amazon. Left: A Jivaro Indian woman near Iquitos.

every passing year, the lives of this region's native inhabitants (like the Shipibo or the Jivaro) are increasingly influenced by missionary stations or fire-clearing practices of new settlers, even though their culture, religion and lifestyle are much better suited to the conditions in the jungle than those of the white and indigenous migrants from the coast and the highlands.

Due to the intense radiation from the sun and the high humidity, the climate in the Amazon region is warm and humid throughout the year. The average maximum daytime temperature is 34°C in October, the hottest month, which is only 2°C warmer than that in July, the coldest month. The nighttime temperatures are between 18 and 20°C. The rainfall is considerable – 3000 millimeters annually. In Iquitos, the largest city in the Peruvian Amazon, it rains more than 200 days a year. Periodical flooding of agricultural land and widespread malaria make the settlers' lives even more difficult.

The Amazon

On February 12, 1542 a Spaniard, Francisco Orellana was the first white man to discover this river in the forest. On the banks, he observed human forms with long hair, armed with bows and ar-

rows for hunting, and was reminded of the mythological female warriors known as Amazons. It didn't occur to him that the men here might also have long hair.

From Iquitos it is still a good 3650 kilometers to the Pacific. Just 100 kilometers upstream, the Río Ucayali and the Río Marañon join the Amazon, the river with the largest flow of water in the world. The **Amazon** has a number of world records to its credit: it transporrts one fifth of the total fresh water on earth and, though it has a maximum width of only two kilometers within Peru, it is an imposing 230 kilometers wide at its estuary in Brazil. At that point, it pours 200,000 cubic meters of water per second into the Atlantic, ten times as much as the Mississippi. Theoretically, this gigantic forest river could fill the huge Lake Titicaca in only 13 minutes.

Above and Right: Peru's luxuriant, but extremely sensitive rainforest eco-system is under threat from clearing by fire, among other things.

The Amazon carries with it massive amounts of mud, and the earth from its steep banks breaks off by the tonne and falls into the river. As the most important traffic artery in South America, it crosses almost the entire continent and with more than 1000 tributaries drains a huge area – larger than any other river in the world. Its most important tributaries are the Río Putumayo (for a long time it was also the border with Colombia), the Río Tigre, the Río Ucayali, the Río Marañon, the Río Napo, and the Río Caquetá (Colombia).

History of the Region

After the end of the rubber boom in the Amazon lowlands, almost everyone lost interest in Peru's largest province. For most Peruvians, their country consisted exclusively of the highlands (*sierra*) and the coast (*costa*). Only the growing poverty among the highland population and the migration from the mountains into the already overcrowded cities turned the attention of Peru's politicians towards the

jungle (*selva*). As early as in the mid-1960's, President Belaúnde Terry had already voiced his thoughts on targeted settlement in the Amazon region. In 1980, at the beginning of his second term in office, he officially encouraged the people of his country to do so.

Thousands of new settlers now suddenly thronged towards the far northeastern region of Peru, established villages, cleared large areas of jungle which had hitherto remained untouched, built roads and tried their luck with cattle breeding and crop-raising. During all this, they disturbed almost 1500 pre-existing Indian communities, which had been there for generations. They – unknowingly – thus contributed to the decline of many native communities, which originate from of 50 different indigenous ethnic groups and today number about 300,000 people.

The expulsion of the natives was soon followed by the expulsion of the new settlers. Large firms laid claims to land and, using mostly dubious means, including

the connivance of corrupt officials, drove away new settlers and erected large, modern cattle farms that produced beef for the US hamburger market. The land, cleared of trees and exposed to the burning sun and torrential rain without any protection, and consequently subjected to massive erosion, can be only be used for grazing for a few years. Afterwards, it is useless for agricultural purposes for many years. The chain-saws of the multinationals then target neighboring forests to create new pastures. In Peru alone, more than six million hectares of jungle have already been destroyed in this manner, and in neighboring Brazil the figures are much higher. In both cases, population explosion and cities that are bursting at their seams are partially responsible for this development, with consequences that are not only local, but also global. No end is yet in sight.

Currently, 250,000 to 300,000 hectares of Peru's rainforest are felled annually. After burning the undergrowth and the roots of the trees, the settlers plant rice,

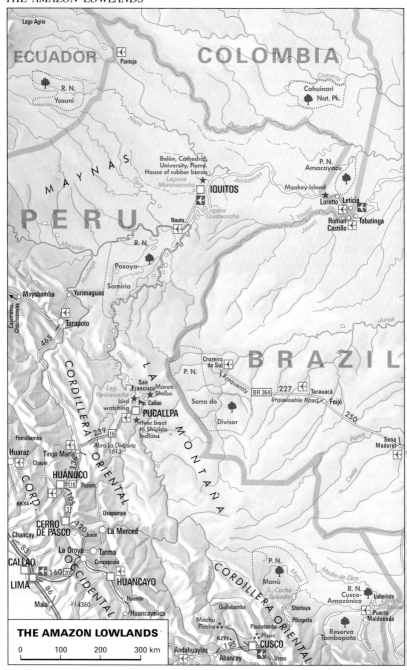

THE AMAZON LOWLANDS

| 0 | 100 | 200 | 300 km |

corn, yucca, groundnuts, and beans, mostly as monocultures. Over the course of the last few years, at the behest of the government, fruit, coffee, and cocoa plantations have helped ease some of the agricultural strains on and break up the monoculturalism of the area. Zebu cattle, which graze on the pastures formed by the clear-cutting, have also been introduced.

At first this type of agriculture gives excellent profits, however, after four or five years of use, the cleared tracts are no longer fertile and the settlers must move on, which is a vicious circle with no end. A thorough reforestation of the cleared areas would cost US $500 per hectare, which in Peru alone would amount to US $125 million per year.

YURIMAGUAS

The small town of **Yurimaguas**, on the Río Huallaga, can be reached by car from Cajamarca via Chachapoyas and Moyobamba, or in a few days by boat from Iquitos via the Amazon and Marañon. Its 30,000 inhabitants call it the "Pearl of the Río Huallaga." Yurimaguas actively experienced the rubber boom around 1900. A few houses from those turbulent times still stand in the Avenida Arica, bearing testimony to the long-gone glory. Today, the cocaine trade and the concomitant guerilla battles against the anti-drug activists from Lima and Washington have taken up the central role. Yurimaguas is the largest port city on the Río Huallaga and offers frequent and quick boat connections to Iquitos.

Peru's illegal cocaine industry, which does an annual business of almost US $2 billion and is concentrated in the Huallaga Valley around Yurimaguas, also contributes to the destruction of the rainforests. Since the end of the 1970s, the cocaine Mafia has cleared thousands of square kilometers of untouched forest and replanted it with coca plants. The "fruit" of these plants is processed at other locations within Peru and the cocaine is then smuggled into the USA and Europe.

Under pressure from the US government, the Peruvian anti-drug agency has been spraying highly poisonous defoliants on the coca plantations since the mid-1980s, in an attempt to put a stop to the coca Mafia. The vegetation and fauna of the region are both damaged by this measure. When the guerillas of the *Sendero Luminoso* began operating against the US "military advisor" in the Huallaga valley (until 1992), the situation worsened even further.

IQUITOS

Named after the Indian race that originally inhabited this region, **Iquitos**, with a population of 450,000, is the Peru's largest city in the rainforests. It lies on the left bank of the Amazon, which at this point is two kilometers wide and only 100 meters above sea level. For the remaining 3700 kilometers to its estuary, it drops only minimally. Iquitos is also the capital of the Departamento Loreto, the largest province of the country, with an area of 350,000 square kilometers. In all, half a million people live in this jungle vegetation. Iquitos, 1000 kilometers from both Lima and Cusco by air, can only be reached via the Amazon or by plane. The cars, three-wheeled taxis, and innumerable scooters that are required for commuting within the city, are transported here by huge ocean-going ships. They have a very limited sphere of action, as outside the city there are no roads to be found anywhere.

In the city itself, established in 1757 as the Jesuit mission, San Pablo, the native Indians fought long and hard against the unwelcome missionaries. The settlement of Iquitos grew very slowly and in 1880 its population was just 2000. But this changed suddenly with the discoveries of

European scientists like La Condamine (1754: latex as sealing material) and Charles Goodyear (1839: vulcanization; 1852: hard rubber) creating a demand for the raw material for rubber, which was collected by the Indians in the Amazonian forests. This demand reached its peak in the form of a rubber boom in the 1880's, which had the city bursting at its seams within months. Rubber barons became fabulously rich overnight; in contrast, their bonded Indian latex collectors did not profit from this development at all. The boom ended in 1912, when cheaper Malaysian plantation rubber came onto the world market. The Britons had cleverly smuggled *hevea* seedlings out of the Amazon region in 1876. With the decline in the demand for latex came Iquitos' economic decline. A short 30

Above: The Amazon and its tributaries are the main traffic arteries in this region – the harbor in Iquitos. Right: Yagua Indians demonstrate how to use blowpipes (near Iquitos).

years later however, the city suddenly woke from its deep slumber. Black gold had been discovered in the vicinity – oil.

Bringing oil derricks with them, thousands of Peruvians streamed towards Iquitos and the city acquired a modern infrastructure. Today Iquitos continues to earn a living chiefly from the oil, and less so from jungle tourism. But for how long? Northern Peru still has deposits of approximately 700 million barrels, but 70 million barrels are currently being extracted annually, which means the deposits could well be completely exploited in just 10 years. At the same time, settlers are clearing huge areas of the rainforest every year. If this keeps up, even the tourists will eventually stay away. The oil extraction also poses another problem for the *selva* and the people of Iquitos. Every day, each drill site pours up to nine million liters of salt-laden water (and some oil) into the forest rivers, putting a severe strain on the plants and animals.

Secondary income comes from timber and agriculture: nuts, tobacco and bananas are cultivated and also wild animals which are exported in considerable numbers to zoos in other countries.

Iquitos is the seat of a university and has a port that is capable of docking ships up to 3000 GRT. It is also the port most distant from the ocean that can be reached by large ocean liners.

In 1981, Iquitos was one of the locations in Werner Herzog's world famous film *Fitzcarraldo*, starring Klaus Kinski and Claudia Cardinale. The story had an authentic model. In the 1880's, the rubber baron Carlos Fermín Fitzcarraldo was able, with the aid of his own military patrols, to completely control the trade along the Río Ucayali and thus become very rich. When he discovered that the catchment area of the Ucayali almost touched that of the Río Madre de Dios he had the first steamship transported across an eight-kilometer-wide isthmus, with the help of thousands of natives. Hundreds of Iquitos' inhabitants appeared as extras in the movie.

The cathedral of Santa Ana and the rubber baron **Carlos Fitzcarraldo's house** are located in the **Plaza de Armas** in the center of the city. In the Plaza 28 de Julio, a **freedom monument** memorializes the struggle for independence, and a small wagon represents the streetcars that once operated in Iquitos. Nearby is the **Casa de Hierro**, a steel structure designed by Gustav Eiffel; the French architect had designed this structure for the 1898 World Fair in Paris. After the fair was over, the structure was dismantled and brought to Peru by the rich rubber baron Anselmo del Aguilla. This was to represent the *dernier cri* of Western architecture deep in the rainforest and it was erected at the corner of Calle Putumayo and Calle Raimondi. It now houses a snack bar.

Many of the **mansions** along Calle Raimondi and the riverbank promenade Malecón (very popular on Saturdays, with entertainers and live music) are dec-

orated with handmade, glazed *azulejos* – faience tiles that were imported from Portugal and Italy at the time of the rubber boom. The *azulejos* were supposed to beautify the "Pearl of the Amazon." Another example of this beautification can be seen in the **Hotel Iquitos** on Malecón Tarapaca. The décor of the hotel, with French reproduction furniture, crystal chandeliers, and luxurious musical instruments from Germany and England, did the rest.

A walk from the Plaza de Armas along the Calle Raimondi, which becomes the Jirón Prospero at Plaza 28 de Julio, enables you to see a large portion of Iquitos' remarkable buildings. Eventually you will reach **Belén**, a suburb at the southeastern end of the city that is known as the "Venice of the Amazon" by the locals. In what in reality is the slum-like tract of huts near the riverbanks, wooden huts float on raft-like foundations. During the drier season, lasting from August to October, however, they are stuck fast in the sludge of the Amazon. Belén looks a lot less idyllic then. Only in March and April, when the depth of water rises by 10 meters, do the traders cruise between the huts and sell food and household equipment from their small boats. Tourists can rent a boat from the huts on the riverbank and take a round trip on the water to get a feel for what the city really looked like at the beginning of the rubber boom.

At the **Mercado Belén**, along the bank of the Amazon, sacks of floor and sugar, baskets, dishes, and tools change hands. Fishermen offer passers-by dried fish, tortoises, armadillo shells, water birds, and the teeth and jaws of piranhas. Farmers sell tropical fruits like avocados, mangos, pineapples, papaya, *grenadille* and *pochote*. Natural medicines (like herbal teas, tree bark, dried flowers, and "magic" beetles) are some of the other products that are in demand at this market.

In the **Museo Regional** on Calle Tavara at the corner of Fitzcarraldo, it is a little less lively. The mounted animals from the Amazon region, some of them in a state of partial decay, and the traditional clothing of the native Indians that just cannot escape the moths.

The nightlife in Iquitos takes place in the movie theaters and discos near Plaza de Armas, and along Calle Raimondi, Putumayo, and Malecón – the riverbank promenade. There are also music bars where you can at least divert your attention, to some degree, from the heat of the night.

A trip to **Laguna Moronacocha** is recommended. This lake is located along the northern periphery of the city and can be reached by a *colectivo* (shared taxi) from the city. The romantic sunset over the lake can be admired from the palm huts that line the lakeshore.

Right: The women of the Shipibo tribe are outstanding potters and carefully guard the secret of their symbolic language.

If you would like something different, you can visit the **Laguna Quistocoacha** is located 14 kilometers west of Iquitos. A small zoo with ocelots, jaguars, anacondas and forest birds is a popular attraction, especially for families. Rowboats and pedal boats can be rented here, and some locals even go for a swim in the lake's murky waters. The *paiche* fish live in the fishponds. They measure up to three meters long, and have external lung-like organs, which mean they have to come up to surface repeatedly in order to breathe. This is a major drawback, because the natives used to catch them with their spears in the Amazon and almost wiped them out. The *paiche* is very tasty, almost a delicacy among the fish of the Amazon. It is eaten as *paiche a la loretana* together with cassava and steamed vegetables.

The 15-day journey on the Amazon to Manaus, in Brazil, is much more than a mere outing. On this trip you can travel as far as the border on the *Juliana*, the romantic riverboat from Werner Herzog's film *Fitzcarraldo*.

PUCALLPA

Pucallpa ("red riverbank" or "red rock") is the second largest city (approximately 200,000 inhabitants) in the Amazon region of Peru. It even has a road link to Lima and is the fastest-growing rainforest settlement in the country. Since 1980 it has also been the capital of the relatively new Departamento Ucayali. Despite the presence of a few modern structures (the Hotel Sol de Oriente, for example), the city still lacks the usual tourist attractions. When building houses for the city's residents, architects seem to have restricted themselves to the use of concrete walls and tin roofs. A large number of young and old women from the Shipibo tribe who live in this region travel to Pucallpa to sell their art and craft work in the Plaza de Armas.

The city also attracts other visitors – flocks of king vultures, magpies, and other hungry birds sit on the roof of the mercado in the hope of getting a half-moldy delicacy. Life in Pucallpa has retained something of its pioneer character. During the dry season swirling red dust from the road penetrates through every crack and gap, during the rains one has to wade through fine, ankle-deep mud. And since the first reports of natural gas, oil and gold deposits, slums – *pueblos jóvenes* – have sprung up even here, in the forest, in Pucallpa's La Hoyada quarter. Huts, on stilts, along the riverbanks or in the form of primitive houseboats testify to this fact.

Ten kilometers northwest of Pucallpa, in the middle of the forest, is the picturesque, U-shaped **Laguna Yarinacocha**; a small canal connects it with the river only when the water is at its highest level, in March and April. The small settlement of **Puerto Callao** has developed near the curve of the lagoon's southeastern end. Here you can find the Amazon's

Albert Schweitzer Hospital, which was founded in 1957 by the German physician Dr. Binder. The friendly, simple Hotel El Pescador, as well as a number of bars and restaurants, happily welcome both locals and visitors. Boat rentals facilitate trips out on the lagoon. Freshwater dolphins live in the lake and you can also observe sloths, iguanas, and thousands of birds, e.g., the colorful Amazonian kingfisher. Day tours into the jungle and fishing expeditions are also available.

While in Pucallpa, you should take the opportunity to visit a village of the **Shipibo Indians** that is near the city. The members of Peru's, possibly best-known, Amazon Indian tribe live along the Río Ucayali and its tributaries and still live a relatively traditional lifestyle in small villages that are only accessible by boat or by narrow mule tracks through the forest. The houses of the Shipibo have only one room, which is open to the outside, with a floor that is a platform of woven bast. It is of special interest to anthropologists that the Shipibo community has a matriarchal form of society – the women wear the pants. The village women also produce ceramic goods and textiles that are decorated with geometrical designs, which tell stories about mythical events and legendary people. The friendly Shipibo village of **San Francisco** lies on the northwestern bank of Laguna Yarinacocha and can be visited as part of a jungle tour. As you would expect, traditional hand crafted items are also produced here.

Anyone who is interested in the *artesanía* (hand crafted items) of the Shipibo should take a good look around the Plaza de Armas in Puerto Callao. Here, Shipibo women sell the handmade ceramic and textile products of their co-operative, which has members from over 30 villages. This market is widely known by the name of **Maroti Shobo**. Small pots, large animal figures, vases, dishes and urns, on which centuries-old traditions, myths and legends are told, change hands here. Trying to haggle over the price of their wares will get you nowhere, as prices are fixed by the co-operative. Unlike many markets, in the Maroti Shobo you can to take your time and really look at all the wares displayed on the different stands without feeling obligated to buy. Anyone who speaks Spanish should also take the opportunity of conversation with one or the other of the co-operative's members.

The University of Oklahoma's **Summer Institute of Linguistics** (SIL) has a mission station located on the outskirts of the city. Here, committed, often totally idealistic members of this fundamental Christian association attempt to translate a few of the more than 20 Indian languages of the Peruvian rainforest region into Spanish and English. Once they make enough progress in one language, their next step is to translate the Bible

Right: The family's gathering-place – the cooking area in a typical house on stilts.

into that Indian language, so these Peruvian "heathens" can finally be guided to the "true" faith.

The Summer Institute of Linguists comes in contact with the Indian tribes through the construction of health centers and schools, and tries to prepare them for life in modern Peru. It also works for a wider acceptance of the rainforest Indians in urban Peru. Despite their good intentions, the work of the SIL is very controversial among anthropologists. To a great extent, the missionaries interfere with the traditional cultures of the tribes and force a Christian-based value system, which is not compatible with survival in the jungle, on them. However, in addition to the US and Peruvian governments, the SIL has a number of noteworthy supporters, among them Mario Vargas Llosa, Peru's most famous author, who recently had some very favorable things to say about the work of the SIL in one of his books.

POZUZO

The small jungle villages of Oxapampa and Pozuzo lie 80 kilometers north of La Merced (via La Oraya). A hundred years ago, **Oxapampa** was a center for timber harvesting and processing. In the meantime, almost all of the area's useful forest has been cut down. Today, the inhabitants livelihood mainly comes from animal farms and coffee plantations. The plantations, at 1800 meters above sea level, yield good harvests of aromatic highland coffee. Oxapampa is still very remote and is rarely visited by tourists. Could that be why the villagers are so friendly and open? The few simple hotels and restaurants offer travelers a German-Tyrolean menu, which contains items like substantial pork knuckle along with pickled cabbage, small sausages, and bread dumplings.

The "Tyrolean" mountain village of **Pozuzo**, is situated 54 kilometers north of

Oxapampa has two districts, Prusia (Prussia) and Tirol; the two parts are connected by a suspension bridge over the Río Huancabamba. Each district has its own church, which the blond and blue-eyed villagers crowd into on Sundays. How did Tyrolean mountain farmers reach the Amazon jungle? In 1885, the Peruvian government asked the German adventurer Damian Baron Schütz-Holzhausen, who was paid to bring emigrants from central Europe to Peru and settle them in the sparsely populated area between the Río Ucayali and Río Huallaga.

In March 1857, three hundred farmers and craftsmen from the Austrian state of Tyrol, and from the German regions of Hunsrück and Eiffel, put out to sea from the Belgian port of Antwerp. Despite the caring leadership of their priest Josef Egg, only 170 of them reached their new home in Pozuzo and took up the fight for survival in the rainforest, at an altitude of 800 meters. Although quite forgotten by the outside world, they succeeded in eking out a livelihood in the middle of the

tropical vegetation, building cottages and farmhouses like those in their Alpine homeland. Their language and the individual elements of their culture, like folk dances and folk music, have been partially preserved; since 1960, the German and Austrian governments have also provided financial support and manpower. A visit to their village can easily be counted among one of the most exotic trips in the Peruvian jungle.

PUERTO MALDONADO

The port city of **Puerto Maldonado** was established around 1900, in the course of the late rubber boom. The inhabitants initially concentrated, in the 1920's, on selling valuable tropical wood. However, when all of the giant old-growth trees in the vicinity of Puerto Maldonado were felled and the forests had been cleared for many square kilometers, work in the sawmills and logging operations on the river came to a standstill. Since then, the town's 30,000

inhabitants survive as gold and oil prospectors, animal breeders, and laborers on Brazil nut and coffee plantations.

The capital of the Departamento Madre de Dios, it also has the province's most important port on the river of the same name. The Río Madre de Dios ("River of the Madonna") is about 500 meters wide here and can be crossed by ferry round the clock. Although hundreds of fortune hunters continue to arrive in Puerto Maldonado every year, the city offers no tourist attractions apart from a trip to the **Lago Sandoval**, which the tour operators often combine with a long walk along the lakeshore.

There are a number of passable hotels and restaurants in Puerto Maldonado. You must try typical local dishes like *castañas* (Brazil nuts covered with sugar and chocolate sauce) at least once. After a lavish, spicy-hot jungle-meal, you can

Above and Right: In Puerto Maldonado you can exchange your nuggets for cash – if you were lucky enough to find some.

enjoy a glass of *mazate* in one of the towns many bars. Locals extract this liqueur from the Yucca palms and enjoy it, often in large quantities, at the end of the day.

There is a flight connection to Puerto Maldonado; it is only four kilometers from the airport to the city. In addition, buses and trucks travel the road (closed to traffic during the rainy season) via the Hualla Hualla Pass (4820 meters), to Cusco.

In Puerto Maldonado there are three options for guided excursions into the rainforest. One is a boat journey of several hours up the Río Tambopata that brings travelers to the **Reserva Tambopata**, which is unique because it is home to such a vast array of species. Over 500 varieties of birds and 1000 varieties of butterflies and dragonflies live here, in an area of just five square kilometers.

Another excursion leads into the large **Cuzco Amazónico Nature Preserve**, which is spread over ten square kilometers. It can be reached by an hour-

long boat trip on the Madre de Dios. The simple **Albergue Cuzco Amazónico** is situated at the entrance to the preserve. From here, you can take a three-day trip into the jungle, where you will see lakes, gold mines, and a saltlick for jungle animals.

A third option allows travelers interested in biology to observe the diverse life in the rainforest from another perspective: from the **treetops**. This system, originally developed in Costa Rica, was brought to Peru by the ornithologist Paul Donahoe, since two-thirds of all animal species in the rainforest live within view of the treetop level. So far, Donahoe has set up **observation platforms** at the Explorer's Inn (100 meters above the ground). More "blinds" are planned at the Manú Lodge and Cusco's Amazónico Lodge.

The small town of **Laberinto**, an hour's bus-ride from Puerto Maldonado, consists almost exclusively of wooden huts and has no sights that are worth seeing. However, from here it is possible to take boat trips along the Madre de Dios to small gold prospecting settlements. Unfortunately, as the mercury that the prospectors use for gold extraction enters the river, it poisons countless number of plants, animals, including the fish that are caught for food!

Hotel Wilson is your only option for lodgings in Laberinto. Here, you can observe the gold prospectors, many of whom are usually more than slightly drunk, as they attempt to drown their rainforest-induced loneliness in yucca liqueur and similar liquid fuels. The bus to Puerto Maldonado also leaves from Hotel Wilson.

MANÚ NATIONAL PARK

In the extreme southeast region of Peru, on the western edge of the Amazon basin, is the largest rainforest national park in the world. Covering an area of 18,000 square kilometers (half as large as Switzerland), it has been a part of UNESCO's World Natural Heritage since 1987.

Even today, a number of isolated Indian tribes live in the largely untouched and almost inaccessible tracts of rainforest.

The **Manú National Park** is best visited with an organized tour; an individual trip can be very expensive and stressful. The Manú agents offer an ecologically tenable program in conjunction with a number of Peruvian environmental protection groups. The (smaller) reservation zone is open to visitors but the actual park is only open to qualified scientists with special permits. The best time to travel here is during the dry season, June to October.

The park can be reached by plane from Lima or Cusco or, for the more adventurous, over land from Cusco via Paucartambo and Pilcopata to **Shintuya**, a small village with simple lodgings and a mission station. Most of the rainforest-tour organizers begin their (generally) week-long jungle expeditions on the Río Alto Madre de Dios, here in Shintuya.

Above: A jaguar in the Manú National Park.

The virgin rainforest begins northwest of the confluence with the Río Manú (known as Boca Manú). If you follow the Río Manú upstream from here, for about half a day, you will reach the idyllic **Lago Cocha Salvador**, the largest lake in the park. The almost impenetrable vegetation hides a lively animal world that is however only discernible to the practiced eye. Eight hundred species of birds, 1200 species of butterflies, 13 species of monkeys, as well as peccaries, tapirs, jaguars, giant turtles, black caymen, giant otters, sloths, and a few of the almost extinct bush dogs populate this area along with its unique flora. One fifth of all the South American plant species are represented here.

A visit to the Manú National Park, with its 360-kilometer-long Río Manú is among the best options available worldwide for exploring virgin rainforest. However, if you are looking for a less expensive and/or shorter rainforest tour, you should try a trip from Puerto Maldonado or Iquitos.

IQUITOS (Area Code 094)
Arrival
Daily flights from Lima, occasionally with a stop in Pucallpa, Chiclayo or Trujillo.

Accommodation
MODERATE: **Real Hotel Iquitos**, Malecón Tarapacá, tel: 231011, formerly state-run, now privatized, near the Amazon and Plaza de Armas. **Acosta II**, Ricardo Palma 252, tel: 231983, fax: 242349, modern, the hotel with the best standard in Iquitos. **El Dorado**, Calle Napo 362, tel: 231742, near Plaza de Armas, air conditioned, pool. *BUDGET:* **Hotel Ambassador**, Calle Pevas 260, tel: 233110, good, with air-conditioning.

Restaurants
La Casa de Jaime, Malecón Tarapacá 246, tel: 239456, Peruvian menu, refined atmosphere, near the Amazon. **Maloka**, Malecón Tarapacá, tel: 233126, floating restaurant on the Amazon, good int'l menu, acceptable prices. **El Mesón**, Calle Napo 116, tel: 231197, typical Amazon menu, fast service, inexpensive lunch menus. **Restaurant El Tuquito**, Calle Putumayo 157, tel: 236770, int'l dishes, near Plaza de Armas.

Museums
Museo Regional, Calle Tavara/corner of Fitzcarraldo, Mon-Sat 8 am-7 pm. **Museo de Loreto**, provincial history museum, near the Malecón, 8 am-6 pm.

Tourist Information
Oficina de Tourismo, Calle Napo 176, Mon-Fri 8:30 am-1:30 pm.

PUCALLPA
(Area Code 064)
Accommodation
PUCALLPA: *MODERATE:* **Sol del Oriente**, Av. San Martín 552, near Plaza de Armas, tel: 575154, fax: 575510, restaurant, bar, pool. *BUDGET:* **Hostal Peru**, Calle Raimondi 636, tel: 575128, simple, cheap. **LAGUNA YARINACOCHA**: **Bungalow-Hotel La Cabaña**, Jr. 7 de Junio 1043, tel: 571120, fax: 573776, eastern side of the peninsula, room and full board, boat transfer.

Restaurants
Chifa Hong Kong/Raimondi, Calle Raimondi, 3 blocks from Plaza de Armas, Chinese, good, cheap. **Don José**, Calle Ucayali/corner of Calle Raimondi, local specialties, good fruit juices.

PUERTO MALDONADO
(Area Code 084)
Arrival
During the dry season, from Cusco by bus or truck (530 km). Flights arrive from Cusco almost daily.

Accommodation
MODERATE: **Puerto Maldonado**, Av. León Velarde 331, tel: 571029, reservations: (01) 2240263, fax: (01) 571323, 1 km from the city center, on the river, air conditioned. **Cuzco-Amazónico Lodge**, 1 hour downstream by boat, tel: Cusco (084) 232161, Lima (01) 4462775, 60 beds, rustic cabins with bath. **Explorer's Inn**, 58 km downstream on the Río Tambopata, reservations in Puerto Maldonado: Calle Fitzcarraldo 136, tel: Cusco (084) 235342, Lima (01) 4313047. *BUDGET*: **Hotel Wilson**, Calle Puno/Jirón Troncoso, tel: 571086, best-known hotel in town, globetrotters' meeting place, cafeteria, pool.

Restaurants
Café Don Pancito, Jirón Velarde/Calle Fitzcarraldo, Japanese and local dishes. **Café Danubia Azul**, Plaza de Armas, fish, local specialties. **Restaurant Califa**, at the pioneer cemetery, Calle Piura/Cusco.

RAIN FOREST TOURS
Tours of the area around **Puerto Maldonado** should be organized in Lima or Cusco (book early). Airplane excursions from **Iquitos** can be booked in Lima, but are cheaper if booked in Iquitos. Reservation offices in Iquitos are between Plaza de Armas, and the banks of the Amazon on Jirón Putumayo. Most tours last 2-3 days, and follow the Amazon at least 50 km from Iquitos. Most of the comfortable jungle lodges are built on stilts. Native Indian guides from the Jivaros or Yaguas tribes quickly trade jeans for war paint, blowpipes and feathers as soon as a tour boat pulls in, and lead tours that give you a feel for what life in the jungle was like before the rubber boom. Hikes through the forest (always accompanied by mosquitoes) include explanations about the indigenous flora and fauna; monkeys, caymen, sloths, ant eaters, pink dolphins, etc. Trips up alternative branches of the Amazon, fishing for piranha and nocturnal photo shoots in search of caymen are mostly optional. Chances of seeing wild animals are best in the Manú National Park or Puerto Maldonado. **IQUITOS**: **Amazonas Adventure Tours**, Freddie Valles Wing, Calle Lores 220, tel: 237306. **Anaconda Lara Expedition**, Calle Pevas 210, tel: 239147, Lima: (01) 4453225, fax: (01) 232978. **Explorama Tours**, Av. La Marina 340, tel: 235471, fax: 234968. **MANÚ NATIONAL PARK**: Tour organizers (excursions with overnight accommodation in the Manú or Tambo Lodge): **Expediciones Manú**, Cusco, Calle Procuradores 50, tel: (084) 226671, fax: (084) 234793. **Cenfor**, Cusco, Calle 235. **Asociación de Conservación para la Selva Sur**, Cusco, Portal de Panes 123, Room 305 (Plaza de Armas), tel: 236200. **Manú Nature Tours**, Cusco, Av. Pardo 1046, tel: 252721, fax: 234793.

PERUVIAN CUISINE

Peruvian cuisine is today still based on four basic foodstuffs: corn, potatoes, beans and rice.

Corn, which is available in many varieties and colors, can be prepared in a number of ways. It is enjoyed as an appetizer, main course, dessert, and even as corn beer. *Choclos*, large-grained ears of corn that are cooked and covered with cheese, are sold as a popular snack. *Humita*, which was also known to the Incas and was popular with them as a kind of fast food, is much older than both the hamburger and the hotdog. It is a very spicy, or sweet, corn porridge that is served wrapped in corn leaves.

Tamales, on the other hand, are cooked in banana leaves. The leaves are stuffed with corn porridge and pork or chicken and small pepper pods make this dish spicy hot.

If you want to round off your meal with a corn dessert, you should order the sweet *mazamorra morada*, which is made from violet-colored corn and lots of fresh fruit.

The most important food in Peru is the potato (*patata* or *papa*). Unlike most countries, however, potato dishes range far beyond French fries and fried or roast potatoes. There are more than 200 types of *papas* with some small farmers cultivating up to 30 varieties in a single field.

Good food is also available in places other than restaurants. Generally the local *mercados* have a hall where numerous food stands offer local dishes at very attractive prices. The atmosphere at these stands, with their counter and bar stools, is much more rustic than in a restaurant. However, before taking this tempting

Previous pages: The llama herds are identified by colorful woolen stripes. Musicians in Arequipa. Right: Chicha, a beer made from fermented corn, is a typical drink among the Indian peoples.

route, keep in mind that your stomach should have had time to get used to the local food – otherwise salads and unpeeled fruit should be avoided.

In the *chifa* restaurants, you will find a wide variety of Chinese-Peruvian dishes, which are usually of very good quality. The *cafeterías* offer menus dominated by local dishes that can be quickly prepared, and have simple decor, and low prices. You will find that food in the coastal regions tends to have been more changed by international influences than has the food in the *sierra* (highlands), where the typical Peruvian vegetables and grains flourish.

A typical Peruvian meal could consist of some of the dishes below. For appetizers, *palta a la jardinera* (cold vegetables with avocado slices), *palta a la reina* (an avocado filled with chicken salad, flavored with salt and pepper) or *palmitos con jamón* (palm hearts with a slice of cooked ham). Other typical Peruvian appetizers include: *chupe de camarones* (a creamy soup made of salt-water and fresh-water crabs); *ceviche de corvina* (white sea bream in a marinade of onions, chilies (*aji*) and lemons, served cold) which is usually served with salted or sweet potatoes (*camote*); and the legendary *sopa a la criolla*, a spicy noodle soup made with pieces of beef, various types of vegetables, eggs, croutons and a dash of milk or cream, which is seasoned in the Creole style.

An *almuerzo*, the main meal of the day, includes a hot main course, which is often one of any number of different variations of *pollo* (chicken), or *lomo saltado* (steak in small, thin slices, roasted with onions, potatoes and tomato slices, served with a side dish of rice). *Corvina a la plancha* (grilled sea bream; a favorite along the coast) is also a popular main course. *Cuy* (roast guinea pig), which is only available in a small number of restaurants, sometimes still seems to be similing at the hungry traveler from the

plate. *Patarasca*, fish cooked in banana leaves, is often served along the Amazon.

Typical Peruvian desserts include *picarones* (dough that is fried in lard and covered with syrup) and *flan*, a sweet caramel pudding.

Naturally, a Peruvian meal can best be enjoyed when accompanied by a suitable drink. In addition to coffee (black or with milk) (*café negro, café con leche*), tea, Inca Cola and other *gaseosas* (soft drinks), fruit juices (*jugos*), and syrup mixtures, *cerveza* (beer) is also considered a thirst-quencher in Peru. In high society they also drink wine from the Ica region, Argentina, or Chile.

An especially popular cocktail is the *Pisco Sour*. It is made with grape schnaps mixed with egg white, lemon juice, sugar, and crushed ice. *Aguardiente*, a high-proof sugar cane liqueur, is the spirit of choice among the poorer classes.

Peru's fruit juices are also excellent and include: *naranja* (orange), *piña* (pineapple), *maracuja* (passion fruit), *mora* (blackberry), *sandía* (watermelon), and *toronja* (grapefruit). The *licuados con leche* (fruit juices mixed with milk), which are like banana, papaya or strawberry milkshakes, are also very popular.

Chicha, a typically Indian drink, is low-alcohol liquid nourishment for traditionalists. The sour corn beer tastes like light, fizzy beer to which a shot odf something stronger has been added, and is sold in markets like Pisac and Cusco. The early method of making *chicha* was very original: Indian women chewed the *maize* kernels until they were soft, then spat them into a barrel where the mixture was then allowed to ferment. Today, however, corn beer is made without the "traditional help" of such women, and as a result, is not dangerous to your health.

There are about 15 different types of beer, Peru's main thirst-quencher. Most of them are produced by master brewers of German origin, or are brewed under German licenses. They include *Pilsen*, *Cusqueña*, *Arequipeña*, and *Bremen*, which are available in bottles and cans in sizes from 330 to 1100 milliliters.

HANDCRAFTED GOODS IN PERU

Almost everyone who visits Peru returns home with carry-on luggage that is bursting at the seams. Friends and family back home are usually delighted to receive much sought-after souvenirs such as alpaca and llama pullovers, woolen vests, dolls, as well as knitted and woven items in the most glorious colors. In Peru you can find the well-known ponchos and patchwork quilts made from pieces of fur, jewelry of pure gold or silver (ensure that it has the hallmark "925") and copper jewelry, which is often decorated with semi-precious stones. Also much appreciated are blowpipes from the rainforest, ceramics, with both traditional and modern designs, clay figures, woodcarvings, and decorated leather goods.

In the largest cities in Peru, there are shops in which fine, hand crafted goods

Above: Women weaving near Chinchero. Right: Typical designs of the Quechua Indians.

are available for fixed prices. One should risk a quick look around one of these numerous shops, even if the prices appear to be high. At the very least, these shops provide one with the opportunity to inspect the various qualities of wool and compare the different brands. Outside Lima and Cusco, it is best to purchase items directly from a workshop or a privately owned shop.

A few of the most popular souvenirs can be found all over Peru. One example is the much sought-after wall hangings, which differ in design from region to region. The largest selection can be found along the Mercado Artesanal in Lima. Here, haggling is an integral part of buying and some knowledge of Spanish is always advantageous.

The handcrafted goods of modern Peru have their origins in very old traditions, as Peru was a land of craftsmen long before the Incas came to power. In Peru's indigenous cultures, which did not have written languages, figures and ornaments depicted episodes from daily life and mythology. Here, illustrated handcrafted items were an important method of perpetuating the religious legends, history, and cultural traditions in the memories of all the members of a tribe.

The Shipibo Indians form a matriarchal society in the Amazon lowlands. Their outstanding craftmanship illustrates the structure of the cosmos as seen from their perspective. The women hold the secrets to the arts of pottery, and the weaving and dying of fabrics. Until about 1900, they decorated everything within the village, including their own bodies, with patterns. Today, they concentrate on the embroidering and appliquéing of womens' skirts and on painting ceramic pots. Under the guidance of the village shaman, the women also paint chevrons, crosses, lattices, body parts, people, Pleiades and Hyades, and mythical events on textiles and ceramics. They use events from everyday life, geographical and astronomical objects, their own family tree, and personal sexual experiences to inspire their themes. The tradition of this craftmanship, according to the shamans, serves, on one hand, to promote the consciousness of the individual self and functions as the personal therapy of the artist. On the other hand, it provides ways and means to accentuate the contrast between the untouched wilderness and the cultured village community.

Clothes today still carry a special message. The richly colored Indian costumes reflect the social status and the regional roots of the wearer. Some elements originated during the time of the Incas, others were adopted by the *indígenas,* not always voluntarily, during colonial times. The Shipibo attach a great deal of importance to having visitors or potential buyers be able to recognize their designs as being clearly Shipibo designs. Today, however, even in the memories of the older generation, the knowledge of the deeper significance of the patterns is fragmentary at best.

Nevertheless, they are very clear about the general significance of craftmanship in the various areas of tribal life. This importance strengthens the social matrix and gives it sense and meaning.

After the great rebellion under Túpac Amaru II was put down, the Spaniards prohibited almost everything that was Indian: their language, their religion, even the traditional clothing. Thus, the wide skirts of the women, the felt hats and knee-breeches of the men, which visitors think of as being typically Peruvian or Indian, were originally a part of the everyday clothes and festival costumes of the rural, 18th-century Spanish population.

Today, traditional costume is worn less and less. Anyone who wants to be "in" and climb the social ladder wears polyester shirts, T-shirts, blue jeans, and even a baseball cap. As a result, Peru's daily life is increasingly losing its bright colors.

However you may prize originality in your search for the perfect souvenir, don't purchase any pre-Columbian artifacts – export of these is forbidden!

THE MUSIC OF PERU

You have probably heard Peruvian music on the radio or seen Peruvian musicians perform on television. Perhaps you have seen one of the numerous groups who, wearing colorful ponchos, regularly perform for spare change on the sidewalks of larger American cities and in the pedestrian zones of European cities.

Peruvian music is characterized by the use of the five-tone, or pentatonic system, and the minor keys, which is a somewhat unusual style for audiences used to more North American/European-style music. Peru's traditional music offers visitors insights into the attitudes and self-images of the inhabitants of the Andes. While having experienced a significant renaissance in many countries during the last few decades, subjecting it

Above: Even in the Paracas culture they had the siku, a kind of panpipe. Right: An Andean harpist in Cusco.

to numerous changes and modernization, Peruvian music has managed to retain its historical core.

To date, Peruvian music has been known abroad predominantly as the Indian music of the highlands, and less as the Creole music (with strong Spanish and African influences) of the Pacific coast or the Amazon. Every region in Peru has its own style of song. Along the coast it is mainly about love and people love to dance merrily to it. This contrasts with the music of the *sierra*, which is often very sad or melancholic. It is, however, songs of the *indígenas* from the Andean villages that have the longest tradition of all the Peruvian music styles.

The many and diverse musical styles that already existed during the time of the Incas, as well as those resulting from the symbiosis with Spanish music, have been carefully recorded and illustrated by the Peruvian historian Felipe Waman Poma de Ayala. In his *Nueva Crónica y Buen Gobierno*, he describes the victory songs of the Inca soldiers, the happy songs of the herdsmen, songs that were sung during the strenuous work on the corn and vegetable terraces, and those that the men and women sang at the end of the harvest in gratitude for the beneficence of the gods. The three most important styles of songs in the Andes are known as *huanca*, *yaraví* and *huayno*.

The *huanca*, a style of song that was composed for religious occasions, was not fostered after the decline of the Inca Empire and has not survived. But in modern Peru, the *yaraví* and *huayno* styles are still very popular.

The *yaraví* stands for simple, short texts with a partially personal background, in which the subject is usually a passionate, happy or unhappy love between two people. The Incas sang *yaraví*s mainly as songs of prayer on the occasion of the ritual sowing of their grain, or at weddings, to pray for blessings and good luck for the couple, though they rarely serve this function any more.

The best-known example of a *yaraví* is probably the internationally renowned song *El Cóndor Pasa*, which deals with the Indian rebellion, initiated by Túpac Amaru, against the Spanish colonial power. The pop duo Simon & Garfunkel made the English translation of this old Peruvian folk song popular all over the world towards the end of the 1960's. For several centuries now, the *yaraví*s that originate in Arequipa have been the most popular and the most respected in Peru.

The third important Peruvian style of song, the *huayno*, uses melodramatic and very poetic language, with musical accompaniment that also makes you want to ge up and dance. Today, *huayno*-style songs accompany the characteristic dance of the inhabitants of the Peruvian Andes, which is always danced in pairs to a 2/4- or 4/4-beat with ever-increasing enthusiasm. According to the reports of local Spanish chroniclers, the Quechua and Aymara Indians of Peru used every available opportunity to make music and

dance. Tragic events and interpersonal relationships are described in the contemporary *huaynos*, but they always include the necessary dash of irony and humor in their narration and descriptions to keep them succinct and entertaining. The ideally suited pentatonic scale gives the entire *huayno* a heartrendingly tragic effect. Today, *huayno*s from the Ayacucho region are usually written and sung in the Quechua language, whereas in the northern Andes they are more likely to be written in Spanish.

While traveling through Peru, you will have many opportunities to become acquainted with the country's typical musical instruments. Often up to ten musical instruments are used in a five- to seven-member *conjunto folklórico*, a musical folklore group from the sierras. The lead instruments in such groups are usually the *charango*, *quena,* and *siku*.

The *charango* is a stringed instrument that is often compared with the mandolin. It was first used in Peru during the 16th or 17th century. Its special feature, typical of many South American instruments, is that its sounding board is made from the armor of an armadillo. This gives the *charango* its unmistakable appearance.

The *quena* is a longitudinal flute that is notched at the top. Historically it was usually carved from llama bones, but today it is carved from special *chuqui* cane and has a body similar to that of a recorder.

The *siku* (also called *anatara* by the locals) is the most typical instrument of the indigenous music of Peru. *Siku* panpipes are made of two rows of reeds and produce the unmistakable music of the inhabitants of the Peruvian Andes. The thin, individual reeds, ten to twenty in number, all have different lengths. Arranged next to each other like the pipes of a church organ and closed at the bottom, they each generate a different note. Minor variations in their construction, or in the material used to make them, can result in an audible difference in the pitch. As a result, every *siku* produces its own individual sound.

Like the *siku*, the *zampoña* is played by blowing air across the upper opening, not directly into the opening, giving rise to a whispered flute tone. Some groups also use the *pinkullo*, a transverse flute, and the *tarka*, a set of panpipes with harsher sound. However, a *bombo* (also known as a *tambor*), should never be missing from any musical group from Peru's sierra. This low-pitched, single-membrane bass drum acts as a kind of replacement for the double-bass. The thicker end of the *bombo* stick is covered with a soft pelt and thus facilitates a low and soft bass note. The *tinya*, a special form of the bombo, has two pelts and is also used as a rhythm instrument. Other instruments used in Peruvian folkloric music include: the *chilchil* (wooden rattles); the *pututo* (sea shell); and the Andean harp, a large instrument with an enormous sounding board.

Apart from the world-renowned music of the Andean inhabitants, there are two further styles of music that are very popular in Peru: the music of the country's Creoles, and that of the Afro-Peruvians.

The *música criolla* developed among the Peruvian upper classes during the course of the 18th and 19th centuries in the urban coastal centers of Lima, Trujillo, Chimbote, and Chiclayo. This Creole-style music was mostly written by authors and composers who were born in Peru, and was originally a mixture of waltzes and polka. Cultural critics and observers consider it to be, without wanting to belittle it in any way, a counterpart or the Peruvian equivalent of North American country music. In the meantime, the entertaining and lively *marinera,* a variation on the Creole-style music, has become well known all over Peru, through radio and television.

When considering the most important musical styles in Peru, one should not forget the music of the Africans. African slaves brought their own musical style to Peru and, over centuries, the rhythms of their music and their melodies influenced the European, Creole and, to a lesser degree, Indian music of Peru. The Afro-Peruvian music often appears to be connected with erotic dances, such as the various forerunners of the *lambada*, which became famous all over the world in the early 1990's. In another form of music, the *habaneras*, the Afro-Peruvians sing about their history as slaves. Not surprisingly, this style of music is much quieter and more melancholic than the Creole style's more upbeat, entertaining and lively *marinera*.

Where and when do visitors to Peru have the best chance to hear the enchanting Andean music, as well as the less-common musical styles? Your best chance, without question, is in the ce-

Right: Drums and sikus are a part of every village band.

meteries throughout the country on All Saints' Day (November 1). This memorable experience is generally most fascinating in the Andean highlands. Keep in mind, though, that despite the apparent cheerfulness of many of the mourners, it is important for tourists to maintain a proper and respectful distance from the family of the deceased.

In the folklore capital of Puno, on Lake Titicaca, hardly a week passes by without some kind of cheerful festival. There are also numerous *peñas* and restaurants here, at these breezy heights. They often have live bands, which play several evenings a week to an international audience.

In Lima, evening folklore programs are scheduled at many of the large hotels. These productions are usually far too professional and far too commercial to give you a real taste of Peruvian folk music. Despite this commercialism, Lima can be interesting for music fans for example on the occasion of the *Señor de los Milagros* festival, which is held every October 18, 19, and 28.

In Cusco, the biggest music, dance, and folklore festival of the year takes place around June 23/24, at the time of the winter solstice and St. John the Baptist's Day. The Cusqueños celebrate *Inti Raymi* in the former Inca fortress of Sacsayhuamán, as well as in the streets of their old city. Indian music and dance groups perform throughout the year in the large hotels and restaurants, and in the university's small theater, where entry is often free.

Musical life in Ayacucho becomes particularly interesting during *Semana Santa*, Holy Week, when the typical folk music of this high Andean region can be heard during the large processions. In Arequipa, on the other hand, it is possible to attend a concert or a folkloric performance by local groups almost every evening in one of the many peñas and restaurants. Peruvian folkloric music can, of course, also be purchased on CD's and cassettes. Numerous Peruvian music groups now live, on the proceeds of their "hits."

PERU'S ANIMAL WORLD

Peru's three very different climatic regions – the coast, mountains and rainforest – allow it to boast of an extraordinarily wide range of animals and birds. In many places, travelers have the opportunity to observe many examples of the indigenous fauna, the most important of which are described briefly below.

The hump-less camels of the New World, several varieties of llamas, are probably the most characteristic animals of Peru. The easily recognizable llamas, alpacas, vicuñas, and guanacos can interbreed. and live between 3000 to 4500 meters above sea level.

The llama *(lama glama)* and the alpaca *(lama pacos)* are domesticated forms of their wild predecessor the guanaco. Up to two meters in length, 125 centimeters

Above: Vicuñas provide the finest wool of all four types of camels found in Peru. Right: Colorful inhabitants of the primeval forest – the bright-red Ara.

tall, and weighing up to 300 kilograms, the llama feeds mainly on grass and leaves. Llamas have a gestation period of 12 months, and their young weigh about 10-15 kilograms at birth. If they are well nourished they can live for 20 years. As early as in the Inca period, llamas were used as pack animals, because they can carry loads of 30-45 kilograms over a distance of more than 20 kilometers. Llama wool has been used by the inhabitants of the Andes for thousands of years to make coarse clothes, grain sacks, ropes, and carpets. Llama meat, though a little tough, continues to nourish those living in the Andes.

The alpaca, the second domesticated llama found in Peru, looks a little smaller and stockier, and has wider and smaller ears than the llama. Alpaca wool is much finer, softer and more expensive than that of the llama.

Of the two wild types of llama, the shy, delicate guanaco *(lama guanicoe)* can be recognized by its much lighter coloring and smaller body structure. Its habitat ranges from the Andes in Central Peru across the deserted stretches of sub-polar Argentina, into Chile and Tierra del Fuego.

The second variety of llama that also lives wild is the vicuña (*lama vicugna*) is the source of the finest wool in all of the animal kingdom. The Incas used this wool 700 years ago. They captured the shy animal every year in the spring, sheared it and released it again. Vicuñas can best be observed in the Pampas Galeras Reserve between Nazca and Ayacucho.

The *cóndor* is the bird that is most typical of Peru. You will be most likely to see one floating through the thin air of the Andes while climbing in the Cordillera Blanca mountains or hiking along the Inca Trail between Cusco and Machu Picchu. The condor, belonging to the vulture family and a distant relative of the stork, lets itself be carried up to heights of 10,000 meters by riding favorable thermals. It is not a raptor that kills live prey, but mainly a scavenger, feeding on carrion.

Its enormous three-meter-wing-span facilitates an incredibly majestic flight. In the older folk art, and even in the contemporary Peruvian folk art, the condor is often the symbol for the Incas, whereas the bull symbolizes the Spaniards. At the annual festivals (*Yawar Fiesta*) in the remote Andean villages, anyone can attempt to prove his courage against a bull, to whose back a condor is firmly tied. Many of the *indígenas* believe that the condor, which is later set free, carries their wishes to the heavens.

Other birds that are very common in Peru, and hence easily observed, are pelicans, cormorants, darters, *jabirus* (giant storks), Inca terns, parrots, starlings and hummingbirds.

Apart from the jaguar and the smaller ocelot, the puma (mountain lion, cougar, silver lion) is Peru's most important wildcat. Up to 1.80 meters in length, 80

centimeters tall, and weighing up to 200 kilograms, the puma is a loner with a very large territory. There are no competitive fights between contemporaries – they stay out of each other's way. They can best be observed at the Manú National Park, in the Amazon, and on the sparsely inhabited eastern slopes of the Andes.

Female pumas give birth to up to four heavily spotted cubs, after a gestation period of three months. They mainly hunt other mammals. In Peruvian religions pumas are often a symbol of strength and power.

The Andes are also home to the High Andean deer, Andean geese, flamingos (found at the lakes), Andean weasels, and white-tailed Andean red deer. The Andean fox kills the sheep and goats of the *campesinos* and is only very rarely seen. Its habitat is in the forests and high steppes up to 4500 meters above sea level.

Viscachas (Andean hares) live in rocky environs and jump like little rab-

bits through the inaccessible terrain. Early in the morning, and just before sunset, they lie in the sun to get warm, and make whistling sounds like marmots. When hiking, you can often see them between 3000 and 4000 meters above sea level, even in the populated regions, especially in crevices and caves. They can be up to 30 centimeters long, with their bushy tails adding up to another 20 centimeters. Through the centuries, *viscachas* were trapped mercilessly for their silky-soft, gray-blue fur. Today there are commercial breeding farms for these animals, which eat grass, the leaves from bushes, and young branches. More than 100,000 pelts are produced annually. The expensive fur, while highly prized, is very sensitive to moisture.

Two other animals that are typical of the Peruvian wilderness are the black *oso con ante ojos* (spectacled bear) and the

Above: The spectacled bear lives in the mid-level heights of the forest. Right: Caymans lurk in the rivers of the Amazon region.

iguana. The *oso con ante ojos* grows up to 1.8 meters long and eats grass, fruits, wild berries, small animals, and tasty cobs of corn from the fields near the forests. They used to be found in the tropical misty forests, at mid-level heights; now they face extinction.

The second typical animal, the iguana, is seen more frequently. Prized by the local gourmets, iguanas are mainly found in dry areas. They can grow to between 10 and 200 centimeters long, and weigh up to 100 kilograms. Their tails are often significantly longer than their bodies. Iguanas, which usually move sluggishly, eat leaves, fruit, and carrion.

The animals that live in the rivers, lakes and near Peru's Pacific coast are no less fascinating. The most famous and notorious of these are the piranhas, which can measure up to half a meter in length and are only native to the tropical northeast of South America, in the Amazon and its tributaries. The sight of their distinctive bodies, which look like they have been flattened from the side, and their

strong, frighteningly powerful-looking jaws filled with razor-sharp teeth has put the fear of death into many a swimmer. Piranhas eat other fish and animals, particularly sick or wounded ones that fall into the water, as well as carrion. It is well known that the blood of a wounded animal powerfully draws piranhas.

Another native of the Amazon and its tributaries is the *paiche* (*Arapaima gigas*), a fish that can weigh up to 150 kilograms and grow up to three meters in length.

Other inhabitants of Peru's tropical rivers include: the electric eel, which anaesthetizes its prey with electrical shocks and drives away its predators "electrically," the fresh-water ray, with its highly poisonous sting, sea cows (manatee), and even pink dolphins.

The king of the rivers is the *caiman* or alligator. The *caiman* waits for its prey in the Amazon and its tributaries, lurking in muddy-bottomed marshes and on soft, sandy riverbanks. The black *caiman* measures almost five meters in length

and females can lay up to 60 hard-shelled eggs. It is capable of killing very large prey, including cattle.

There is, however, one animal in Peru that can challenge the powerful, adult *caiman*: the anaconda. This gigantic constrictor snake, which can reach 9 meters in length, can strangle powerful *caimans* to death. Equally dangerous are the boa constrictors, which also strangle their prey, as well as the extremely venomous bushmaster snake, the *chuchupe*.

The most common fish splashing about in the cold mountain lakes and rivers is trout. In the Pacific, near the coast, there are millions of *anchoas,* a kind of small small anchovy, which feed on plankton. Anchovies which haven't fallen prey to birds or the *bonito* tuna are harvested by the tonne, and processed into fishmeal. Other animals living along the Peruvian coast include penguins, sperm whales and sea otters. Sea lions can be easily observed at the Islas Ballestas, off the coast of the Paracas Peninsula.

COCA DES INCAS
VIN TONIQUE & DIGESTIF
DÉPÔT GÉNÉRAL·26·Rue de Pontoise·PARIS

Que faites vous ma chère pour rester aussi belle
Je bois chaque jour du COCA DES INCAS

COCAINE - A DREAM IN WHITE?

The cultivation and consumption of coca leaves have a long tradition in Peru. A considerable time before the Incas, presumably even before the flowering of the Chavin culure (around 1000 BC) people from many and varied tribes and regions chewed coca leaves in order to feel less hunger, thirst, and tiredness and altitude problems. If you travel in Peru today by overland bus or on the back of a truck in the company of native Peruvians you will see many older men and women (with the necessary equipment in their pocket) who bear the scars of prolonged use of coca: dark green stains on the teeth and large gaps between the teeth.

The coca leaf also played an important role in the prophecies of the shamans (and still does today): the magician threw a handful of coca leaves into the air and

Above: Around 1890 soft drinks containing cocaine were very popular in Paris. Right: In a coca plantation.

from the way they lay when they had fallen to the ground he was able to predict the future. Healers of the cultures along the coast already used this method 5000 years ago to diagnose illnesses and for treating mental and physical sicknesses in members of their tribe; this has been proved by archeological finds.

The Spanish conquistadors attempted to forbid the use of the leaves but soon had to admit that the farmers and the mine workers could not endure their hard labor in the fields and mines without this sedative.

The Spanish then laid out proper coca plantations in the jungle and brought Indians from the Andean highlands to slave for them in inhuman conditions in the heat of the Amazon lowlands, causing them to die in huge numbers. Many a Spanish knight made his fortune by cultivation of the leaves and by transporting them 1000 kilometers in long llama caravans to the silver mines in Potosí in Bolivia. And even the church grew rich because of coca: it demanded a tenth of the profit from the sale of the plant which the priests simultaneously denounced from the pulpit as a devil's weed.

In the culture of the time coca was a generally accepted "luxury" good, consumption remained within certain limits – similar to coffee or tea – and use of it was in no way a criminal offence. When coca, mixed with chalk, is chewed, only a very minute amount of the actually reaches the bloodstream. Doctors have proved that this kind of use certainly does not lead to addiction.

It was not until the demand for cocaine grew rapidly – principally in the USA, later in Europe – forming a large market, that canny entrepreneurs in Peru, Bolivia and Colombia understandably wanted to make large amount of capital with cocaine. In this they were hugely successful. In the 1990's the illegal cocaine exports from Peru constituted approximately one third of the entire exports of

the country. The cultivation of coca is thus an economic factor of eminent importance in the economy of Peru, even more so than tourism.

In Peru almost one million people today live from the cultivation of coca and in the poorer neighboring country, Bolivia, a further 500,000. In the valley of the 1100-kilometer-long River Huallaga (in northeastern Peru) the tender one to two meter high bushes of the coca plant, grow in an area of about 220,000 hectares which produces 100,000 tonnes of coca leaves annually. This is more than one third of the total world-wide production.

Only one tenth of this harvest is used by the indigenas in the traditional way. The leaves are mixed with chalk and chewed to diminish feelings of hunger and thirst; a small percentage is sold to the pharmaceutical industry. In the restaurants and hotels of the altiplano travelers can freely partake of coca tea to help counteract the symptoms of altitude sickness.

The cocaine trade hit the headlines of the world's press at the end of the 1980's because of measures taken by the Colombian government. Mafia-like plots, numerous assassinations, cold-blooded murders, gang wars and corruption scandals on the highest political level did the rest. US presidents Ronald Reagan and George Bush Senior attempted to fight the narcotráfico (drug dealing) with publicity measures – but in vain. The majority of cocaine users are still to be found in the USA.

The US government made grants of US $40 million annually available to Peru, Bolivia and Colombia at the beginning of the 1990's to assist in the struggle against the cultivation of coca. But even the conversion of coca plantations to fruit orchards with subsidies from the USA could not balance out the enormous financial losses to Peru. These measure have not brought in even one tenth of the profit from coca; a solution to the conflict is therefore not likely within the foreseeable future.

THE SLUMS OF LIMA

Extensive slums surround the Peruvian capital like a wide belt. The number of huts increases daily and there is no end in sight. However, this development did not just start yesterday.

After 1950 there was an unparalleled migration from the Peruvian countryside, mainly into Lima, and within a few years dozens of slums (*barriadas*) stood on the edge of the city. Unlike similar settlements in the USA or Brazil, in Peru these shantytowns are not called slums or *favelas*; the euphemistic official term *pueblos jóvenes*, or "young villages," is used instead.

The causes of this migration from the countryside included miserable conditions for *campesinos* working for the owners of large estates, the lack of progress outside the cities, and unsatisfactory rural infrastructure. In addition, one farm could often no longer provide for the ever-increasing number of family members. The hostile attitude of the influential Catholic Church toward family-planning measures only aggravated the problems that were caused by enormous population growth.

Terrorist activities of the *Sendero Luminoso* – the Maoist Shining Path movement – and the counter-terrorist measures of the army and police also drove thousands of highland Indians from the *sierra* into the suburban areas of the coastal cities.

Today, the tracts of low, gray huts made from straw, wood, cardboard and sheets of corrugated iron have expanded outwards, almost 30 kilometers from Lima's city center. Ten people often live in a single 15 square meter room. Only the older *barriadas* have sanitation, a safe water supply, streetlights, garbage collec-

Right: Immigrants from the countryside settle on the outskirts of Lima in "Púeblos Jóvenes."

tion, electricity and paved roads. Hospitals, schools and grocery stores are rare, especially in the *pueblos jóvenes*.

Taking the bus from the *barriadas* to the industrial areas or downtown often takes several hours and further burdens the traffic that already crawls through the capital. Today, an impoverished migrant from the countryside occupies, as far as possible, Lima's parks, schoolyards or unused industrial areas within the city center rather than looking for a place in the suburbs. Otherwise, the commute to work simply takes far too long.

During the 1990's, 250,000 migrants made their way to Lima every year. According to the estimates of city planners, more than 50 percent of Lima's more than eight million inhabitants live in *pueblos jóvenes*.

Generally, the father of a family or one of the older sons will leave the village and look for accommodation in the pueblos jóvenes, which he constructs himself with materials such as bast mats, plastic sheets, cardboard, wooden crates and boards.

The rest of the family, also frequently the entire extended family in the village, follows within the next few months with what few possessions they have. All of the family members, even the children, then begin to search for work in earnest – in the factories, as maids, as saleswomen, as street traders or lottery ticket sellers. The money that is not directly required for supporting the family and oneself is immediately invested in purchasing (mostly used) stones, wooden beams and the roof tiles of houses that have been torn down. Thus, with time, slowly but surely, a solid house with concrete pillars and brick walls is built. This house is always expandable, so that, even after a number of years, it is possible to add another story. It is precisely for the purpose of expansion that, on many houses in the poorer suburbs of the large cities, rusted steel reinforcement rods can be seen pro-

jecting out of the oncrete columns, which are necessary because of the danger of earthquakes.

If the inhabitants of the slums are asked what they think of life in the *pueblos jóvenes* as compared to their earlier existence in the countryside, the answer is almost always that the move to Lima was the correct decision and was certainly worthwhile.

This belief that they made the correct decision may hold particularly true for the inhabitants of the *Villa El Salvador* (named after the Savior Jesus Christ – El Salvador) in the south of Lima. In 1971, more than 10,000 highland Indians left the region around Huaraz in the Cordillera Blanca after a devastating earthquake and moved to Lima, in the hope of being able to start a new and better life in the city.

Following violent clashes with Lima's administrative officials and the police, during which one of the migrants was shot, the people of Villa El Salvador were successful in their attempts to establish a functioning city, which now has a population of 350,000!

By setting up an artificial irrigation system they have made the arid desert soil fertile again. They are now able to plant corn, alfalfa, cotton, and citrus fruits there. In their own industrial area, numerous small factories, built by owners and employees, provide jobs for more than 1000 people. These accomplishments, along with a busy cultural center and several libraries prove that the people here have transformed the unyielding desert into a "flourishing landscape."

The inhabitants of Villa El Salvador maintain several partnerships with cities abroad, such as the German university town of Tübingen on the Neckar. Third-world and "one-world" groups enthusiastically support such promising models in Peru; they collect money, and support projects financially, even personally. This kind of help and international cooperation is much more than just the proverbial drop in a bucket.

237

METRIC CONVERSION

Metric Unit	US Equivalent
Meter (m)	39.37 in.
Kilometer (km)	0.6241 mi.
Square Meter (sq m)	10.76 sq. ft.
Hectare (ha)	2.471 acres
Square Kilometer (sq km)	0.386 sq. mi.
Kilogram (kg)	2.2 lbs.
Liter (l)	1.05 qt.

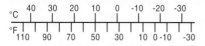

TRAVEL PREPARATIONS

Arrival / Immigration

Citizens of the US, Canada, and the United Kingdom must have a passport that is valid for a period of six months beyond the date of entry, but do not need a visa in order to enter Peru. At the time of entry, an Immigration official will stamp your passport allowing you to stay for 30, 60, or 90 days. The specified duration can be extended several times, three months at a time; occasionally extensions are given only upon presentation of the return air ticket and payment of US $50. The *Migraciones* office is located in Lima in the Av. España, Cuadra 6, and is open on workdays from 9 a.m. to 1 p.m. If you want to save yourself the hassles of the extension procedure, you merely have to travel to a neighboring country for 72 hours then re-enter Peru.

When entering Peru by land travelers with backpacks are sometimes asked to produce a return air ticket, or to prove that they have sufficient funds for the intended duration of stay. All non-Peruvian travelers will be given a *Tarjeta de Ingreso* (tourist card) in the plane or at the border post, which you have to fill out. In addition to your personal information you will be asked the reason for entry, the probable duration of stay, and the address of your hotel.

There are no restrictions on the amount of money that tourists may carry into Peru. An International Certificate of Vaccination for yellow fever is required if you are arriving from an infected area, e.g., Central America and northern South America.

Customs

The *Declaración de Aduana* (customs declaration; Spanish and English versions) asks about objects you are bringing into the country. You may bring up to 400 cigarettes, 50 cigars or 250 grams of tobacco, and three liters of wine or spirits. The value of these goods should not exceed US $300. If you intend to export coca leaves for making coca tea (*Mate de Coca*), keep in mind that their importation into most countries is prohibited under the Narcotic Substances Acts!

Climate / Travel Seasons

All of Peru is located in the tropics and has the corresponding climate: small seasonal changes in temperature, but large variations between day and night, especially at the higher altitudes. Peru's great variations in climatic conditions are due to the non-uniformity of rain distribution and the extremely large differences in altitude.

Pacific Coast (Lima, Trujillo, Arequipa): dry throughout the year, temperatures between 20 and 30°C; in the immediate vicinity of the ocean, from May to December, it can be very foggy and temperatures can drop to 10°C. Best time to travel: December, March, April.

Northern Mountains (Cajamarca): Day temperatures at 3000 meters between 15 and 25°C; rainy season; December to April.

Southern Mountains (Cusco, Lake Titicaca): Day temperatures at 3500 meters between 10 and 20°C; rainy season: December to March.

Northern Amazon (Iquitos): Day temperatures 30°C; some rain throughout the year, rainy seasons in November/December, and mid-March through mid-May.

Southern Amazon (Puerto Maldonado): Day temperatures 30°C; rainy season: December to March.

Clothing

For the coastal areas, between December and April, summer clothing is advisable. The rest of the year in Lima you need light woolens and a thin jacket.

In the Andean Highlands it can be comfortably warm during the day. In the shade and during the night, it is much cooler. Especially from May to September, warm, windproof clothing is necessary. Don't forget sunglasses and a hat. For excursions involving large differences in altitudes (Arequipa - Cañón de Colca; Cusco - Machu Picchu), it is best to dress in layers, since you will have to count on extreme temperature differences. The same applies for hiking; here, you additionally need hiking boots, warm underclothing, a fleece sweater, and a waterproof jacket.

For the Amazon region, light cotton or linen clothing that breathes and provides protection from mosquito bites is recommended. Good rain gear is particularly important.

Currency / Exchange

Since July 1, 1991, the Peruvian currency has been named for Sol de oro, Inti and Sol, and is known as the *Nuevo Sol* (new sun; plural: Nuevos Soles) It is designated by the character "S." One hundred céntimos equal one Sol.

It is advisable to exchange money in Peru, rather than at home, and it is best to travel with US$. Cash can be exchanged easily. Exchanging traveler's checks in banks often requires a lot of patience; in some rural areas it can be very difficult to find a bank that is willing to cash them. However, because of the high risk of theft, it is nonetheless recommended that you carry a part of your travel budget in the form of US$ traveler's checks. Cash and traveler's checks in other major currencies are not accepted as readily, and usually only in large hotels and individual exchange bureaus in the larger cities. The black market exchange of money is officially prohibited, but still exists, especially in Lima (Plaza de Armas), Cusco (Avenida del Sol), Puno, and Arequipa. In addition, there is a so-called "parallel market" (also on the street), in which currency traders try their luck, but take care: the rate is hardly better and the risk of getting cheated when exchanging on the black market, e.g., with counterfeit notes, is high.

Before going on an excursion of several days into more rural areas, make sure you have a plentiful supply of *soles* in cash; exchanging money in a provincial bank can be a long, tedious process. Banks are open weekdays from 9 a.m. to 4 p.m. and the currency exchange counters in the large tourist centers are usually open longer. Large hotels, restaurants, and travel agencies accept most major credit cards. Caution: never lose sight of your credit card while paying! Certain tricky maneuvers can result in very unpleasant surprises when you receive your next bill.

TRAVELING TO PERU

By Air

Many airlines offer international flights to the Aeropuerto Jorge Chávez in the capital, Lima, but they are usually not direct flights. When leaving Peru you are required to pay an airport tax of (currently) US $25.

By Car

Tourists don't usually drive into Peru from Ecuador (Tumbes/Aguas Verdes) or Bolivia (Desaguadero). The border crossings are described in the relevant chapters and are often closed during the afternoon and after sunset. In any case, it is highly advisable that you ask your embassy about the current regulations regarding taking your own automobile into Peru.

By Ship

Individual cruise ships occasionally dock for a few days in the harbor of Callao near Lima, but there are no regular sea connections worth naming.

TRAVELING WITHIN PERU

By Air

The domestic airlines, Aero Continente and TANS, have good networks and serve all of Peru's larger cities almost daily. Flight details are listed in the relevant Guidepost located at the end of each chapter; ticket prices are quoted in US$.

In March 1999, the former national carrier AeroPerú, with most of its stock now in private Mexican hands, canceled all flights because of bankruptcy. At the time this book went to press it was not known when or if flights would resume. As the demand for domestic flights is high all year, it is advisable to book early. An airport tax of (currently) US $4 is charged for all domestic flights.

Rental Cars

Local and international car rental companies (Avis, Budget, Hertz) have offices in all of Peru's large cities, and at the larger airports. In the more rural areas, it is best to rent a car with an experienced chauffeur. The (low) cost of hiring a chauffeur is always worthwhile. The most common rental cars, e.g., VW Beetles and VW Golfs, are both manufactured in Mexico.

There are large price differences between local rental companies and large international rental companies. When comparing prices, however, you should always check that taxes and insurance (in Peru, there is no insurance against theft of objects from inside the vehicle) are included and the extent of your exposure in case of damage. The pre-requisites for renting a car are: a minimum age of 21 years, a credit card, a valid driver's license and a passport.

If you want to drive on dirt roads in more rural areas, you should rent a four-wheel-drive (a Nissan Patrol is one of the most common); the rental contract does not allow you to travel on the dirt roads with a regular rental car. If several people plan to take turns driving the car, it should be noted in the contract, otherwise, there can be problems during a police check.

By Bus

The public bus system has a good network. Buses continually leave in all directions from the bus stations in Lima, Trujillo, Chimbote, Arequipa, and Cusco. However, connections become less and less frequent as you move away from the densely populated highlands into more rural areas.

By Train

There are two independent railway networks in Peru. One runs from Lima, via La Oroya, to Cerro de Pasco or Huancayo (there are currently no passenger trains!). The other network connects Arequipa with Cusco and Lake Titicaca (Juliaca and Puno).

A trip with the Peruvian railway over the *altiplano*, along rushing mountain rivers and through narrow mountain gorges, is a unique experience that shouldn't be missed. The most spectacular routes are those between Puno and Cusco, as well as between Cusco and Machu Picchu. Unfortunately, there are only night trains on the extremely picturesque route from Arequipa to Puno. The details of departure locations and times are given in the Guidepost located at the end of each chapter.

Two important tips: buy your tickets one day in advance and be sure to keep an eye on your luggage and your valuables both in the station and on the train!

By Ship

A boat trip along the Pacific coast or on inland waterways can be as interesting as a train ride. An expedition to the Islas Ballestas off the peninsula of Paracas, a tour on Lake Titicaca, with a visit to the islands of the Uros, or several days spent cruising on the Amazon, via Pucallpa and Iquitos towards Manaus (Brazil), is an unforgettable experience. Departure locations and times of the ships are given in the Guidepost at the end of each chapter.

Organized Tours

Apart from organized group-tours, travel agencies, especially in Lima and Cusco, offer a large number of package deals lasting anywhere from one to several days, or even several weeks. Led by an English-speaking guide, these tours usually begin with a trip to a nature reserve, and include hotel pickups, transportation, entrance fees, and all meals. The range of tours offered by such tour operators in Lima and Cusco is very large. Most operators have their own offices, as well as agents in the larger hotels. Lima Tours has offices in Lima and Cusco, and is a reliable firm.

PRACTICAL TIPS FROM A TO Z

Accommodation

The hotel categories in the Guidepost located at the end of each chapter correspond to the following price classifications: *LUXURY:* From US $100 to above US $200; *MODERATE:* US $30-100. *BUDGET:* US $10-30.

Only a few hotels meet the requirements of the highest international hotel category "Luxury"; such hotels can only be found in Lima, Miraflores and Cusco.

Most hotels in Peru are privately operated. The hotels belonging to the erstwhile national Turistas chain are being privatized and some are being sold to Peruvian hotel chains.

Simpler hotels are often more "intimate"; the owner is usually the operator and can give you insider tips and offer help if you run into problems.

Alcohol

Buying and consuming alcohol is no problem in Peru. Drinking alcoholic beverages is permitted in public, but here as in most countries, there are restrictions on drinking and driving. The Peruvian *cerveza* (beer), the good, sun-drenched wines from the Ica region, and *Pisco Sour*, Peru's national cocktail, are definitely worth trying.

Business Hours

Most businesses and shops are open Monday through Friday from 9 a.m. to 12:30 p.m. and from 3-7 p.m. Many shops are also open on Saturdays from 9 a.m. to 6 p.m. Not all shops adhere to the hours above; the numerous street vendors who sell groceries, tobacco, alcohol, and all kinds of knickknacks are often actively engaged in selling their wares even outside these hours. Government offices close as early as 3:30 or 4:30 p.m.; government employees also enjoy a siesta from 11:30 a.m. to 1:30 p.m. During the summer, between January and March, government offices are only open in the mornings. Banks are generally open Monday though Friday 9 a.m. to 4 p.m.

Camping

Camping is not at all as popular in Peru as it is in Europe or in the USA. The equipment at the few camping sites near Lima is very modest. However, putting up tents is permitted outside the archaeological zones and off private property, and is common during the Christmas holidays, especially on the beaches. Camping is unavoidable when mountain climbing in the Cordillera Blanca, or hiking, especially on the Inca trail and around Lake Titicaca. Several local tour operators even offer organized expeditions (the necessary equipment can be rented). In remote places, camping alone or in small groups can sometimes be dangerous.

Dangers / Crime

The Pacific coast and the highlands of Peru are particularly earthquake-prone areas, and before embarking on your trip, you should learn what you should do in case of an earthquake. Trips into the isolated interior are not recommended from January through March because of continuous rainfall. The disputed border with Ecuador leads to occasional incidents in the Amazon province. Terrorist attacks cannot be ruled out, even today.

As in many countries, pickpockets mainly practice their skills on foreign visitors. In large cities, tourist centers, and the larger towns along the Pacific coast especially, they take advantage of the bustle and the crowds to steal wallets, cameras, and bags. They sometimes use violence if necessary, and often work in two's and three's. In addition, they often use the element of surprise. For example, one pretends to have fallen and skillfully takes advantage of the tourist's helpfulness, to relieve him of valuables.

Photocopies of travel documents and credit cards are very helpful in event of loss or theft. You should also note the numbers of your traveler's checks and keep them separately. Pickpockets normally look for the easiest prey. In Lima stay alert in the city center and in the markets, and in Cusco and Puno be especially careful at the train station. In addition, all crowded places draw criminals (including bands of youth and even children). Hikers have also been mugged.

Drugs

In the last few decades, Peru has increasingly become the place of drug manufacturing and trade between North and South America, but the government in Lima, together with the US enforcement authorities continue to fight it. Not just selling drugs, but even drug consumption is prohibited and subject to severe punishment.

International drug trafficking carries a prison sentence of up to 15 years; the use of marijuana, cocaine and heroin also carries sentences of several years. You should be careful, especially in the Río Huallaga valley, not to get involved in the business of other people. There is no specific "drugs district" in Lima.

Electricity

Power is supplied at 220 volts and 60 Hertz. Plugs and sockets are the same as in North America; travelers from Europe should take an adapter along. Not all of the remote jungle lodges have electricity from the national grid.

Emergencies

There are no specific emergency phones in Peru, but you can dial 105 to contact the nearest emergency service.

Guides

Local guides are available in some National Parks, nature reserves, archeological sites, and cities. They are often biologists, ecologists, archeologists, tourist guides, and entertainers all rolled into one and many can speak several foreign languages. Good *guías* (local guides) can do more than just point at animals and plants and identify them; they can share countless details in a gripping and fascinating manner. If you are traveling alone and are interested in knowing specifics about an area, hiring such a *guía* is highly recommended. It is worthwhile to at least test the foreign language skills of the *guía* when agreeing to a time, route, and price.

Health

Health services are better in the larger cities than in the country, but even in some small villages, you can find well-organized pharmacies that carry various medications against the most common ailments encountered during travel – diarrhea, insect bites, sunburn, and colds.

No specific inoculations are prescribed for a trip to Peru, but it is better to consult a specialist in tropical diseases or an inoculation advisory service well before your departure. There hasn't been a cholera epidemic since 1991. In the Amazon region, however, there is some danger of malaria. It is advisable to consult a tropical medicine specialist before taking any malaria prophylaxis (e.g., Larium, chloroquine, or doxycycline). In the different regions of Peru, especially in the *pueblos jóvenes* (slums) of the large cities, there have been cases of tuberculosis and typhoid in the last few years. Private overseas medical insurance is advisable.

You can take some preventive precautions against diarrhea. Avoid at all costs: salads, ice cream from street kiosks, unwashed or unpeeled fruit (also because of pesticides), and dirty water that hasn't been boiled (e.g., from the tap).Insect repellent and a sunscreen are also musts.

If you want to travel in the mountains, i.e., at altitudes above 3000 meters, you should have your heart and blood pressure checked by your doctor, because altitude sickness (*soroche*) should not be taken lightly. If the don't take time to get properly acclimatized, e.g. after a direct flight from Lima to the highlands, you may experience headaches, dizziness, cramps, earaches, heart palpitations, and vomiting. The basic rule of altitude acclimation is: for every 1000 meters of altitude, one should, strictly speaking, give the body one week to adjust. The locals swear by a daily consumption of several cups of coca tea (*mate de coca*); even *Coramina Glucosa* (well-known in the Peru's highland pharmacies) or *Diamox* can help. Plenty of rest makes it easier for your body to adjust to the altitude. In critical situations, never hesitate to visit or call a doctor. On a mountain, the best thing to do is to immediately descend, be carried if necessary, to a lower altitude.

Holidays

Peruvians celebrate the following holidays across the country:

January 1: New Year's Day (*Año Nuevo*).

Holy Thursday: from noon onwards.

Good Friday: processions.

Easter: *Pascua*, only one day.

May 1: Labor Day (*Día de los Trabajadores*).

Corpus Christi: processions.

June 23/24: Inti Raymi Festival, in Cusco.

June 28: St. Peter and St. Paul.

July 28/29: Independence Day/Day of the Republic, national holiday with parades.

August 15: Assumption of the Virgin Mary (*Asunción de la Virgen Maria*).

August 30: *Santa Rosa de Lima*, processions.

October 9: Day of National Dignity (*Día de la Dignidad Nacional*).

November 1/2: All Saints' Day/All Souls' Day (*Día de Todos los Santos*).

December 8: Immaculate Conception.

December 25: Christmas (*Fiesta de la Navidad*).

December 31: New Year's Eve

Hospitals

Payment must be made in cash before you are discharged from clinics; foreign health cards or coupons are not valid. It is advisable to have foreign travel/medical insurance that will reimburse you upon production of your receipts.

If you need medical attention in Lima the following are recommended: **Anglo-American Hospital**, Av. Salazar, San Isidro, tel: (01) 2213656. **Instituto de Medicina Tropical**, Universidad Particular Cayetano Heredia, Av. Honorio Delgado, San Martín de Porres, tel: (01) 4823903.

Pharmacies

Farmacias are usually open from 9 a.m. to 7 p.m. and stock a wide range of common medications. On weekends and at night one pharmacy remains open in every community. Most antibiotics and similar drugs are mostly available without a physician's prescription.

Photography

You should buy film, spare batteries, flash, tripods and special lense filters (UV and polarization) before leaving home. These things are usually more expensive in Peru, are rarely available, and if you do manage to find them they have often (in the case of film) not been stored correctly, or been stored for too long.

Apart from an adequate number of rolls of 100 ASA film, it is advisable to take along a few 400 ASA rolls for excursions to the tropical rain forest and for interior photography (when permitted) in museums and churches.

If you buy film in Peru, it is absolutely essential to check the expiry date. While traveling it is also very important to ensure that rolls of film are not exposed to too much heat and (when reloading) to naked sunlight. When traveling by boat or exploring the rain-soaked jungle, photographic equipment should be stored in watertight cases if at all possible.

Photography in Peru is best in the early morning hours and late in the afternoon, when the light is the most appealing and, in the National Parks, the animals are at their most active. In the dense rain forests, there will be times when you cannot manage without a tripod or a flash; this is also true when taking pictures of dark-skinned people, e.g., on the Pacific coast.

In any case, before taking photographs, it is essential to ask for permission: *¿Con permiso?," ¿Me permite?"* or *¿Puedo tomar una foto?"* For some years now, in the places heavily frequented by foreign tourists such as around Cusco and along Lake Titicaca (especially on the islands of the Uros), the locals have been demanding some compensation for photographs, usually US $1. If you need accessories for your photography equipment, the camera shops in the pedestrian zones of Lima (near Plaza de Armas) and in Cusco (opposite the cathedral) are currently the best places to go.

Post / Telephones

The *correos* (post offices) are mostly near the Plaza de Armas or in the city centers. Peru prints very pretty, colorful and original stamps. There are no mailboxes on the streets; mail must be taken to the post office. Almost every hotel has arrangements to accept stamped mail. A card or a letter from Peru to Europe or the US usually requires 8-14 days to reach the addressee. Poste restante mail must be marked as *Correo Restante* and sent to the General Post Office in Lima or another big city; the family name of the addressee must be clearly visible. When picking up such mail, you will have to produce your passport.

The private telephone company is called Telefónica del Perú. Telephone numbers in Peru are usually 6 or 7 digits; area codes are 3 digits, with the exception of Lima (01). Public telephone directories are rare, but a call to directory assistance (*operadora*) is usually enough. In addition to the Telefónica del Perú offices, most larger hotels allow you to place direct overseas calls. Peru's country code, for calls from abroad, is +(51). For domestic calls from public telephones, you can pay with coins or telephone cards, which can be bought at kiosks and from street vendors.

Press

In Lima and other large cities, newspaper boys, and bookshops sell the common Peruvian newspapers as well as some larger foreign newspapers like the

International Herald Tribune, USA Today, and other US daily newspapers.

Restaurants

Most restaurants in Peru are open from mid-day to midnight, often with a break between 3 p.m. and 6 p.m.; many are closed on Sundays or Mondays. When paying it is advisable not to let your credit card out of your sight. More and more frequently, crooks make a copy, which they use to "earn" several thousand dollars extra, often in an expensive jewelry shop. Restaurant recommendations are given in the Guidepost at the end of each chapter; this book also includes a special feature (see page 222) providing information about the most important specialties of the Peruvian cuisine. The language guide (see page 247) should be helpful when studying the menus.

Shopping

Apart from the usual shops, shopping at the stalls of the mercados in the larger communities can be a lot of fun. In numerous cities and villages, mercados are held outside, sometimes there is even a weekly market on a specific weekday. The most interesting markets in Peru are in Lima (Av. Petit Thouars in Miraflores, or along the Av. de la Marina towards the airport), Huancayo, Cusco, Chincheros near Cusco, Pisac, Juliaca and Puno. Souvenirs can be bought at many places in Peru. In addition, you can find well-stocked souvenir shops in all the larger hotels.

Taxis

Taxis are an inexpensive means of transportation in Peru. In 1997, a trip within Lima or Cusco generally cost US $1-3. Most taxicabs are Japanese- or Korean-built, but there are also some 2-door VW Beetles. The dark limousines that wait for passengers in front of the more expensive hotels and at the airport often cost twice or even three times the normal fare.

You can easily hire taxis even for an entire day at a price of US $30-50. Shared taxis (*colectivos* or *micros*) are not quite as fast, but are even cheaper than taxis. The colectivo network in the cities is well developed and is an excellent supplement to the public buses.

Time

Peru is five hours behind *Greenwich Mean Time.* (When it is 2 p.m. in London it is 9 a.m. in Peru.) It is the same time zone as Eastern Standard Time (US East coast and Central Canada). It is three hours ahead of Pacific Standard Time (US and Canadian West coast). Since Peru lies so close to the equator, the sunrise and sunset times hardly vary during the year – day in and day out, it gets light at 6 a.m. and is dark by 6 p.m.

Tipping

In hotels and restaurants the cashier generally adds a tip (*propina*) or service charge (*servicio*) of 10 percent to the bill. In such a case, additional tips are not expected, but waiters and cashiers are always appreciative if you round up the total when you pay.

The prices quoted on the menus are the net prices; over and above these, there is an 18 percent tax and 10 percent service charge. In rural areas and smaller restaurants, tips and service charges are often not included and a *propina* is expected.

It is not necessary to tip taxi drivers if you have already negotiated a price.

Tourist Hotline

The Ministry of Tourism has set up an office Servicio de Protección al Turista that you can call round the clock in case of emergency. From Lima: tel/fax: 224-7888, outside Lima: tel: 0-800-4-2579 (toll-free); in Cusco: tel: 252974. [http://www.concytec.gob.pe/rural/turista-i.htm

Tourist Police

For the last few years, the Peruvian government has been deploying special uniformed (and armed) tourist police in Lima, Cusco, Puno, Arequipa, and other tourist centers country-wide. Currently there are more than 2000 of them. Most of these policemen speak a few sentences of English, can provide information to foreign visitors and are supposed to protect them from criminals at hot spots such as train and bus stations, airports, mercados, Plaza de Armas, etc.

Trekking

The Peruvian Andes are a paradise for trekkers and mountain climbers; especially the Cordillera Blanca (e.g., Santa Cruz Trail), the Cordillera Huayhuash, and the region around Cusco (e.g., Inca Trail and Cordillera Vilcabamba, treks around the Auzangate).For safety it is advisable to travel with a group, or at least with local guides. In Huaraz and Cusco, there are many local agencies that organize trekking tours, rent equipment to their customers (stoves, tents, sleeping bags, crampons, etc.) and arrange for pack mules with drovers (*arrieros*).

Women Traveling Alone

Although women are respected in Peruvian society, some of the classical *machos* appear to assume that foreign women traveling without a male companion are fair game and much easier to conquer than Peruvian women. Such women are often referred to by the feminine form of the disparaging "gringo," *gringa*. A woman traveling alone in Peru is likely to experience smutty remarks, meaningful looks or suggestive movements, as well as the internationally known whistle. Peruvian women themselves ignore these remarks and hold their heads high; however, sometimes, a very definite, verbal rebuff to these insinuations is unavoidable, e.g., with a forceful *Déjame en paz!* (Leave me alone!). To avoid drawing additional unwanted attention to yourself (you'll probably get enough by the simple virtue of being an "exotic" female foreigner), try to wear clothing that keeps within the norm.

ADRESSES

Peruvian Embassies and Consulates

Australia: 43 Culgoa Circuit, O'Malley, ACT 2606, tel: (02) 6290 0922, fax: 6290 0924. Mailing address: PO Box 106, Red Hill, ACT 2606

Canada: 130 Albert Street, Suite 1901, Ottawa Ontario, K1P 5G4. Tel: (613)238-1777. Fax: (613)232-3062. Telex: 053-3754. E-mail: emperuca@magi.com

New Zealand: Level 8, Cigna House, 40 Mercer St., Wellington, tel: 499-8087, fax: 499-8057. Mailing address: P.O. Box 2566, Wellington.

UK: 52 Sloane St., London SW1X 9SP, tel: (020) 7235-1917, fax: (020) 7235-4463, web site: www.peruembassy-uk.com.

USA: Washington DC: 1700 Massachusetts Ave. NW, Washington DC 20036, tel: (202) 833-9860, fax: (202) 659-8124, web site: www.peruemb.org. New York: 215 Lexington Ave., 21st Floor, New York NY 10016, tel: (212) 481-7410, fax: (212) 481-8606. Chicago: 180 N. Michigan Ave., Suite 1830, Chicago IL 60601, tel: (312) 782-1599, fax: (312) 704-6969. Los Angeles: 3460 Wilshire Blvd., Suite 1005, Los Angeles CA 90010, tel: (213) 252-5910/9795, fax: (213) 252-8130.

Embassies and Consulates in Peru

Australian Consulate General: Av. Victor Andres Belaúnde 147, Via Principal 151, Torre Real Tres, Of. 1301, San Isidro, Lima 27, tel: (01) 222-8281, fax: (01) 222-4996.

British Embassy: Edificio el Pacifico Washington, Natialo Sanches 125, Piso

12, Lima, tel: (01) 433-4738, fax: (01) 433-4735. Mailing address: P.O. Box 854, Lima 100.

Canadian Embassy: Calle Libertad 130, Miraflores, Lima, tel: (01) 444-4015, fax: (01) 242-4050. Mailing address: P.O. Box 18-1126, Miraflores Post Office, Lima. E-mail: lima@dfait-maeci.gc.ca

New Zealand Consulate: Camino Real 390, Piso 17, Torre Central, San Isidro, Lima 27, tel: (01) 442-9317, fax: (01) 421-3194.

Embassy of USA: Av. La Encaladacdra 17 S/N, Surlo, Lima 33, tel: (01) 434-3000, fax: (01) 434-3037, http://ekeko.rcp.net.pe/usa/wwwhmain.htm

Tourist Information in Peru

Specific tourist information offices (government- and state-organized) are mentioned in the Guidepost located at the end of each chapter. There you will be able to get the latest information about the conditions of the streets and hiking trails, National Parks, transportation connections, private guest-houses (*pensiones*) and hotels. The tourist information offices can also arrange for local guides (*guías*) in various cities, nature reserve areas and archeological sites.

Tourist Information Abroad

Peruvian embassies and the general consulates in particular can provide you with specific details as well as informative brochures.

LANGUAGE GUIDE

Monday	*lunes*
Tuesday	*martes*
Wednesday	*miércoles*
Thursday	*jueves*
Friday	*viernes*
Saturday	*sábado*
Sunday	*domingo*
today	*hoy*

tomorrow	*mañana*
yesterday	*ayer*
morning	*por la mañana*
evening	*al mediodía*
afternoon	*por la tarde*
evening/night	*por la noche*
0	*cero*
1	*uno, una*
2	*dos*
3	*tres*
4	*cuatro*
5	*cinco*
6	*seis*
7	*siete*
8	*ocho*
9	*nueve*
10	*diez*
11	*once*
12	*doce*
20	*veinte*
21	*veintiuno*
22	*veintidós*
30	*treinta*
40	*cuarenta*
50	*cincuenta*
60	*sesenta*
70	*setenta*
80	*ochenta*
90	*noventa*
100	*cien*
200	*doscientos*
500	*quinientos*
1000	*mil*

single room	*habitación individual*
double room	*habitación doble*
– with bath	*– con baño*
– with shower	*– con ducha*
toilet	*baño / sanitario*
men	*hombres/señores*
women	*mujeres/señoras*
check (bill)	*la cuenta*
Where is the....?	*¿Dónde hay...?*
closed	*cerrado*
open	*abierto*
Does this road go to...?	
	¿Por aquí se va a...?
straight	*derecho*
right	*derecho/a*

left . . . . *izquierdo/a*
street . . . . *calle*
highway . . . . *autopista*
bus . . . . *camión, ómnibus*
1st-, 2nd-class . *primera/segunda clase*
ticket . . . . . . *pasaje, boleto, ticket*
How long does it take...? . . . .
. . . . ¿*Cuánto dura...?*
Where does (e.g., this bus) go...? . . .
. . . . ¿*Adónde va...?*
Where has (e.g., this bus) come from...?
. . . . ¿*De dónde viene...?*
Good morning, good day . *buenos días*
Good day, good afternoon (noon-6 pm)
. . . . *buenas tardes*
Good evening, good night . . . .
. . . . *buenas noches*
yes/no . . . . *sí/no*
good-bye . . . . . *hasta luego, adiós*
sorry/excuse me . . . . *perdón*
May I? . . . . *con permiso*
please . . . . *por favor*
thank you . . . . *(muchas) gracias*
you're welcome . . . . *de nada*
I need . . . . *necesito*
Is there / there is . . . . *hay*
How much? . . . . . . ¿*Cuánto vale?*
I don't understand . . . *yo no entiendo*
Leave me alone! . . . .
. . . . *Déjame en paz!*
What time...? . . . . ¿*A qué hora?*
What time is it? . . . . . ¿*Qué hora es?*
Summer (Dec.-April) . . . . . *verano*
Winter (May-Dec.) . . . . *invierno*
Spring . . . . *primavera*
Post Office . . . . *correo*
letter . . . . *carta*
postcard . . . . *tarjeta postal*
stamp . . . . *sello, estampilla*
airmail . . . . *correo aéreo*
money exchange bureau *casa de cambio*
money/coins . . . . . . *dinero/monedas*
bank . . . . *banco*
church/cathedral . . . . *iglesia/catedral*
signature . . . . *firma*
doctor . . . . *médico*
help . . . . *ayuda*
hospital . . . . *hospital*
police . . . . *policía*

sick . . . . *enfermo*
friend m/f . . . . *amigo/a*
husband/wife . . . . *esposo/a*
gas station . . . . *grifo, gasolinera*
gasoline . . . . *gasolina*
airport . . . . *aeropuerto*
train station . . . . . *estación de trenes*

In a Restaurant

ají . . . . Chili
ajo . . . . garlic
albondigas . . . . meat dumplings
alcachofas . . . . artichokes
arroz . . . . rice
atún . . . . tuna
botella . . . . bottle
camarones . . . . crabs
carne . . . . meat
cebolla . . . . onion
cerdo, chancho . . . . pork
cerveza . . . . beer
chivo . . . . goat meat
choclo . . . . corn on the cob
chuleta . . . . chops/cutlets
coco . . . . coconut
coliflor . . . . cauliflower
cordero . . . . lamb (meat)
desayuno . . . . breakfast
dulce . . . . sweet
empanada . . pastry stuffed with meat
. . . . or cheese
ensalada de fruta . . . . . . fruit salad
espárragos . . . . asparagus
flan . . . . caramel custard
frijoles . . . . beans
helado . . . . ice cream
hongos . . . . mushrooms
huevos fritos . . . . fried eggs
huevos revueltos . . . . scrambled eggs
jamón . . . . ham
leche . . . . milk
lenguado . . . . sole
lomo/lomito . . . . steak
mantequilla . . . . butter
naranja . . . . orange
palmitos . . . . palm hearts
palta . . . . avocado
pan . . . . bread
pan integral . . . . . wholewheat bread

papas fritas . . . . French fries
pato . . . . duck
pavo . . . . turkey
plátanos . . . . bananas
piña . . . . pineapple
pollo . . . . chicken
pulpo . . . . cuttlefish/octopus
queso . . . . cheese
queso frito . . . . fried cheese
res . . . . beef
salchicha asada . . . . . grilled sausage
salsa . . . . sauce
sandía . . . . water melon
seco . . . . dry
sopa . . . . soup
tortilla . . . . omelet
trucha . . . . trout
verduras . . . . vegetables
vino . . . . wine

AUTHORS

Dr. Klaus Boll studied cultural science, ethnology, and ancient history. For several years Dr. Boll worked as a journalist for the art magazine *Art Aurea* and lived abroad, especially in Latin America. Today he gives seminars for an international development cooperation and is a freelance author and a study-tour guide. He is also the author of the *Nelles Guide Costa Rica* and co-author of the *Nelles Guide Corsica*.

Heike Mühl, art historian and Romance scholar, has been traveling in South America for many years and wrote the features about Peruvian hand crafted items and cuisine. She is also the senior author of the *Nelles Guide Corsica*.

PHOTOGRAPHERS

Archive for Art and History, Berlin
35, 70, 96, 234
Bach (Montanus)   184
Boll, Dr. Klaus   36, 56,150, 197, 226
Bousquet, Claude   200/201, 213

Braunger, Hans-Peter   229
Bruder, Eugen   205
Busch, Oskar E. (Montanus)   15, 182
dpa   25
FLPA (Silvestris)   232
Frangenberg, Johannes   8/9,23, 24,
    29, 84, 100, 101,105, 107, 113,
    120, 123, 126, 128, 209, 223, 237
Gassner, Andreas   131, 183, 196
Gross, Andreas   14, 17, 18,28, 30
    33, 42/43,49, 51, 57, 65, 77, 82/83,
    87, 91, 92, 93, 114,116, 134/135, 138,
    139, 151, 152, 159, 162/163,
    169, 174, 176/177, 178,
    185, 186, 193,
    220/221, 225, 227
Hendrichs, Nelly   198
Herion, Peter   127, 211
Janicke, Volkmar E.   19, 40/41, 44,
    54, 64, 86,95, 106, 118/119,
    168, 170, 235
Jennerich, Herbert   76
Kiepke, Günther (Photo-Press)   59, 79
Kirst, Detlev   27, 39, 58, 68/69,
    74, 75, 80, 97, 108, 109, 136, 142,
    156, 157, 171,
    188/189, 190, 216, 231
Kozeny, Günther (Silvestris)   143
Lahr, Günther   cover, 50, 90,
    94, 104, 115, 124,129, 132
Müller, Ernst (Mainbild)   153
Schwarz, Berthold   145
Silvestris   204, 233
Vautier, Mireille   10/11, 12,
    16, 20, 21, 22,
    31, 32, 34, 37, 38,
    48, 55, 61, 62, 63, 66, 78, 102,
    103, 125, 130,
    140L, 140R, 144,148, 149, 158,
    164, 192, 202,208, 214, 215,
    218/219, 224, 230

Explore the World

NELLES GUIDES

Nelles Guides – authoritative, informed and informative.
Always up-to-date, extensively illustrated, and with first-rate relief maps.
256 pages, approx. 150 color photos, approx. 25 maps.

Explore the World

AVAILABLE TITLES

Afghanistan 1 : 1 500 000
Argentina *(Northern),* **Uruguay**
1 : 2 500 000
Argentina *(Southern),* **Uruguay**
1 : 2 500 000
Australia 1 : 4 000 000
Bangkok - *and Greater Bangkok*
1 : 75 000 / 1 : 15 000
Bolivia - Paraguay 1 : 2 500 000
Burma → *Myanmar*
Caribbean - **Bermuda, Bahamas,**
Greater Antilles 1 : 2 500 000
Caribbean - **Lesser Antilles**
1 : 2 500 000
Central America 1 : 1 750 000
Central Asia 1 : 1 750 000
Chile 1 : 2 500 000
China - *Northeastern*
1 : 1 500 000
China - *Northern* 1 : 1 500 000
China - *Central* 1 : 1 500 000
China - *Southern* 1 : 1 500 000
Colombia - Ecuador 1 : 2 500 000
Crete - Kreta 1 : 200 000
Cuba 1 : 775 000
Dominican Republic - Haiti
1 : 600 000
Egypt 1 : 2 500 000 / 1 : 750 000
Hawaiian Islands
1 : 330 000 / 1 : 125 000

Hawaiian Islands – **Kaua'i**
1 : 150 000 / 1 : 35 000
Hawaiian Islands – **Honolulu**
- **O'ahu** 1 : 35 000 / 1 : 150 000
Hawaiian Islands – **Maui - Moloka'i**
- **Lāna'i** 1 : 150 000 / 1 : 35 000
Hawaiian Islands – **Hawai'i, The Big**
Island 1 : 330 000 / 1 : 125 000
Himalaya 1 : 1 500 000
Hong Kong 1 : 22 500
Indian Subcontinent 1 : 4 000 000
India - *Northern* 1 : 1 500 000
India - *Western* 1 : 1 500 000
India - *Eastern* 1 : 1 500 000
India - *Southern* 1 : 1 500 000
India - *Northeastern* - **Bangladesh**
1 : 1 500 000
Indonesia 1 : 4 000 000
Indonesia **Sumatra** 1 : 1 500 000
Indonesia **Java - Nusa Tenggara**
1 : 1 500 000
Indonesia **Bali - Lombok**
1 : 180 000
Indonesia **Kalimantan**
1 : 1 500 000
Indonesia **Java - Bali** 1 : 650 000
Indonesia **Sulawesi** 1 : 1 500 000
Indonesia **Irian Jaya - Maluku**
1 : 1 500 000
Jakarta 1 : 22 500
Japan 1 : 1 500 000
Kenya 1 : 1 100 000

Korea 1 : 1 500 000
Malaysia 1 : 1 500 000
West Malaysia 1 : 650 000
Manila 1 : 17 500
Mexico 1 : 2 500 000
Myanmar (Burma) 1 : 1 500 000
Nepal 1 : 500 000 / 1 : 1 500 000
Nepal Trekking **Khumbu Himal -**
Solu Khumbu 1 : 75 000
New Zealand 1 : 1 250 000
Pakistan 1 : 1 500 000
Peru - Ecuador 1 : 2 500 000
Philippines 1 : 1 500 000
Singapore 1 : 22 500
Southeast Asia 1 : 4 000 000
South Pacific Islands 1 : 13 000 000
Sri Lanka 1 : 450 000
Taiwan 1 : 400 000
Tanzania - Rwanda, Burundi
1 : 1 500 000
Thailand 1 : 1 500 000
Uganda 1 : 700 000
Venezuela - Guyana, Suriname,
French Guiana 1 : 2 500 000
Vietnam - Laos - Cambodia
1 : 1 500 000

IN PREPARATION

South America - The Andes
1 : 4 500 000

Nelles Maps are top quality cartography!
Relief mapping, kilometer charts and tourist attractions.
Always up-to-date!